LION OF SCOTLAND

Neil Robinson

This edition published in 1999 by
Birlinn Limited
Unit 8
Canongate Venture
5 New Street
Edinburgh EH8 8BH

First published in 1952 by
Hodder & Stoughton

Cover design by James Hutcheson

Cover image *Dawn, Canisp and Suilven* © David Noton Photography

ISBN 1 84158 009 0

British Library Cataloguing-in-Publication Data
A catalogue record for this book is available from the
British Library

TO THE MEMORY
OF THE
PIONEERS

Printed and bound in Finland by WSOY

CONTENTS

The publisher would like to dedicate this book to the memory of Jean Gough without whom Ullapool and Scotland are poorer places

ACKNOWLEDGEMENT

The quotation on page 125 from 'Roamin' in the Gloamin' by Sir Harry Lauder is made by kind permission of Messrs Hutchinson & Co. (Publishers) Limited, London, under whose imprint this biography appeared in 1928.

INTRODUCTION

Norman MacAskill

It is appropriate that Neil Robinson's *Lion of Scotland* should be reissued at this time.

When first published in 1952, it coincided with the celebrations to mark the arrival at Waipu, one century before, of Rev Norman McLeod and his followers. It was, and still remains, an important brick in the structure of the dramatic history of a remarkable man and his people. Neil's second book on the subject, *To the Ends of the Earth*, published in 1997, complements his *Lion of Scotland*. Plans are being laid for the celebration of the 150th anniversary in the year 2003.

The arrival, in the 1850s, of some 800 of the Rev Norman's followers in New Zealand completed the final leg of the migrations which began at Clachtoll, in Assynt, in the year 1817. In Assynt, as in many places, the mention of his name is still good for a civilised argument. In his life his personality repelled many but attracted many more.

In any attempts to analyse or unravel a character so intricate and controversial, it is well to recall that most of those who arrived in New Zealand followed him voluntarily. He had left Cape Breton before them. They were not driven. They chose to follow their accepted leader.

My people have been in Assynt for many generations. I was born and raised here and continue to live in what many claim is one of the most beautiful parts of the world. My paternal grandmother was born in a house less than a mile from the site of the crofter-fisherman's cottage which was

Norman McLeod's family home. My maternal grandmother was born nearby also. In spite of this the details of Norman's life, especially after his departure for Canada, were little more than scraps, and some of these grossly inaccurate, for example 'Didn't he cut off a boy's ear for stealing an apple?'

Within our own family he was remembered as forward and full of pranks. An ancestral relation was a schoolboy from Loch Crocach who met Norman, then a youth, driving some cattle. Norman asked the boy to assist him but the lad refused, claiming that he would have to learn part of the second Psalm to recite in school the following day. Norman assured him that there would be no problem as he would teach him the psalm as they went. When the time came for the lesson, Norman had taught the boy some nonsense verses which began with the first line of the metrical psalm that he was to learn. The verses were not strictly a parody. They began with only one line of the psalm and then went on so as to be much more easily remembered than the lesson that was to be learned. The boy was duly thrashed for the sacrilege the following day.

Early publications, like Macdonald's *The Highlanders of Waipu*, published in 1928, were restricted to small numbers of copies, few of which reached these parts. The Rev John McLeod of Inverness in 1930 published the booklet 'The North Country Separatists' in which he records some 'stories that tradition has preserved about this remarkable man'. He also gave a full description of the life and works of the young Norman in the Highlands:

> There was a forwardness and masterfulness about him that he could not hide or hold in check. He was no moderate. He was rather inclined to be immoderate in his polemic against the ruling party in the Church Courts. He began to preach while he was still not even a licentiate, a grave irregularity.

He describes Norman's famous journey through the Highlands to find out how many real Christians there were.

His quest, the man from Clachtoll claimed, produced only two.

The Rev Dr John Kennedy, minister of Dingwall Free Church until his death in 1884, was the son of the Rev John Kennedy, whose evangelical prowess was claimed to have effected the conversion of many of the young men of Assynt (including Norman McLeod) while he was assistant to the infamous Pastor William MacKenzie. Dr John wrote *The Days of the Fathers of Ross-shire*, first published in 1861. In it he paints a vivid picture of Pastor William, the drunken minister of Assynt. He was frequently absent for long periods. A visit to Ross-shire 'would be an affair of a month's length at least and the people never clamoured for his return'.

During one such absence he was accompanied by the beadle, who also happened to be his ghillie, and the local piper to boot. A local, when asked when the minister would return replied, 'I don't know and I don't care. If he had only left the piper he could have stopped away as long as he pleased.'

The Rev Dr John claimed that Norman McLeod was suddenly converted and 'began at once to prepare for the ministry'. But Norman separated from the Church to found a sect for himself. Kennedy admitted that 'the anxiety and disappointments of this trying season were particularly painful to my father'.

The iniquitous Highland Clearances, where the indigenous people were removed to make way for sheep, lasted for more than ten years. Assynt, which was cleared mainly between 1812 and 1821/22, belonged to the Sutherland Estate owned by the Marquis and Marchioness of Stafford. Those 'cleared' were the pastoral people who bred hardy black cattle in the glens in the hinterland mainly. Drovers took their surplus cattle to the markets in the south and returned with the money, perhaps a year later.

An elderly man giving evidence to a Government Commission in 1883 claimed that over 50 townships in Assynt 'were made desolate and the tenants sent hither and thither over the face of the earth and when they found a resting place at all, it was on the poorest scraps, rocks and bogs, and often put among the poorest crofters, intensifying their poverty'.

The landlords had the right to impose ministers of their choice, who were paid high stipends and lived lives of relative luxury and often, as in the case of Pastor William of Assynt, debauchery.

Norman McLeod railed against the patronage ministers and the general injustice of the social order.

In 1803 the Marquis of Stafford, married to the Countess of Sutherland, inherited a vast fortune. The clearances were not carried out from financial necessity but were examples, sadly seen world-wide, even to this day, of the poor being brought to suffering and greater poverty through the greed of their wealthy superiors. The marquis was a member of the House of Lords and his commissioner, Loch, an MP. There was no recourse for the dispossessed.

So it was not until the arrival of the *Lion of Scotland*, and later *Watchman Against the World* by Flora McPherson, that the rounded picture of the amazing adventures and voyages became available to those of us in his native parish.

In the early 1960s I was approached by two New Zealand girls, driving an old car. They wanted to be shown the birthplace of the Rev Norman. They said they were from the district of Waipu where he and his people settled. They mentioned that there were memorials to them in Cape Breton and Waipu. I willingly took them to Clachtoll to show them the then bare ridge where his family home had been. It surprised them that his birthplace by the rocky edge of the seashore was unmarked. From that meeting was born the determination that one day the place would be suitably marked. Thirty years later, in 1994, a goodly gathering of some 400 people, including a Canadian pipe band, attended the unveiling of a memorial on the rocky headland at Clachtoll. A large, rough-hewn block of Assynt marble was chosen for the monument. The inscription ended with the Gaelic sentiment – '*Lean iad e gu iomall na talmhainn* ('They followed him to the ends of the earth'). The speaker representing New Zealand was none other than the author of this book, Neil Robinson, who has used part of the inscription 'To the Ends of the Earth' as the title of his second book, published in 1997, which brings the story of the various communities involved in the migrations up to date.

The Hon. Roland Thornhill, former Deputy Premier of Nova Scotia, represented that part of the world, and spoke of the epic film waiting to be made on the migrations.

The formalities over, everyone was invited to the large hospitality marquee where Gaelic songs of Assynt were soon being sung. More than one local said, sotto voce, 'What would he think of this *himself*?' And the same question was posed later at a superb, crowded international ceilidh in Lochinver Village Hall.

Since the erection of the monument there is an increasing number of visitors from Canada and New Zealand each year, seeking their roots. The twinning arrangement between St Anns and Waipu has been extended to form the Assynt/St Anns/Waipu connection.

Norman A. MacAskill, OBE, JP
Lochinver, 1999

FOREWORD

In August 1951 Miss Mary Sutherland and her kinsman, Roderick Finlayson, visited the annual Gaelic Mod, or assembly, held at St Ann's on Cape Breton Island in the province of Nova Scotia. Miss Sutherland had come from Waipu, a little village in New Zealand, a six months' journey by sailing-ship, as her grandfather had proved, although she herself had covered the distance by aeroplane in less than a week.

One day when Miss Sutherland was at the Mod, two men came up and greeted her. " We are your cousins ", they said. Linking arms with her, they explained in more detail just who they were. One of them, it seemed, had come over from Scotland for the Mod; the other had lived all his life on Cape Breton Island. All three were cousins, but it was necessary to go back a hundred years and more to prove their relationship.

Miss Sutherland was delighted at the encounter, but not as surprised as one might think. For the Gaelic Mod at St Ann's that year had a special significance for families living in Scotland and New Zealand as well as in Nova Scotia. Part of the reason was given when the Hon. Angus L. Macdonald, Premier of Nova Scotia, unveiled a memorial built of granite from an old grist mill in the Norman McLeod Memorial Park at St Ann's. The inscription read as follows:

" Rev Norman McLeod, 1780–1866 ".

> " As clergyman, schoolmaster and magistrate he moulded the character of this community for a generation. He emigrated to Pictou in 1817, led his band of Scots to St Ann's in 1820 and remained here until 1851, when he again led his followers first to Australia and finally to New Zealand."

For New Zealanders, the most important fact is that, largely through the example of Norman McLeod, over 800 men, women and children sailed in their own six ships to new homes across the world nearly a century ago. Nova Scotians, especially the residents of the conservative Cape Breton district, where he had spent thirty years, remember him as the dour, iron-hard man whose personality has gained a place in the island's folk-lore. In Scotland, when still a young man, he was the stormy petrel whose activities gave warning of the religious upheaval that, thirty years later, was to disrupt the Church of Scotland.

There are photographs and pictures of Norman McLeod still in existence. They show a stern, powerfully built man, with an arrogant eye and a hard mouth. In New Zealand, too, there are stories still current of his last years and of his death. Whether they were told by his followers or by his enemies, they all testify to his unusual qualities. There was, for example, the man who, when the minister arrived at church, would kneel before him to take off his knee-boots. He would tell, with pride in his own abasement, how on one occasion Norman McLeod jerked his leg impatiently and upset him on the floor. When he died, he was buried across the foot of McLeod's grave—a retainer watching loyally, even in death, over the chief of his clan.

During his lifetime, he was hated and admired with equal intensity. When Hugh Sutherland took a wife, she was unwise enough to appear in church shortly after the wedding wearing a gay crinoline gown. Norman McLeod changed the subject of his sermon immediately. In fervent, frightening language, he spoke about the foolish woman who showed her lightness and frivolity by appearing, so soon after the solemn sacrament of marriage, in a dress that had been inspired by the agents of Satan. "And", he added, "no doubt you are pregnant. What sort of children do you expect to bring into the world if this is your attitude?"

The girl, quivering with shame and fear, sat dazed beside her husband. The congregation itself was overwhelmed, the inhumanity of the minister's words fighting with the respect and trust that he had won over many years. No one spoke up in her defence, but the minister made many lifelong enemies that day.

A man of indomitable will and great physical strength, Norman McLeod did not lightly give up his earthly life. As he lay dying, the people came to the window of his room, and he would speak to them.

" I would gladly lie here for a hundred years ", he said, " if I thought I could save one soul."

Even after his death he could still arouse an almost fanatical devotion or an equally positive dislike. The pulpit in which he had preached was removed from the church by some of his followers, for they did not want anyone else to take his place. And while his coffin was being carried on the shoulders of his friends on the long road to the cemetery, one man, who had not been friendly with the minister during his life, offered to relieve one of the bearers. At such a time emotions run high, and sympathy can often turn suddenly to passion. The bearer looked at the volunteer and said: " Do you think I would allow you to touch his coffin? " The other, his anger flaring, replied as he turned away: " Then you can take him to hell yourself."

But such stories do not give the key to the power of this remarkable man. At times he provoked hostility, but for the most part he fostered, by his own example and compelling argument, the simple Christian virtues. He lived in a different world from that of today, and there is no doubt that he was suited to his environment.

One tribute to him was written by a man who, not quite accurately, perhaps, classed himself as an unfriendly critic of the minister. What he probably meant was that he took a more objective view of him than did some contemporaries.

" He was a big man of leonine countenance, a giant mentally and physically, and recalled to one's memory the character of the great cardinal—

> 'He was a scholar, and a ripe and good one,
> Exceeding wise, fair spoken and persuading,
> Lofty and sour to those that loved him not,
> But to those men that sought him, sweet as summer.'

" He ought indeed to have been a cardinal or a pope, for in that position he would shine; while with us he was lost. I have heard him in church castigating one of his parishioners at a dreadful rate for a trivial offence of which we thought little; yet this man was one of his special friends. Next day we visited him at his hospitable home, and while sitting around the table he was full of youthful talk, simple and sweet as a child. He played the part of father to the whole community, and like a good father he bore no malice to anyone who came under his lash. If anyone attempted to dictate to him, he flung defiance in his face. If they assumed airs of superiority, he quickly levelled them. He always preached man's innate dignity, which neither riches nor learning could add to nor labour, poverty nor weakness degrade. He taught all men to trust each other as brothers. He himself would help anyone in their most menial tasks, and he never assumed any airs or sought any reward."

This book attempts to tell something of the story of Norman McLeod and the other Highlanders, nearly all of them from the West Coast of Scotland and the Inner Hebrides, who during more than fifty years of pioneering and arduous travel preserved their identity and brought, first to Nova Scotia and then to New Zealand, the atmosphere of a Highland community. They were a closely knit community, accepting changes slowly in their homes. Nearly one hundred years after their forebears had left Scotland, it was still a commonplace for children to chatter in Gaelic, although they might forget it when they went out into the world. Like most Highlanders, too, their racial memories were long, and tradition meant much to them. And so, when Mary Sutherland visited Nova Scotia for the Gaelic Mod; when she listened to an eminent scholar, Dr Alexander Kerr, of Dalhousie University, extol the virtues of Norman McLeod to an audience that included Chief Flora McLeod from the Island of Skye; when she watched the people of St Ann's re-enact in pageantry the sailing of the minister and his followers for the far lands of the south—while all this happened, she was not very surprised to meet kinsmen from two widely separated parts of the world. And to discover that, although their paths had led in different directions, she still had much in common with them.

The stories told in the following pages came from many people in many different places. Some of these who helped me are mentioned in the text. To them, and to all the others whose kindness, warm hospitality and good humour made my work a pleasure, I give my thanks. The settlements that the Scottish Nova Scotians founded in New Zealand a hundred years ago are still united by the old tradition of " Ceud Mile Failte "—" A Hundred Thousand Welcomes "; and those who have gone to live elsewhere have taken the same spirit with them.

My thanks go also to Malcolm McCharles, Esq., of Pictou, a cousin to many New Zealand Nova Scotians; to the librarians at the Auckland Public Library, and at the Mitchell Library, Sydney, Australia, for their prompt and able assistance; to the proprietors of the *Weekly News*, Auckland, and to its editor, H. I. Macpherson, Esq., for his encouragement and generous help.

And finally, I should like to mention that, while the book was in the printer's hands, death claimed two of those who helped me greatly with this story—Mrs Willina Lang, aged 89, and Mrs Norman Finlayson, aged 90. Their passing will be regretted, but their lives were rich beyond ordinary measure. I hope that something of their character is caught in these pages.

NEIL ROBINSON

Campbell's Bay,
Auckland.
June 18, 1952.

CHAPTER ONE

THE LION OF SCOTLAND, AND HOW IT WENT TO A FAR COUNTRY

" QUICK, here he comes! " an excited voice called. Like a flock of sparrows the small boys scattered from the door that opened on to the street.

From our hiding-places we watched an old man walk by. He had a bristling beard that might have inspired fear, but the eyes that he turned in our direction were mild and merry, as though he himself was sharing in our fun.

" What was his name? " I whispered, trying to recapture that first exhilarating moment of terror.

" The Ooorrsh," my friend replied. He dwelt on the opening sound, rolled the ' r ' tremendously, and subsided in an explosion of hissing, as if the kitchen tap had been turned on suddenly. So grand was the effect that his eyes widened and his cheeks almost popped with delight.

" But what does it mean? "

" I don't know. You'll have to ask the grown-ups that."

By now the man was out of sight, and we were free to play once more on the footpath outside the store. Its dark interior smelt of home-cured bacon, cough lollies and leather. The road was empty, except for an antique motor-car parked near the church. There was no sound on that mild summer's day, not even the clicking of the old man's boots.

Cottages tucked away behind hedges, a few old-fashioned shops, empty sections where bees rioted in the long meadow-grass. Except for one thing, it might have been any of a hundred small country villages, centres that came to life for a few hours on occasional days, and then lapsed back into slumber.

There was, of course, the war memorial, a simple obelisk that was repeated in many parts of the country. But the

Monument for Pioneers was something different. Along the road from where we played, a tall granite pillar rose into the sky. Twenty feet high it was, although to us it seemed much higher then. On its top balanced a defiant lion, poised on two sturdy legs. His face had something of the benevolence that one associated with God. I used to think that he was studying a book held in his two front paws, and that was the reason for his sublime and thoughtful expression.

" That is the Lion of Scotland," my mother explained to me; and then she showed me something that I had not noticed before. On the six sides of the monument's base, names were deeply carved in the stone. " You see," she went on, " your grandfather and his people came here from Scotland. They lived for a little while in a place called Nova Scotia, and these are the ships on which they sailed to New Zealand."

And there they were, sure enough. Handsome little boats, with fine sails, all carved in the Aberdeen granite.

" You should be very proud of them," my mother continued, " and be kind to your grandfather."

The logic, I suspect, escaped me; but there may have been a remote connection with my next question.

" What does the Ooorrsh mean? " I asked, dwelling on each sound with a fearful joy.

My mother looked a little surprised, but answered patiently. " It is a Gaelic word," she said, " the nickname given to one of our men. Gaelic is the true language of Scotland, although it has been replaced to some extent by English. Your grandfather could speak it before he learned English, and your grandmother, although she was born here in New Zealand, still thinks of it as her native speech. It is a very expressive language. Here in Waipu, most of the old people prefer to use it when they are very happy or very angry; or when they are in church."

Gaelic; the Lion of Scotland; the quaint figure of the Ooorrsh, not so fearful as his nickname; I could not have explained why, but they all left in my mind the impression that Waipu was, in some way, different from other places where we lived when I was a small boy. There were other impressions, too. New Year's Day, when the green, bare sports-ground near the school suddenly filled with people; kilted figures, such as I had never imagined, strutted majestically about in beautiful boots and gaiters, producing music that stirred and bewildered the mind. A splendid tartan disguised many a pleasant old man who, in other days, had stopped to talk to me. Now they were as remote as gods.

I remember, too, the beaches that seemed so white, the crashing waves and the sound of birds; the magic blue islands whose ragged profiles broke the horizon. The gig bowled smoothly along a quiet country road, down through a red cutting in the hillside and there, curving gracefully round to Bream Tail, was the beach. Spreading pohutukawa trees made a cool shade against the glare of the sun; and out beyond the waves crashed endlessly.

The road to Waipu from the railway station passed through the Gorge, an ominous place when first encountered, for the journey was usually made at night. The service car turned and twisted, its engine roaring as we pulled up a hill. The lights flickered on the road, and then shone out over a dizzy black drop where trees and tall ferns showed up like fleeting ghosts. Below us, the roar of water could sometimes be heard when the engine ran quietly.

An ominous place at night, but how different when visited on a cheerful summer day! The mystery had gone, the sun picked out a cool pattern on the road. The waterfall, so fearful when heard in the darkness, now sparkled in sunshine. It no longer thundered like Niagara, but its size and sound diminished, dropped down between banks that were covered with a lusty tropical growth.

From the entrance to the Gorge a wide valley—the Braigh—ran towards the sea. The bush had disappeared from here. Green fields, rectangular outcrops of pine and macrocarpa trees showed where the pioneers had been at work. The houses were sturdily built of wood, for larger families than in most cases now tenanted them. But, I remember, they still bore traces of their earlier life. The kitchen, with its worn step and open door, was still the centre of the house. It faced the sun; the fowls, a cat and a dog or two enjoyed the warmth and the scent of cooking that drifted out. Even then, I could feel that here were homes that had mellowed as people lived out their lives in them.

There was the church, with rows of discreetly black-bonneted women. Although I did not know it at the time, they had brought their own version of the Presbyterian Church with them, a church that one remarkable man had established from his study of ecclesiastical history, plus a large proportion of personal theology. No one-day Christians were they. With many of them religion entered into every thought and action, and helped to frame the distinctive character that was one of the most abiding impressions of Waipu. Grace before meals was no loud invocation. It was whispered unobtrusively by the head of the house; and a stranger was often confused to find that it had ended before he realised it had started. Nor, when I first knew the people, was there any ostentation about Bible-reading. The New Testament was read, often in Gaelic, and its lessons formed the subject of silent meditation. Although old friends, in the Highland tradition, would argue with amazing profundity over various interpretations.

My grandmother had a three-legged cooking-pot that, with the passing of time, had fallen on evil days. It stood out on a back porch holding grain for the fowls. Then one day a visitor from Scotland happened to notice it and remarked: " You don't see many of those in Scotland now, outside museums."

My grandmother did not say anything, but not long after the visitor had departed the family noticed the pot, shining with unaccustomed polish, standing in a place of honour in the hall.

Every-day articles of one generation become the treasured heirlooms of the next. But in the transition much is lost. An old man dies, his sons or relatives destroy as " junk " the litter of papers, books and correspondence that, in fifty years time, might have given a valuable clue to the ways of life of a lost age. Timber is stripped from the old house to build barns or cowsheds. Rain, rats and time hasten the destruction of homes that, with care and interest, would have survived usefully for many years.

In the same way, in Waipu, time brought a touch of romance to every-day actions of the pioneers. Neither they nor their sons and daughters saw anything unusual in the fact that, with little but faith in themselves and a good practical knowledge of life, they built and sailed ships across the world from Nova Scotia to New Zealand. Or in the fact that, buffeted by strange circumstances, they remained a closely linked community through difficult days until they found a permanent home on the land at Waipu.

Independence, the ability to turn their hands to many tasks, an invincible belief in God and their own future, were part of their birthright. Lack of these qualities would have been more remarkable than their possession. For life in those days made them necessary for survival. If, in the eyes of the present generation, they have been invested with a touch of glamour, does that rob them of their merit?

As men and women grow older, old times, old ways begin to have a greater appeal. Those who left Waipu in their youth, expecting never to see the place again, find their minds turning back, their memories holding pictures of scenes that they had not thought to remember. They become more curious about the background to the settlement in which their fathers took part, and also more interested in the legends that grow up around people and places. History becomes a mingling of fact and fantasy; and out of this combination there often comes a truer picture than could be gained from a bare recital of events.

Talking to the surviving members of the first generation after the pioneers arrived, you get fact and fancy in full measure. With them, as with generations of Highlanders before them, a story is not something to be set down in cold print, but a living thing. It gains character with each telling until it becomes a legend or an epic.

They are skilful talkers, humorous, deft at underlining character, sympathetic with human frailties of which, they have learned, almost everyone has his share. As they relax comfortably and talk, they take you on a journey that may touch on many far-distant places. You learn about the Waipu sea-captain who, though over seventy, tackled bare-handed a

Malayan running amok on his ship near Singapore. Disdaining to use the pistol in his pocket, he was killed for his pains. You will be told of feats in the kauri forests and on the football fields by men from the Nova Scotian settlements.

You will be told, as I was, of some who went away and became wealthy, controlling fleets of ships, establishing businesses that are still flourishing. Their conversation will range through more than one hundred years, recalling tales that had been passed down to them in much the same way.

As I listened, the Waipu of my childhood memories became the background for something richer and more varied. I learned that, while Waipu was the centre, there were sister-settlements that built up their own traditions of sea-faring, ship-building, timber-milling and farming. I began to know the men who had led the migration from Scotland to Nova Scotia, to Australia and finally to New Zealand. They took their place in the general story of a period during which Britain was discovering the world, and sending her people to colonise many parts of it. Numerically, they may not have been very important, but in other ways their story was unique; a chapter in the history of colonisation that was never repeated.

Ties with Scotland and with Nova Scotia have remained strong. One man will write letters to a kinsman and, when he dies, his son or daughter carries on. Every now and then someone will pack up for a trip to visit " cousins " they have never met before, although letters may have been exchanged for many years. They come back and tell stories of the Hebrides, Lochalsh, St Ann's and the Bras d'or Lakes that stretch deep into Cape Breton Island. Probing with enjoyment into family history, they will, in the fashion beloved by Highlanders, have established relationships after going back six or more generations. They will have gained knowledge to strengthen the verbal traditions of a century and more. Ian Matheson, for example, member of a family that built fast sailers still remembered in New Zealand, is delighted to discover, on the West Coast of Scotland, vessels with all the marks in their design of the Matheson ships.

In some cases, notably that of my friend Hector Clark,

verbal traditions do not need a great deal of outside support. For Hector, as he demonstrated the first time I met him, has a confident mastery over the broad lines of family history. He sat in the living-room of his Auckland house, a sparely-built man with a white moustache and brown, sinewy arms. He looked at me thoughtfully.

"I think I'll tell you something you may not know," he began, "about Duncan McKenzie, whom they called the Prince, and his brother Murdoch, the Captain; and how they learned their seamanship. My grandmother, their sister, married Hector McDonald. He was the greatest seaman of them all, and they were his pupils.

"But we must start, I think, with my great-grandfather, another Duncan McKenzie. Not to his face, but everywhere else, he was known as the Smuggler. A strange name, you think? Not so strange, perhaps, when you consider the times in which he lived.

"After the '45, conditions were very difficult in the Highlands, and on the coast where the McKenzies had their home. There was much restlessness among the young men. Instead of improving, life became worse, and Duncan decided to see if America held out a better chance for him. He made a home on Prince Edward Island, but I fancy did not see much of it. The War of Independence was over, and there was an honourable living to be made overcoming tariffs, and similar man-made barriers. There was no stigma attached to his action. The free-trader was a benefactor in most people's eyes.

"All this may seem a long way from Duncan, the Prince, and Murdoch, the Captain, who were to help found a settlement on the coast of far-away New Zealand. I did not meet their mother, the Smuggler's wife. But I remember my elder brother John telling how he once went up to Hector McKenzie's house at Waipu. There was a fire burning in the big fireplace, and beside it a rocking-chair with a very small, very old, bright-eyed lady sitting in it. She was nearly a hundred when she died, long after the Smuggler had gone to his rest.

"But at the time of which we're talking she was young, with much travelling ahead of her; and her husband a vigorous man with sons growing up around him—when he was home. It may have been for their sake that, some time before the Battle of Waterloo, he decided to return to Scotland; or it may have been that America was growing uncomfortable for him. The family settled at Applecross, in Ross-shire, and there the boys were educated.

"It was there, too, that they met Hector McDonald. He was interested in young Duncan and Murdoch, partly because they were near his own age, and from a strange country, but also because he had his eye on their sister Ann, whom he later married. They, for their part, were interested in him, and the handy little vessel in which he traded with England, Ireland and the main Scottish ports. On alternate voyages he would take the boys with him, and he taught them much of what they knew about navigation and the other crafts of the sea.

"I remember Hector well, for he was my grandfather. When we asked him his age, he would never give the year of his birth, but would say instead: 'The year after the Battle of Trafalgar.'

"But the McKenzies were restless, and Scotland still not a great place for a man with ambition. The Smuggler, leaving Ann with her husband, returned with his wife and three sons—now young men—to Canada. They had been away too long; his abandoned farm was in other hands. But the boys did not worry about that. With their base at Baddeck, on Cape Breton Island, they built ships, made trading voyages and eventually established themselves as merchants. They became part of an isolated but alert community. Its spiritual centre—and that meant something to those people at that time—was at St Ann's Bay. . . ."

When the McKenzies arrived, the settlement at St Ann's had been established for little more than ten years. Cut out of the forest that stretched north to the Gulf of St Lawrence, it was a halting-place for thirty years in one of the strangest migrations in British history. Its leader, Norman McLeod, is still remembered nearly one hundred years after his death—in Scotland, where he was born; in Nova Scotia, where he spent the years of his maturity, and in New Zealand, his final resting-place.

"Prophet, priest and king of the northland", was one description applied to him in Nova Scotia. In physique and in mental power he was above the ordinary. Fisherman and farmer; magistrate, schoolmaster and preacher; graduate of Aberdeen University and student at Edinburgh until theological differences with his professors abruptly ended his stay there, Norman McLeod had a dominating, often harsh personality, a sudden, unexpected tenderness and a gift for oratory that made willing slaves of many with whom he came into contact.

He was over seventy when, after thirty-four years in Nova Scotia, he once again decided to take his followers to a new land, to subdue yet another wilderness. Until his death in his eighty-sixth year, he retained his strength, his eloquence, his respect for the old ways and his hatred of cities and other disruptive influences. He caused the colony established in New Zealand to resemble, in many respects, a section of the Scottish Highlands set down in a strange land, modified to only a minor degree by the years in Nova Scotia.

This and much else did Hector Clark tell me as we sat in his quiet Auckland home.

The days when the Smuggler crossed the Atlantic have long passed away. Hector McDonald, born the year after Trafalgar, has been dead a good many years, although he was a fresh-faced, clean-shaven man of ninety when Hector Clark last saw him. There is little written material to give a clue to the complex personality of Norman McLeod. But to Hector and his diminishing band of contemporaries these men are as alive as they ever were. Slightly more than life-size, perhaps. Their sayings and their actions are magnified in the glass of unwritten history, but retain their essential perspective.

Before I left him, Hector added a footnote to the story of his grandfather. In the early 1860's, Duncan McKenzie, the Prince, wrote to his brother-in-law, Hector McDonald, suggesting that he should come out to New Zealand with his family from Scotland; and adding that a 100-acre farm awaited him in the Braigh. As the ship took him south on the long run round the Cape of Good Hope, the thought may have struck Hector that now at last he would see the final stage of the long migration. He may have thought, too, of the quiet little village in Applecross Bay, from which he had sailed so often with young Duncan and Murdoch McKenzie. Soon he would see them again.

His mind may have gone back to the letters which he had received from his kinsfolk as they adventured round the world. Letters that told first of the desire of the people at St Ann's for another home in the warmer lands of the south; of the building of ships and the voyage to Australia; of the search, there and in New Zealand, for land where they could once again establish themselves as a self-supporting community; of the other ships which had followed until more than 800 Scottish Nova Scotians were living on the beautiful coast north of Auckland that runs down from Bream Bay to Omaha.

Perhaps, as he settled down on the farm with his family, he marvelled at all that had happened. It is more likely, however, that he accepted it as the natural course of events. To those of his time and race, the orderly pattern of life was not so fixed that it could not be altered at will. Man the individual was still the most important thing in his Creator's eyes. If several hundred men, women and children, many of them speaking only Gaelic, decided to move half-way round the world to a land they had never seen and of which they knew little, God, and their own ingenuity, would see that the journey would be safely accomplished.

When plans for celebrating the hundredth anniversary of the settlement's foundation were being discussed, there was a suggestion that the Government should be asked to subsidise any funds that were collected for a permanent memorial. This, it should be added, is a common practice in New Zealand.

"Would you go begging among your neighbours for money to put a headstone on your father's grave?" growled one sturdy old pioneer's son. "If the Government is asked for help, the committee sees none of my money!"

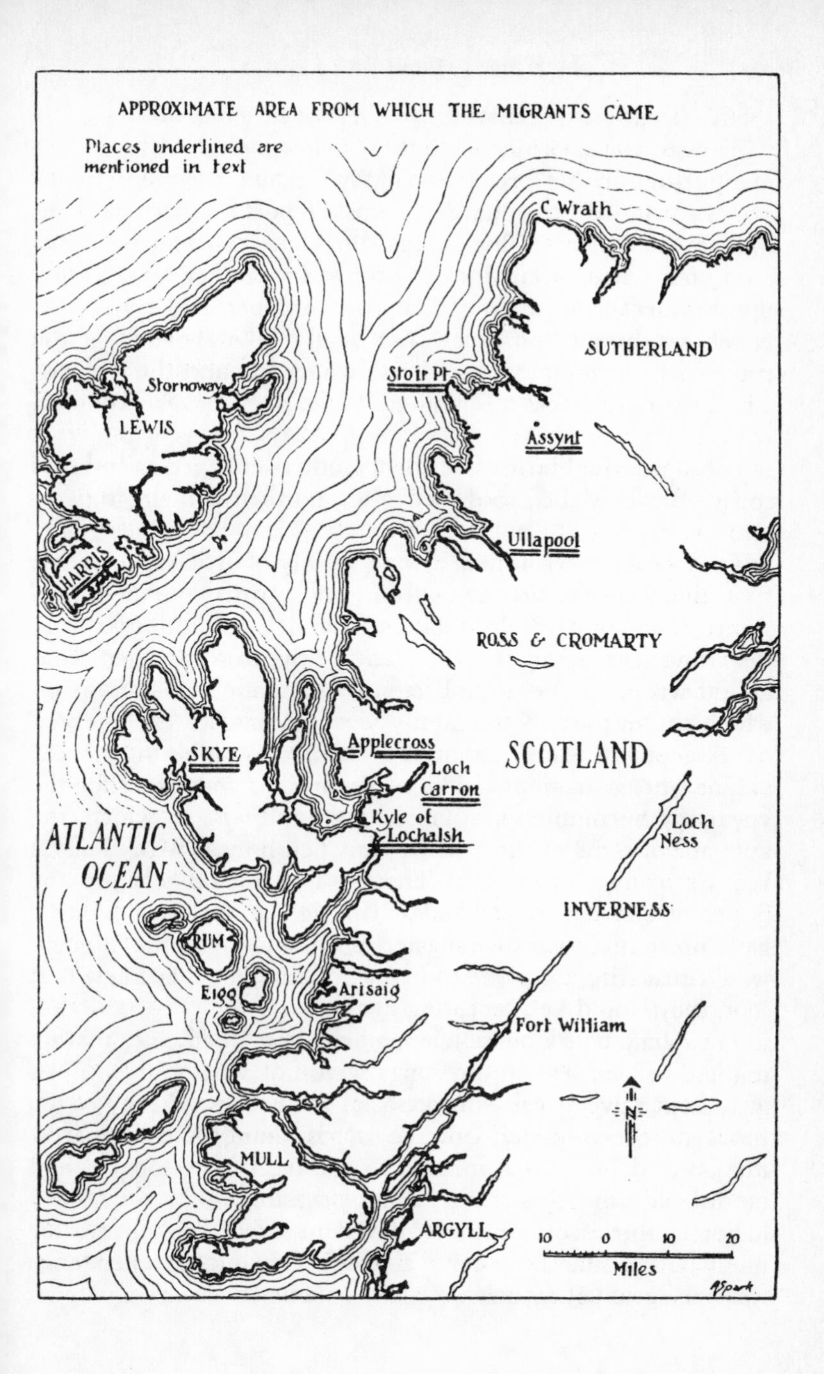
APPROXIMATE AREA FROM WHICH THE MIGRANTS CAME
Places underlined are mentioned in text
C. Wrath
SUTHERLAND
Stoir Pt
Stornoway
LEWIS
Assynt
Ullapool
HARRIS
ROSS & CROMARTY
SKYE
Applecross
SCOTLAND
Loch Carron
Kyle of Lochalsh
Loch Ness
ATLANTIC OCEAN
INVERNESS
RUM
Eigg
Arisaig
Fort William
N
MULL
ARGYLL
10 0 10 20
Miles

His viewpoint was shared by others of his generation.

He was, perhaps unconsciously, following the independent line pursued by his forefathers. When they were preparing to migrate from Nova Scotia, there was a report that free passages were available from Britain to Australia. No one was very interested. Men went into the forest for timber, and skilled ship-builders from among their own number laid down two vessels—of about 300 tons—that would take the first of the emigrants. They provided their own crews, and the women-folk prepared stocks of food and clothing for a six-month voyage.

Those who had farms sold them; others engaged in business collected their debts, paid their bills and turned their property into useful goods or gold.

They brought with them a wide variety of articles; blankets that the women had made from wool grown on their own sheep; leather made by their own tanners; stout casks from their own craftsman cooper. There was iron salvaged from an old wreck on the Cape Breton coast, made into a crane on which the mother of the family would hang her three-legged cooking pot in a new country. There were spinning-wheels, violins but no bagpipes, sides of bacon and corn-meal for the voyage; a combination knife, fork and spoon which the ancestor of some of them had used when he was with General Wolfe's army at Quebec. There was a medal won by the father of one family at Ciudad Rodrigo, in Spain, before he gave up soldiering and went across the wide Atlantic. There were cultivating tools and tools for building, for they knew that soon they would be pioneering again.

They had books on religion, navigation, medicine, mathematics. Their stories and songs were not written down, but were kept alive at ceillidhs or social gatherings. Many of the tunes were traditional, but the words changed. The bards, mimics and humorists, in their expressive Gaelic tongue, had no difficulty in improvising for any occasion.

For centuries before they arrived in Nova Scotia, and for many years after they came to New Zealand, independence was a by-product of their way of life. There was no shop down the road, no well-stocked warehouses were within easy reach. This situation produced leaders, on whom the less assertive members of the community leaned, but it also fostered to an extraordinary degree the self-reliant spirit.

There was plenty of scope for self-reliance, as well as for good leadership, in the new colony. Deliberately, they had selected an area covered in heavy forest and scrub, rejecting in its favour an offer of pastoral lands farther south. Alone among organised bodies of settlers up to that time, they were already skilled timber-workers; the forest which daunted and repelled many others anxious to establish farms was no enemy to them. Land that would grow crops and yield timber for boats and houses, a coastline where fish could be caught—these were the chief requirements of the new area.

They knew, from past experience, that they could produce sufficient food and a surplus of saleable goods even in the first years; and it was an old-established custom that, when returns were small, the young men could go and find work in a variety of occupations until they were wanted again on the farm.

But, for the great majority, in the early years, subsistence farming was the rule. A wide variety of produce was grown. Cattle, sheep and pigs were raised as much for home use as for sale. No one dreamed that by the end of the nineteenth century New Zealand's farm economy would be geared to a huge export system, with entire districts producing vast quantities of butter, cheese and meat; and little else. With the change, money became more plentiful, but life lost something of its variety and simplicity. The pioneers' economy was primitive; their need for money not great. But their larders were usually full of home-grown food, and their hospitality was open-hearted.

In another way, too, the Nova Scotian settlement differed from those in other parts of New Zealand. The founders had no desire to develop a city, or even a town. In Otago, Canterbury, Nelson and Wellington an urban area was laid out before the migrants arrived. But the Nova Scotians, with memories of their way of life in the Scottish Highlands, looked only for a continuation of their traditional habits in a more pleasant land. Their opinions were confirmed by what they had seen of Melbourne, seething with the turmoil brought about by the gold-rush.

As Duncan McKenzie, the Prince, now a responsible man charged with the negotiations for acquiring land, wrote to the Governor of New Zealand: "We speak the Gaelic language, and there are many of our old people who speak that language only, so that it becomes a matter of the greatest importance that our people should, as far as possible, be located in the same place; and more especially, we unite with our Pastor, Mr McLeod, in desiring that this should be so, on account of devotional purposes."

"A settlement not only for ourselves, but also for those to follow us from Nova Scotia, so that we may form a community, and be as near to each other as practicable." That is how Duncan specified their aims. And that is why Waipu was never more than the centre of a farming and fishing community, although its settlers were as numerous as those who founded many a flourishing town in the South.

The church and school were established there; it was as convenient as any part of the coast for the small vessels likely to call; and stores naturally opened at the Centre, as it is still known to most of those born in the district.

And so, never far from a sight of the wide-spreading Pacific Ocean, clearings began to appear for the first time on the bush and scrub-covered shores of Bream Bay. Small marks in a universal and varied greenness, they were linked by tracks that became the life-lines of a community. It was in these clearings, that gradually grew larger with the passing of years, that the Highlanders built their last homes. To many of them the days of their youth became a long-gone dream. The Hebrides, the strange and beautiful coast running up from Lochalsh to the craggy forehead of Sutherlandshire—memories of these places were overlaid with stronger memories of Cape Breton. Its long winters and brilliant summers were dimmed by thoughts of the voyage to another land, of precarious settlements on the rim of the empty Australian continent.

Now, once again, their cherished possessions were set up

about another hearth. They had land of their own. The children grew up, married, and brought into the world grand-children who still spoke the familiar Gaelic tongue more fluently than the English they learned at the schools. The young men, many of them, went away; for as in Scotland and Nova Scotia there was not enough land to support them all. The sea still attracted the more adventurous among them; and these would come back at intervals with stories of strange meetings with cousins, or relatives of friends, in the busy ports of the world. Later, as often as not, they would retire to the farm where they had been born.

Life was uneventful, but not dull, in the land where they now lived. For then, more so than today, work and pleasure were closely linked. Community effort made light tasks that would have daunted a single man. And when men and women met together for work, the routine would be made pleasant by songs and cheerful arguments. Many of the stories that are still repeated in Waipu seem to come from another world.

" They were all individuals," one man told me, reaching back into his memory for a description that would fit his recollections of the men and women who were old when he was young. " They acted in whatever way seemed right to them; they worked out their own destiny, in small matters as well as in big. The community was held together not by uniformity, but by the varied efforts of varied men and women. For them, in their quiet district, life took on a rich and colourful pattern."

Inevitably, as New Zealand's agricultural revolution gained force, the pattern of life at Waipu, Omaha, Kauri and the Whangarei Heads changed with the changing times. The old people died, farms were sold, young men and women looked elsewhere, as Scots always have done, for fields in which to employ their talents. But still, after a hundred years, much of the land is occupied by descendants of the pioneers. Young McKenzies, in the sixth generation since the Smuggler, are now farming land which had never felt a white man's tread when their ancestor crossed the Atlantic so long ago; and there are many others in the same category.

Hector Clark introduced me to the Smuggler and his family. Talking with other men and women, I became acquainted with a host of colourful characters, all of whom had played some part in the shaping of a settlement. There were rigid Calvinists, and there were others who had retained their ancestors' love for music, dancing and whisky. Many were staunch followers of Norman McLeod, conforming to his autocratic control of their domestic, religious and public affairs; but others reserved the right to choose for themselves, and tolerated but did not obey the leader. There were men and women who made themselves slaves to duty and their code of life; but there were others, too, who would not be stampeded into a departure from their established routine. Sublimely uninterested in money or material success, they worked when it was necessary. A tight roof over their heads, enough plain food to satisfy their bodily wants—this they required; but more important was good conversation, time to sit and think.

For all these there was a place in the transplanted Highland society of Waipu. The indolent, the unworldly or the unambitious, living their serene lives on a few half-cultivated acres, proved by their own example that wealth was not the only standard by which a full life could be judged. Their rejection of the material world, their independence and cheerfulness, helped to fashion the character of younger generations.

It is of all these that I write in the following chapters. The written word may be a poor substitute for the varied inflexions, the apt mimicry, the subtle phrasing of the experienced story-teller; and of this class there are still a considerable number abroad in the north. But the story-teller's art is a fleeting one, and even the pale shadow of his skill, caught in cold prose, may be better as a record than nothing at all.

The search for an understanding of their character took me back a long way, and became as fascinating as discovery itself. The men and women who came to Waipu were fashioned by their unusual environment; but their story would not be complete if it did not take into account the restlessness, the half-remembered griefs, the lost loyalties that sent them wandering across the world.

For Scotland, one era had ended with the breaking up of a highly-organised clan system, a feudal way of life. Another was to begin as Scottish men and women adapted themselves to new conditions in new lands. This, too, is part of the Waipu story.

CHAPTER TWO

SHEEP, RELIGION AND A LIFE THAT HAD GONE

At the age of twenty-three, James Sutherland swore that he would never again eat mutton or keep sheep. He respected his vow for the remaining seventy years of his life.

His hatred of the animals was well known. Thus, when a friend visited him on his Waipu farm, towards the end of his life, he was surprised to see some sheep grazing in one of the fields. He asked his host whether he had changed his mind.

Sutherland drew himself up to his full height of six feet and several inches. His voice came from the depths of a magnificent beard, above which glittered a pair of frosty eyes.

"No, those are not my sheep," he replied. "They belong to my neighbour. The fence is weak down there at the corner, but I do not propose to repair it. I let the brutes through," he roared, "just for the pleasure of dogging them out again!"

In most respects, James Sutherland was a judicious man, strong in his opinions, but capable of seeing most sides of a question. There must, I felt, have been some good reason for his attitude to what is usually considered a harmless and useful animal. And there was.

As a young man, James Sutherland took over his father's farm in the Highland county which gave him his name. It was freehold land, I was told, adjoining the estates of the Duke of Sutherland. The year was about 1818, a date not without significance in the history of the Highlanders.

There, in that quiet but well-populated glen, James saw something that made him decide to leave Scotland forever; and moreover, caused the sight of sheep to fill him always with hatred. His neighbours were evicted, and their land given over to southern sheep.

Here, in the words of the Rev Donald Sage, is a description of what James Sutherland may have seen: "Summonses of ejectment were issued and despatched all over the district. These must have amounted to upwards of a thousand. The summonses were distributed with the utmost preciseness. They were handed in at every house and hovel alike. All were made to feel the irresponsible power of the proprietor.

"The middle of the week brought on the day of the Strathnaver clearances. At an early hour of the day Mr Sellar, accompanied by the Fiscal and escorted by a strong body of Constables, Sheriff, Officers and others, commenced work at Gunmore. Their plan of operations was to clear the cottage of its inmates, giving them about half an hour to pack up and carry off their furniture, and then set fire to their cottage. To this plan they ruthlessly adhered."

A week later the disconsolate minister passed down the evicted strath. "The banks of the lake and river, formerly studded with cottages, now met the eye as a scene of desolation. The thatched roofs were gone off all the houses, but the walls remained. The flames of the preceding week still slumbered in the ruins; and sent up into the air spiral columns of smoke, whilst here a gable and there a long wall, undermined by the fire burning within them, might be seen tumbling to the ground. The sooty rafters of the cottages, as they were consumed, filled the air with a heavy and most offensive odour. In short, nothing could more vividly represent the horrors of grinding oppression, and the extent to which one man, dressed up in a little brief authority, will exercise that power without feeling or restraint, to the injury of his fellow creatures."

The events that roused the indignation of the good Mr Sage had already cast their shadow on many other parts of the Highlands. What happened to the dispossessed? Some were moved to new settlements near the coast, leaving behind them land where a few shepherds, their flocks and in many cases deer were the sole inhabitants. Others, in crowded migrant ships, went across the sea to Canada, many of them to Nova Scotia. For that was the nearest place to their homeland.

Among the Highlanders who eventually went to Waipu,

there was no bitterness, and in fact little talk about the clearances. The attitude of James Sutherland was rare enough to be remarked upon by others of his generation, and remembered by those who came after him. Many of those who settled in New Zealand had already left Scotland before the evictions reached their climax in the years following Waterloo.

There were a host of reasons for the move. Norman McLeod, the minister, departed because he sought a religious freedom that his country and the Church of his day denied him. The power of his personality induced many others to follow him. The Mathesons, from Lochalsh, were connected by marriage with the minister. But they were seamen also, and saw their livelihood dwindling on the Scottish coast. The McKays, the Campbells and many others were tenant-farmers in varying degrees of prosperity in Skye and the glens of the Western coast, chiefly in Ross-shire. Their rents were being raised steadily. They decided to go where they could buy land of their own and stay clear of a landlord's exactions.

Others, among them the Frasers, had seen service in Canada with the Highland regiments that took part in the capture of Quebec and Louisburg. They had settled on Prince Edward Island and in Nova Scotia long before the mass movement from Scotland began. Reports on conditions in Canada from them and their friends were one of the chief reasons why so many Scots went to North America.

A host of reasons for migrating, all of them inextricably bound up one with the other. Religion, economics, the sense of defeat that came with the breaking-up of the clans—all were linked with a melancholy period in Scotland's history. A period that nevertheless established Scotsmen in parts of the world that otherwise might have remained a wilderness for many more years.

Few echoes from the past disturbed the lives of the Waipu Scots. The present was too urgent for them to harbour old grievances. And yet individual families nursed traditions that went back to the days when the clans were all-powerful; and feuds, or alliances, might last for centuries. In Waipu, Campbells might marry McDonalds. But it was still possible for sturdy Tormod Mhor, otherwise Norman McDonald, to remember a black day in his family's history. Norman was the descendant of a man who escaped from the Massacre of Glencoe in 1692. One day, when he was many miles from home, a Campbell offered him dinner. Rather than accept hospitality from a member of that clan, Norman went hungry. Nor would he willingly have dealings with any who bore the name of Campbell. Even in Norman's case, however, time had succeeded in softening an ancient wrong; for, in discussing the offer of a meal, Norman admitted that there must be some good in the man!

The clan, as it had flourished in the centuries before Culloden, was a unit organised primarily for war. The position and power of the chief depended on the number of clansmen he could muster. Accordingly there arose an elaborate system of recruiting. Kinsmen or followers of the chief were given "tacks" or leases of land, and in turn took under-tenants who were counted on to provide the necessary number of men for the field. By systematic raiding, the population was efficiently maintained at an artificially high level. But once the days of cattle-lifting passed away, the people of the Highlands had to learn to support themselves on its scanty resources, and very often in isolated communities.

The unsuccessful rising of 1745 sounded the death-knell of their old way of life. But even if it had succeeded, the clans could not have continued to exist in defiance of changes that had already transformed England and the Lowlands. The rising was, to use the words of a sympathetic Englishman, "the last despairing rally of the Celt, the final romantic desperate revolt which began in the Hebrides and ended in 1746 in an April snowstorm on Culloden Moor".

The people who settled at Waipu came from an area where the inhabitants were as neutral as any Scot could be in a dispute. The coastal districts of Ross-shire and northern Inverness-shire, the islands dominated by Skye sent few warriors to aid the Stuart cause. Yet, when the Prince was a fugitive, it was in these same districts that he was loyally sheltered and helped in his escape. And their future was decided just as firmly as if they had themselves taken part in the march towards a throne.

It is a vague period in history. Novelists and romantic painters have conspired to give the picture that most people carry in their minds: A Celtic twilight, through which stumble the shadowy figures of Prince Charlie and his men, with kilted pipers sounding a sad lament. A twilight that allows no sharp outlines to be seen, as mysterious and formless as a misty Highland glen, where long-haired cattle peer shaggily through the fog.

The power of the chiefs was broken; although, as Sir Walter Scott noted, " the spirit of clanship subsisted no longer indeed as a law of violence, but still as a law of love. The Highlanders maintained, in many instances, their chiefs at their own expense; and they embodied themselves in regiments, that the head of the family might obtain military preferment." And this is still one of the chief impressions that can be gained of the little-documented period following Culloden. The English garrisons moved in, tartans and many other features of Highland life moved out. Prompted by loyalty, restlessness or economic necessity, young men in great numbers joined regiments recruited to fight Britain's wars. A staunch Hanoverian raised 500 men from his tenants and followers for the 42nd Highlanders—the Black Watch—in 1754. And it is calculated that between 1793 and 1815 forty battalions of the line and seven of militia were raised in the Central Highlands, a total of 37,600 men. In addition, there were many volunteer regiments.

While these men were fighting in North America, in India and on the expanding battle-fronts of Europe, the people who remained behind had another war on their hands, a war of attrition that could not be countered with weapons. A less glamorous war, but one which was to have a vital effect on their lives.

It had begun even before the '45. For centuries their life had been simple and primitive. " The tenantry in general ", wrote Sir John Sinclair, " have their lands intermixed with their neighbours, in what is called run-ridges. They have no enclosures, and prefer during the winter months an universal commonty of each other's lands for pasture, rather than be at the expense of herding, otherwise than by precarious attention of their numerous families of children." Before 1745, however, the new system of agriculture, which wrought such damage in even the settled rural life of England, had begun to penetrate the Highlands. A higher standard of produce was demanded. The old starveling cattle, the natural hay, the very light grain and inferior butter would no longer find a market. Cattle had been the basis of their economy. Too valuable to kill for meat, they had provided butter, milk, cheese, leather for boots and harness; while even the horns were used for spoons.

Many years before large-scale sheep-farming was introduced, reports of an easier way of life, a higher standard of living, were drifting into the remotest glens. Barefooted boys, runaways from poverty-stricken homes in the north, began to appear in the streets of Glasgow. Many of them could not speak English, but such was their tenacity that large numbers mastered their new environment. Soon there were few districts where the mothers of families did not receive help, either in money or in goods, from their devoted though absent sons.

And now we come back to James Sutherland and the sheep. Whatever tendencies may have been leading towards the break-up of the Highland feudal system, the increased value of wool was the decisive factor. There had always been sheep in the Highlands. Their wool and milk helped to provide food and clothing. They were yarded closely at times to fertilise land designed for crops. But for the most part they gained sustenance in the hills that were of no use for anything else. As the ewes produced lambs with remarkable infrequency, their numbers were not very great.

When wool prices rose in the young manufacturing towns of the south, it required little to set a new revolution on its way. Hungry, far-ranging southern sheep came into the glens. In the summer they found their pasture in the hills, but they needed also sheltered feeding during the autumn and the spring. And much of this fertile land was occupied by the cottages and fields of the clansmen. Where grouse-moors had been strictly preserved by the zealous factors of new owners, the need for sheltered grazing in the straths was even more urgent. The inevitable happened. The coarse-woolled, hardy, black-faced sheep, with their south-country shepherds, soon had their way. Large-scale sheep-farming had begun by 1784, and as it spread the sad story of the clearances was repeated throughout the Highlands.

The bloody feuds, the cattle-rieving had ended; and with them had disappeared much of the poetry and romance that was part of the people's heritage. Something had to take their place, for the Highlander, although his life might be hard and narrow in the material sense, nevertheless had a fervent imagination and an intellectual energy that demanded nourishment. Education and religion largely supplied the want.

Here, to show the conditions that existed towards the end of the eighteenth century, we cannot do better than detail the early life of Norman McLeod, the man who was to lead his followers to Canada, to Australia and finally to New Zealand.

Stoir Point juts out towards the Hebrides and the open sea from Assynt, southernmost parish in Sutherlandshire. It had been McLeod country for generations, but young Norman, born in 1780, found himself in a swiftly changing world. The villagers manned the herring fleet and cultivated the soil, but a sense of impending change now made them restless. The world was moving in to end their centuries of comparative isolation.

To the people of Assynt, religion had long been little more than a pleasant accompaniment to their daily routine. The old Highlander, with his delight in witches, fairies and ghosts, brought equal belief and much more interest to the stories and songs that were the clan's mental heritage. The centre of their life was not the church but the ceillidh; when neighbours would gather in the evening in one of the huddled, turf-built cottages. While the peat glowed and the candles glimmered through wreaths of smoke, old stories would be re-told against the comforting drone of the women's spinning-wheels.

The Church of Scotland, in this area at least, had lost the high zeal of its early days. The parish minister at Assynt, from

1768 to 1816, was the Rev William McKenzie, of whom John Kennedy, a church historian, wrote as follows: " Mr McKenzie was almost all that a minister ought not to be, and yet he continued to occupy his charge until his death. Always accustomed to regard his pastoral work as an unpleasant condition of drawing his stipend, he reduced it to the smallest possible dimensions, and would not infrequently be absent without reason and without leave, for many weeks together. During the latter part of his life, Parson William was much addicted to drink. This was well-known to the Presbytery, but could not easily be proved. The people were unwilling to complain and to give evidence against him. As a man and a neighbour, he was rather a favourite."

There was, indeed, a vacuum in life at Assynt during Norman McLeod's boyhood and youth. The closely integrated clan system, in which everyone had a place and a purpose, had gone, and nothing had come to replace it. Norman, having finished his years at the parish school, had gone back to help his father with fishing and farming. The description of him as " a clever, irreverent, forward youth " is a key to one with a restless spirit and an inquiring, unsatisfied mind. His irreverence rose from the feeling that the careless life of his parish minister was an indictment of religion itself.

Then, in the year 1806, the appointment of the Rev John Kennedy as Mr McKenzie's assistant brought to Norman and his contemporaries a glimpse of a new world. While McKenzie drank with his friends in Ross-shire and remained to those in his parish a vague but cheerful figure, Kennedy sought them out with the fervour of a true evangelist. To him, religion was a personal matter; his mission, to " awaken, regenerate and save sinners ". Those to whom he brought his message could no longer remain neutral. They had to come out on the side of God or remain prey for the Devil.

Tall and powerfully built, hardened by his strenuous life as a fisherman in Atlantic waters, Norman McLeod might seem at first sight an unlikely convert. But he had in full measure the hunger for knowledge and truth so often found among those whose physical background is harsh and demanding.

For us today it is almost impossible to imagine what religion meant, on its first impact, to men of his time and place. Restless, searching for something that would satisfy mind, heart and spirit, he found it in the doctrines of the Presbyterian Church. Not as it was then, but as it had been in the days of Knox. Faith, sudden belief, hit him with the force of a blow. He felt that, as with Paul, there had been something miraculous in his conversion. And then, with the conscious feeling that he was one of the chosen, he refused to believe that the same experience could come to others.

The scorn that McLeod later poured on revival meetings with their frenzy and fervour, the suspicion he had of mass conversion of sinners, may have been partly caused by the quality of honest common-sense that gave balance to his own mind; but even more than that it stemmed directly from the iron-hard, rigid belief of the Calvinist in his own salvation and in the damnation of almost everyone else.

Religion, without the distractions that might encroach on the time and thoughts of other men in other places, became the burning force in McLeod's life. He turned to it all the power of his brilliant, narrow intellect. It was the measuring-stick for moral conduct, but in addition he found in the Bible, through his own interpretation, standards for dress and for general demeanour. He obeyed rigidly himself and, being a man of eloquence and personality, succeeded in persuading many others that his judgment was correct.

Norman McLeod was twenty-seven when he decided to prepare for the ministry. He studied at the University of Aberdeen during four sessions, graduating in Arts in 1812 and gaining the gold medal for moral philosophy. Then he married Mary McLeod, from his native parish, and embarked on the final stage of his preparation for the church—a theological course at the University of Edinburgh.

The crisis was at hand. His own individual beliefs had hardened into an unyielding pattern. He could not reconcile his formidable conscience with the lack of discipline, the want of zeal and energy that was everywhere apparent in the Church, not the least at the University itself. He studied there for two sessions and then, feeling that he could never accept a licence to preach from any presbytery in the Church of Scotland, left after a series of stormy interviews with the professors.

He was still a man without a vocation. He began to teach at Ullapool, a fishing village in the parish of Lochbroom, not very far south of his birthplace. And in addition to teaching he also preached, for that was now part of his life. He bowed to none of the Church's mandates; the doctrines he outlined were stark, simple and uncompromising. They soon brought him a host of adherents, and one powerful enemy.

Dr Ross was the minister of Lochbroom parish, a wayward man, addicted to law-suits and easy living, with a casual attitude towards religion that enraged and provoked McLeod. But he could not remain idle while the schoolmaster's unofficial preaching disrupted a large part of his parish. Already Norman and his wife had taken their young son, John Luther, forty miles " over moss and mountain " to have him baptised by a different minister at Loch Carron. The journey was fruitless, for Dr Ross also happened to be there, and forbade such an action. Now, however, the doctor called him to conference, with outward cordiality, to discuss terms for an armistice. He suggested that all would be well if McLeod would only appear at church, even once in a quarter, and show by his conversation his approval of the doctor's ministry. McLeod said he could not be taxed with unlicensed preaching, for he was merely explaining the Scriptures; a subtle distinction that led to a long argument without either giving ground. In the forthright manner that was part of his nature, Norman McLeod spoke of the " dead hearts, and deceitful tongues of wily and worldly ministers ", and justified his conduct in a way that left no doubts about his intention to continue on the course he had begun.

Everything about Dr Ross irritated the uncompromising young man: the luxury of his manse (silver candlesticks and blazing fires); his smooth good nature that refused to be ruffled even in argument; the casual, heartless pretence at family worship that ended the day. The meeting could have only one ending. Norman went back to Ullapool. Shortly afterwards his school was closed and his salary, payable through the parish minister, no longer arrived. To pay his debts, he went to Wick and served for a season in the " dangerous and troublesome Caithness fishing ". Even after his return Dr Ross continued to harry him; although, to judge by a remark of the doctor's which Norman quoted later with some satisfaction, it was no one-sided affair. " He returns to torment me! " the doctor exclaimed when he heard that McLeod, disappointed in obtaining a passage for Canada, intended to go back to Lochbroom.

The torment, on both sides, was now near an end. Within a year Norman McLeod was to leave Scotland for ever. It was a step that he never regretted. He was going into a wilderness, but creature comforts had not played any great part in his life. More important, he felt, was the chance to bring up his family away from the deadening influence of the Church of Scotland. Leaving his wife and three children to follow him the next year, he sailed on the barque *Frances Ann* from Lochbroom, bound for Pictou, Nova Scotia, in July 1817.

Many of his fellow-passengers were already his friends and held similar opinions about the Church. These were forerunners of the men and women who, in 1843, were to found the Free Church and precipitate a religious war that was no less bitter because no blood was shed. Although, when that event took place, McLeod was to thunder with equal fervour against the lack of spirituality among the Free Church ministers.

The voyage of the *Frances Ann* was long and tedious. But one occurrence on board the barque was to be remembered, and possibly magnified, until it firmly established the power and authority of Norman McLeod among a growing number of followers. During a mid-Atlantic gale, the *Frances Ann* sprang a leak, and the captain began to consider turning back to Ireland. But Norman, so the story was told in later days, had seen a vision. " If we turn back," he said, " we are lost." Furthermore, he backed his opinion with evidence that the vessel was nearer to the coast of Nova Scotia than to Ireland. The captain blustered and threatened to put him in irons, but finally took his passenger's advice, and the ship reached Pictou in safety.

And there for a few years Norman McLeod stayed; a natural leader who had not yet gained his full following. While he was there, many more Highlanders from the districts where he himself had lived were to disembark at Pictou. Another Lochbroom was built on the river not far from where McLeod took up land, and that may have been the reason why he did not stay there long. A leader of his type must have raw material to work on. For him, Pictou was too set in its ways, too much a replica of the Scotland he had left. He could not build a community there that would satisfy his exacting standards. He was to try again in a few years with greater success on the remote, thinly-populated east coast of Cape Breton Island. And there, over thirty years, the colony that would later be transplanted to New Zealand grew in strength and numbers.

Meanwhile, however, he and his friends were busy on the land they had taken up near Middle River. In the thirty years since the first Highlanders had come to Pictou, most of the good land near the port had been occupied. McLeod, although determined not to remain near Pictou, was still gaining a greater influence, particularly among the new arrivals who discovered that, in spite of their hopes, Nova Scotia was a long way from being a paradise. Because of the highly individual nature of his preaching, his followers became known as Normanites. McLeod had lost nothing of his vigour in a new land.

" Torrents of abuse against all religious bodies, and even against individuals " is one recorded description of his manner at that time. " Though so wildly fanatical, he was a man of great power, and gained an influence over a large portion of the Highlanders such as no other man in the country possessed."

He also wrote, in the manner of Paul, to friends in other parts of the American continent. And these letters probably gave rise to a legend that gained wide belief in later years.

McLeod received a call from a settlement of Highlanders in Ohio. He was anxious to accept it, but unwilling to leave his

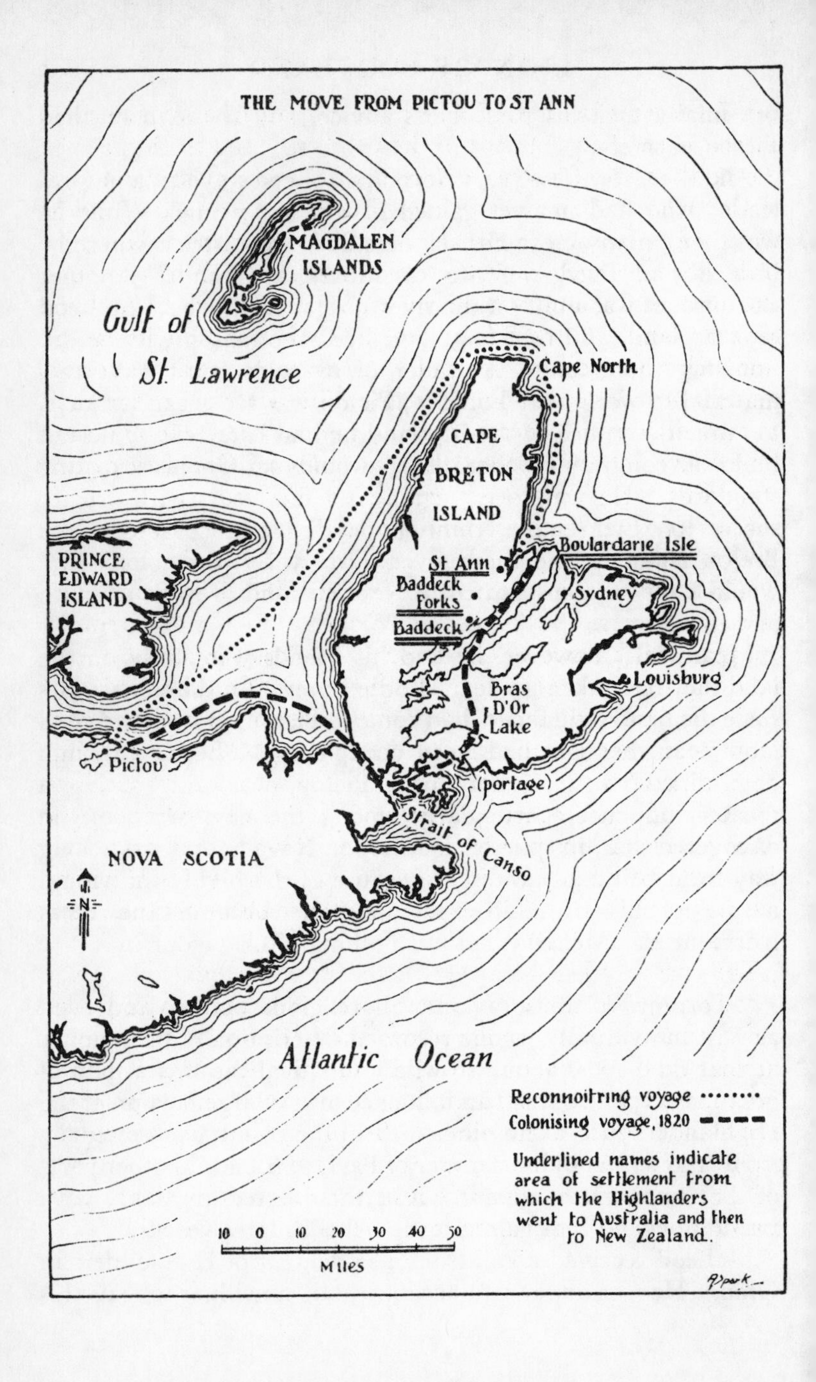
THE MOVE FROM PICTOU TO ST ANN
MAGDALEN ISLANDS
Gulf of
St. Lawrence
Cape North
CAPE BRETON ISLAND
Boulardarie Isle
St Ann
Baddeck Forks
Baddeck
Sydney
PRINCE EDWARD ISLAND
Louisburg
Bras D'Or Lake
Pictou
(portage)
Strait of Canso
NOVA SCOTIA
N
Atlantic Ocean
Reconnoitring voyage
Colonising voyage, 1820
Underlined names indicate area of settlement from which the Highlanders went to Australia and then to New Zealand.
10 0 10 20 30 40 50
Miles

faithful friends behind. They built a boat, of about 20 tons, named the *Ark* in defiance of the mockers; and in this, so the story goes, about forty of them set sail on a voyage to the mouth of the Mississippi River. From there they planned to make their way through the heart of the continent. The tiny craft was never to reach there. When they gained the open sea, it is said, a terrific storm arose and forced them back towards land. After a long ordeal, they found shelter in St Ann's Harbour, on the coast of Cape Breton Island. The sea-weary men looked about them. The waters of the bay teemed with fish. There was forest and farmable land waiting for settlers. They decided that the hand of God had drawn them there, and that they would go no further. The *Ark*, sailing back to Pictou, was lost; but the rest of McLeod's followers eventually joined the pioneers at St Ann's.

It is a picturesque story with a good Biblical flavour. The more likely version, while not so colourful, gives more credit to the practical common-sense of those who took part.

Ohio may have been the ultimate destination, but it is unlikely that the *Ark* would have sailed farther than New York. From there, the immigrant trail led to the Great Lakes. But these men also knew that much of Cape Breton Island was uninhabited, for settlement had not been allowed there for many years. As they sailed round Cape North, they examined the coast thoroughly; and in this manner St Ann's Harbour was discovered. They landed and, after a short consultation, decided to go no further.

The party then returned home for the winter. They negotiated with the Government for land, and awaited the spring thaw which would allow them to move with their families and possessions away from the neighbourhood of Pictou, a lively little seaport that, for its frivolous ways, their leader likened to the cities of the plain, and on which he promised the same destruction would fall.

At St Ann's there would be a better opportunity to create a simple world on his own pattern, founded on God's will.

CHAPTER THREE

CAPE BRETON: A LETTER FROM THE PAST, AND THE DAY-BOOK OF JOHN MUNRO

In autumn it was a serene and beautiful land. Mists, that gave warning of heavy winter fogs, crept around the hills. Below them the water was like a mirror, quietly reflecting the many-hued trees.

Arms of the sea ran deep into the land—Bras d'Or, the Arm of Gold, was one. Its literal translation was poetically true, although the name was a corruption of the word, probably Indian in origin, that appears also in Labrador. St Ann's Harbour itself was a deep indentation, with a fertile glen running down to meet it. And then there were North Gut and South Gut, where the country was hilly, with outcrops of gypsum and strong red granite. Over the hill from St Ann's, Big Bras d'Or stretched inland to form a lake that almost cut the island in half. In its mouth, like a green-glass bottle-stopper, was the flat and fertile island of Boularderie; and Baddeck, a tiny village, lay on its northern shore. Above it, the country blazed with colour in the autumn, dark clumps of fir and spruce framing the lighter tints of maple. Good hunting country, with partridge in the woods, duck in the ponds, and bear plentiful enough to provide excitement for the more daring. One man who went to Waipu inherited the nickname "Bear" from his father, a memorial to a famous encounter.

In spring, too, the colonists found it a good land. Crops flourished in the ground when its forest cover was cleared and the accumulated wealth of the soil put to use. It seemed something of a miracle to them that such land, such fishing, such trees for building ships and homes, should have been held in reserve until they came.

But, they soon discovered, the winters were long. Snow and ice closed up the harbour for several months in normal years. They could at such a time, hunt and take out timber, but farming was restricted. Much of the year's growing period was spent in preparing to keep themselves, and their stock, alive until the following summer.

It was a life that made even more prominent the qualities that they had brought from the Highlands. Self-reliance was carried as near as possible to self-sufficiency. And at the same time their devotion to Norman McLeod, on whom they drew for spiritual and mental sustenance, became even more deeply rooted.

The minister had taken up a block of land two square miles in extent at South Gut. Here his home was built, and later a church that held 1,200 worshippers, replacing the small building that served the needs of the first arrivals. From twenty miles around the people came to hear Norman McLeod lay down, in no uncertain way, the path they should follow in their lives. McLeod had inherited the prestige of the chief as well as the reverence due to a servant of God. He was not paid a stipend, nor did his people contribute money for his maintenance. Such an action would have diminished his dignity and power. But they served him in other ways.

Mrs Norman McKenzie, whose lively mind and ninety-eight years bridge a long period, told me how her mother, a great friend of the minister's daughter Margaret, would spend much of her time at the minister's house helping with domestic tasks. Such help by the women of the district was voluntary, and unpaid, but it was part of the service that the minister expected and was gladly given. In the same way, the men helped to clear his land and build his house. The minister's life as spiritual warden of the people, as magistrate, schoolteacher and adviser, was a full one; too full to allow him to expend his energies on the trivialities of making a living. He did not spare himself for his community's sake, and his followers repaid his efforts cheerfully and whole-heartedly.

He went away to Genesee, in the western part of New York State, where he was ordained. The Presbyterian Church there was acceptable to him, for it was not linked with the secular State, as was the Church of Scotland. He visited friends and converts in other parts of Nova Scotia. And before long he entered upon the most strenuous part of his career.

The church at St Ann's was the first on Cape Breton Island. But, as migration from the Highlands swelled the population, other ministers were appointed to districts near that where McLeod ruled so strictly. The minister looked upon them with a suspicion that was soon confirmed by their actions. They were, he considered, missionaries seeking worldly praise for their work in the " wilderness " of Cape Breton, or else they were evangelists, bringing about shallow conversions by the hundreds at revival meetings that were marked by emotional and physical excesses. And so he stormed against them. One in particular, the Rev James Fraser, of Boularderie, became his enemy.

The key to McLeod's invective is found in a sentence he used in his book, " The Present Church of Scotland and a Tint of Normanism ", a volume that, not without humour, pugnaciously defends his beliefs against his opponents. " Distinguish between speaking evil of men and speaking necessarily of their evil ", he wrote. With this premise, he could formally address Mr Fraser—in print—in these terms: " Of all fools I consider religious fools, at the pinnacle of their profession, to be the most dangerous to deal with. . . . I have certainly from time to time professed myself, as in my own estimation, a poor and unworthy member of the once venerable and glorious Church of Scotland; but the meagre, the pitiful and degenerate thing that now passes under the pompous and boasted sanction of that name, I utterly and indignantly disclaim. . . . I heartily regret that your unfortunate, offensive and confirmed insolence and pride, so conspicuous in your letter, as a true specimen of your general disposition and conduct, towards all who dare object to your measures, render it morally impossible for me to answer you in a more agreeable way."

Many features of Cape Breton life, outside his own sphere of influence, attracted Norman McLeod's outspoken criticism.

"Extravagance in dress", he writes, "is, and has been now for a long time, one of the crying sins of our times. . . . Her Majesty Victoria is not half so proud of her royal robes, her diadem and diamonds, as our mushroom maids are of their own belts and beads, busks and bonnets, combs and crisping-pins, rings and ringlets, lace and lockram, locks and linings."

But it was for revival meetings that he reserved his most vivid denunciations: "Some are screaching and screaming—others peeping and tooting—or snuffling and snorting—and that truly in a mood far beyond the utmost ordinary pitch of their pulmonary power; others falling down prostrate, monkey-like spring from place to place with surprising agility. Another sort sit still, statue-like, in a wild and vacant gaze."

Norman McLeod, it must be admitted, had a poor opinion of mankind in general, and of women in particular, to judge purely from his writings. But there were other aspects of his character. The cold exterior, the piercing eye, masked a warmth that spread from his family to his intimates; but even there it was often repressed, and it was never visible to those who knew him only slightly.

The number of these was growing rapidly in the districts near St Ann's, for Cape Breton Island was swiftly filling up with new arrivals from McLeod's own country, from Lewis, Harris and the rest of the Hebrides. Some of them came under his spell, partly because they liked a dynamic leader, partly because they realised that the violent utterances of McLeod came from a man who was single-minded in his desire for their welfare, and completely unselfish. But many of them, not liking what they saw, held aloof.

Even among those who went to New Zealand there were families or individuals who had refused to yield complete allegiance to Norman McLeod. Their friends were McLeod's friends, but between them and the minister there existed a state of armed neutrality. They went to New Zealand because they felt that, in this community whose ways they knew, there was a better chance for their families' welfare; but they objected to the minister's rigid control of the private life. If they wanted to dance or to sing the old songs, they would do so.

If they wanted to drink whisky, no edict from the minister would prevent it.

But in spite of personal differences and religious controversy, which, after all, sharpened their wits and gave them food for thought during the long winter evenings, life on Cape Breton Island in the districts near St Ann's had a basic stability. The same problems faced them all, the best solution came from a community effort. It was a primitive land, showing few signs that for more than a century it had been fought over by the armies of England and France. At one time, St Ann's itself had been a French settlement, and if the harbour had been freer of ice it would have become a fortress. Instead, the French built their citadel at Louisburg. After its capture in 1758 by a force that included ancestors of the families that later went to Waipu, insurance rates on vessels bound for America dropped from 30 per cent to 12 per cent. The French hold on the gateway to a continent had been broken.

Even then, settlement was not allowed by the British Government until 1784, and the first arrivals from the Highlands reached Sydney in 1802. Until 1816, the revenue needed to maintain the Government was raised from the lessees of the coal-mines, and from the not insignificant duty of one shilling a gallon on rum. Four years later Cape Breton was re-annexed to Nova Scotia, and the stream of migration rose to a flood.

The new arrivals were to retain many of the characteristics of the Highland Scot, but Cape Breton, and America in general, set its mark on them. A Fraser who took his discharge from the army in Canada after Quebec, married a Red Indian princess. Their descendants in New Zealand still occasionally show, with their high cheek-bones and aquiline noses, a trace of this alliance. Others, chiefly boys who spent periods away from home, learned something of the Indian language and also of French. For the French settlement of Acadia, which gave us Longfellow's " Evangeline ", was still a lively memory at the time when the first Highlanders arrived.

From this period also date a number of the folk-tales, almost legends, that some of the Nova Scotians brought with them to New Zealand. One tells of a French ship that had been wrecked, forgotten years before, on the rocky coast not far from St Ann's. A crane, made from iron taken from the wreck, still hangs in the fireplace at Alex McKenzie's Waipu home; and it was Alex Bill, as he is sometimes called, who told me the fragment of story.

" The wreck ", he said, " was supposed to have treasure in it, but it was also haunted. One Scottish party went to search, and climbed down into the broken hulk. Then suddenly, they heard the sails flapping on masts that were no longer there, and the wind whistling through rigging that had long since disappeared. They fled, and never returned."

A boy with a gift for comedy helped to keep another story alive; a story that, however garbled it may now be, illustrates the contemporary attitude of these staunch Presbyterians to Frenchmen and Catholics.

The boy was feeding the fowls outside a Waipu home. As he scattered the grain in front of him with many a flowery gesture, he spoke in Gaelic words that could be translated like this: " It might not do you any good, but it won't do any harm ".

Perhaps a hundred years before, a boatload of Highlanders had been forced ashore on the Nova Scotian coast in an area populated largely by the French. They were hungry, I was told, but knew that there would be no food for them in the French village if their nationality was discovered.

" They decided, therefore, that one of their number would pose as a priest, and the rest as his escort. The ' priest ' could speak French fluently. The stratagem worked. They were plied with food and drink, and the ' priest ' entered wholeheartedly into the spirit of the day. He knew no Latin, but decided that Gaelic would satisfy the villagers just as well. He said some notable graces and, as they moved in procession out of the village on their way home, he sprinkled the water to left and to right, calling out in fluent Gaelic, ' It might not do you any good, but it won't do any harm! ' "

The Highlanders near St Ann's developed many interests. They shared in the ship-building boom which made the name of Nova Scotia famous on the world's oceans. They shipped timber to Europe, and brought fish from the Newfoundland

Banks to Halifax and to the United States. Ambitious youths went off to work on the mainland, and others, taking advantage of the opportunities for gaining a good education, became doctors, lawyers and administrators.

But Nova Scotia, and Cape Breton Island in particular, was still a quiet backwater, out of the main stream of what we know as progress. During the thirty years that Norman McLeod remained there, the fishing-boat and the farm were the chief material elements in the life of the people. Changes came slowly, and were accepted with a natural caution. During the latter half of the nineteenth century, after McLeod and his followers had sailed away, the Cape Breton way of life stayed smooth, strong and almost unchanged. Until recently, long after the Waipu settlement had merged in most respects into the New Zealand pattern, St Ann's and Baddeck retained many of the qualities that marked them a century ago.

More than twenty years have passed since Bill Craig was posted to the cable station at Halifax. His mother, a McMillan, had left Nova Scotia as a girl in the late 1850s. As soon as he could, he visited St Ann's and wrote his mother a long letter describing what he found. To the young New Zealander it was an exciting experience, and his letter revived many of his mother's childhood memories. As also did the photographs that he collected and neatly titled in his album.

Mr Craig soon made contact with relatives and friends. " Wherever I go ", he wrote, " they at once start to prepare a meal, and inevitably try to persuade me to stay a few days or, failing that, to come back again. Nearly everyone in the Baddeck district has or had relatives in New Zealand, while Angus McKay showed me numerous farms from which the folk sailed away to Waipu. All the old folk, and most of the young ones, speak Gaelic. Christie McMillan, an old identity living up Big Glen, gave me a most dramatic welcome. Christie, who is eighty-eight years young and quite active in doing her household duties, was a cousin of grandpa's; and when Angus explained who I was, she embraced me and started off on a few paragraphs of Gaelic. Fairly took my breath away until Angus explained that I couldn't speak the old tongue. Whereupon he took the part of interpreter, but I'm sure she said far more than he translated.

" Everyone seems to know everyone else's business—where he or she went, what they did, how many barrels (not bushels) of oats they had, etc., etc. If a person is seen going down the road, they all know where he is going, why he is going there and when he will come back. At first, I felt a little out of things, folk referring to me as ' the Stranger '. When I went shooting, or threshing, or doing little odd jobs round the farm, everyone seemed to know. In the post office they seemed to know just exactly what mail to expect for each family in the district and in fact the whole place is just like one big family.

" As at Waipu, the second growth of timber covers a lot of the old cultivated land. On this farm, for example, there are 1400 acres (400 cleared), carrying thirty cattle (nine cows), twenty-one sheep and five horses. Farming would be a paying proposition but for the winter, which takes away all the profits. Everything produced on the farm seems to be consumed in the winter."

Harvesting, country dances, an occasional visit to the little town of Baddeck added variety to his experiences. And then came the " milling frolic ". It was held at the house of another McKay in Big Glen, a little two-storeyed cottage into which crowded about one hundred people from many miles around.

" We were packed in the house like sardines," Mr Craig told his mother, " children of nine and upwards to old folk of seventy or more; and to make matters worse the shy country people seemed to gather in the passages and doorways just ' looking and looking '. As I passed to and fro I could hear vague whispers of ' New Zealand ', but I daren't turn round to look at them because they would be fearfully embarrassed."

Milling, he explained, was the process of thickening blankets manufactured on a hand-loom from wool, made locally on spinning-wheels, and cotton warp. A long table built of plain rough boards stood in the room, and round it the millers sat in chairs. There were eighteen or twenty of them, of both sexes, and all had their arms bare to the elbows. The newly-made blanket was dipped in warm water and then laid lengthwise on the boards. Usually, two blankets were joined together so as to make a complete circuit of the table.

Then, while steam filled the warm room, someone began to sing in Gaelic, and the rest joined in. Each miller grasped the blanket with both hands, gave it one rub over the boards, and passed it to his neighbour on the left. No one seemed to know what the words they were singing meant. They referred to forgotten incidents that occurred in Scotland long before, but the songs had remained alive because their rhythm helped the work.

The frolic continued for many hours, young and old taking their place at the table while the snow fell silently outside and a gramophone in another room supplied music that contrasted strangely with the old Gaelic songs.

The long winter evenings in Cape Breton caused many of the old crafts to be followed when they had been discarded by those who went to Waipu. In both places the spinning-wheel was retained for many years, and hand-knitted socks made by Waipu women were keenly sought by seamen and by workers in the bush. But the hand-loom, which helped to make the Cape Breton home a hive of industry, soon dropped out of use in New Zealand. Blankets were never made there, although some that were brought from Nova Scotia were to remain in use for many years.

On a misty October day Bill Craig and some of his McKay cousins made the pilgrimage from Baddeck to St Ann's. The log cabin which his great-grandfather, Donald McMillan, built on his arrival from Scotland in the early 1820s, had long since been replaced, but he discovered its site on a hill overlooking North Gut, and directly opposite the spot where Norman McLeod built his church.

" Immediately below the house, at the head of a lovely little cove, was the place where grandfather built his house and forge. Such a lovely spot, mum," he wrote. " A little cove perhaps 100 yards long and 50 yards wide, with a stream running into the head of it. Of course the old house has been pulled down, and only a deep hole—the cellar—remains;

still, the outline is almost visible. Of the workshop, only a mound where the forge stood reminds one of the hard work these pioneers had to do. Just fancy a modern blacksmith making nails!

"As I stood on the old spot, I began to wonder how grandpa could leave such a pretty place—how often he must have gazed on these same waters when the work for the day was done. I believe tears came to Angus McKay's eyes when he told of the swimming races the McMillan brothers used to have across North Gut, and the weight-lifting competitions in the smithy. 'Here is the spot', he said, 'where Norman McLeod picked me up in his hands and held me high above his head. How I was frightened of him!'"

A little way down towards the mouth of the cove he was shown the spot where the *Margaret* was built to take the first of the migrants to a southern land. Angus, who remembered the days when the ship was being built, showed him where the bow had rested. Two rotting logs lay by the water. These, Angus believed, were part of the slipway. Fir trees had encroached on the land, but grassy roads along the beach in front of the smithy were still clearly formed. Along these roads, oxen had dragged the huge logs which were to make the ships.

They drove back through Englishtown. As they went along the main street, where a few cows were grazing, the car's engine seemed to make an overwhelming noise. There were few inhabitants, and the calm water reflected empty buildings and trees, and a few old schooners rotting on the shore. Goldsmith's deserted village, the writer added, was rowdy when compared with Englishtown.

And so, after stepping back into the past, Bill Craig returned to the modern world.

"Would you be interested in seeing the day-book of John Munro?"

William McKenzie Fraser, good companion, experienced teller of tales and ardent collector of curiosities that range from a mummified Maori chief's body to Norman McLeod's sextant, had a twinkle in his frosty eye when he asked me this question.

He knew that the number of relics of the migration had been sadly diminished, and that anything connected with John Munro would be of interest.

For John Munro, known as the Diplomatist, was a remarkable man, around whose name numerous stories have gathered. His nickname probably arose from an incident that occurred when he was bringing his own ship, the *Gertrude*, from Nova Scotia to New Zealand in 1856. The first of the migrants were already on the land, but a long dispute between James Busby, who claimed that the Maoris had sold it to him, and the Government, had complicated the title. And the Government, as such bodies are known to do, was moving slowly and deviously in no certain direction. The Government's hand must be forced, John Munro decided. When the *Gertrude* arrived at Capetown, he interviewed the Governor, Sir George Grey, and obtained from him a promise in writing that, if the Nova Scotian Highlanders were not satisfied in New Zealand-they would be welcome in South Africa.

Fortified with this, he interviewed Governor Gore Brown in Auckland on his arrival there, and was told to see the Auckland Provincial Superintendent, John Williamson. The super, intendent, an adept politician, explained his own dilemma. The Council, he said, was hostile to him and to his land policy. There was a vacant seat in the Council, however, which Williamson suggested Munro should contest. He did so, and was duly elected as representative for the Northern Division. Not long afterwards the Auckland Immigration Act was passed, giving the Nova Scotians all the advantages of a special settlement at Waipu.

That anecdote is history. A second one, while it may not reach that elevation, reveals another side of John Munro's formidable character.

By this time he was established with his family at Whangarei Heads. There were many children in the district, and he decided it was time something should be done about educating them, and also teaching them English. Accordingly, he sailed for Auckland to find a teacher.

Down by the Queen Street wharf he saw a young man, well

dressed, and obviously not long in the colony. John asked him what he was planning to do.

"I should like to work in a bank," the young man said, "as soon as they get a bank started here."

"Would you perhaps be interested in school-teaching?" John asked.

The young man admitted that he was not.

But John Munro was a guileful man with great determination. He excused himself for a few minutes and, going along to where the boat to the Heads was waiting, requested the captain to put off his sailing time for an hour. "I'll have a passenger for you," he added. Then he went back to convince the young man that his future lay in teaching.

The persuasion took nearly the full hour, but at the end of that time the young man was delivered on board—in a handcart, some say—and the boat put to sea. Whether it required very much whisky, John Munro never revealed.

When the would-be bank clerk came to, a little while later, he asked where he was, possibly wondering who he was.

"I hope you enjoy teaching at the Heads," the captain remarked. "They are a fine lot of children, and it has been a shame to see their education so sadly neglected just for the want of a talented young man like yourself."

The captain did not think it necessary to add that John Munro himself had once been a school-teacher in far-away Nova Scotia.

The young man realised that destiny had him in her grip, and raised no further protests. He had nothing to complain about in his subsequent treatment. In one of the Heads families there were several charming daughters. From these he chose a wife, and later rose to a respected place in the teaching profession.

I looked at John Munro's day-book, thinking how well its sturdy cover and firm, century-old paper symbolised the man whose business transactions it recorded. The store at St Ann's, where the book had been kept, was only one part of Munro's life. After teaching for a few years near Caribou, he had gone into business, exporting timber and other produce to

Glasgow, Aberdeen and Greenock, and importing goods for his store. He built his own ships for fishing, and owned two grist-mills. By the time this volume of the day-book began, on January 1, 1852, he was well established in the small business world of Cape Breton, the seal having been placed on his career by his election, as representative of Victoria County, to the Nova Scotian Legislative Assembly.

There are only glimpses of his larger business life in the day-book. It records the purchase of supplies for the grist-mill; timber is bought for export; butter shipped to Halifax and cattle to St John, New Brunswick. Prices were good for cattle in that part of the world. An ox brought 237*s.* 6*d.*, and a cow 72*s.* 6*d.* The millwright's pay, on the other hand, was 5*s.* a day, and his assistants received 2*s.* 6*d.* and 3*s.* Which shows, not that men were badly underpaid, but that beef was hard to raise and correspondingly expensive.

But these transactions are not the most significant in John Munro's day-book. The pages, filled with names and prices, give a clue to the everyday life of a frugal people.

The names themselves are revealing, for these entries were made by no imported clerk or shopman, but by a man or youth whose own home was at St Ann's. Many of them are in Munro's own hand. The *Margaret* had already sailed for Australia, but the district was still inhabited by McLeods, McKenzies, McInnes and McKays in bewildering number. They had to be distinguished, and the distinction was made by writing down their nicknames. There is Donald McLeod Og, Donald McLeod Neil Son, Angus McLeod Kenett Son, Alex McLeod Mason, Angus McLeod Murdo Son. John McNeil Piper rubs shoulders with John Finlason Cooper and Alex McKay Tailor. There is Phillip McDonald Foolish, whose name does not necessarily carry any stigma, while the presence of Neil McDonald Poet gives the clan some compensation. John Charleson has lost his surname completely. Malcolm McInnis Blacksmith carries the mark of his sturdy trade, and Donald McAuley Teacher would be recognised even if his purchase was not " 1 qr paper, 1*s.* 3*d.*"

Another name in the day-book, that of Angus McAskill,

was well known to the pioneers. Angus McAskill toured Europe and America under contract to the famous Barnum, being known to thousands of marvelling onlookers as the Nova Scotian Giant. There was nothing freakish about Giant McAskill except his size. He was 7 feet 9 inches in height, his weight was 425 lb., and his chest measured 80 inches. Unlike most giants, he had prodigious strength and a keen brain. It was his strength that became his downfall. On the rare occasions that Barnum would allow him to walk about unescorted and with no charge being made to see him, he would gravitate to the water-front, for, like most of his compatriots, he had the spell of the sea upon him. On the New York water-front he showed an admiring crowd of dockers how he could carry an anchor that weighed at least 2,000 lb. While he was setting it down, a fluke caught his side and caused a troublesome, undiagnosed internal injury. He returned to St Ann's, where, with the money he had saved, he bought two grist-mills and a general store, which he ran with considerable business ability until his death a few years later in 1863. The store and mills may have been those previouslv owned by John Munro.

For his good humour and kindliness, as well as his spectacular feats of strength, Giant McAskill has won a permanent place in Cape Breton folklore.

Life at St Ann's, as seen in the day-book, followed a little-changing routine. Each season of each year had its own requirements. Money played a small part in the household economy. Towards the end of winter, housewives could earn a small sum—3*d.* a lb.—carding wool for John Munro, and others did weaving for him. The enterprising farmer would have potatoes for sale in May. In June, July and August, home-made butter would be brought in to the store and usually exchanged not for money but for goods. Its value varied from 8*d.* to 10*d.* a lb. An occasional bullock's hide would be sold at 1*s.* 8*d.* a lb.; for the same price the customer could buy 6 oz. of sole leather. In August, too, the day-book records the purchase of herring, a substantial cash-earner for those near the sea.

The thrifty residents of St Ann's did not lavish their earnings on trifles. Yet John Munro did well in July with a line of glazed hats, which proved popular at 2*s.* 8*d.* each. If the customer wished, she could buy a " riband " for 8*d.* to grace her new headgear. Winter was the time for sewing. Moleskin at 5*d.* a yard, lining and trimming for coats, buttons which varied in price from 4*d.* to 10*d.* a dozen—these and other items appear as a witness to the women's industry. Boots were often made to order by local experts, but if necessary they could be bought from John Munro for 20*s.* and 17*s.* 6*d.* But razors were cheap—1*s.* 2*d.*—a scythe would cost 5*s.* 6*d.* and a candlestick, snuffer and tray 5*s.* 3*d.*

Tea was a luxury at 2*s.* 8*d.* a lb. It was, apparently, no national drink, for the only record of its sale is in the summer months. Not many years before, an ancestor of Nova Scotian Highlanders had brought home from India, as a present for his mother, in Skye, a choice little chest containing 1 lb. of tea. His mother, much to his sorrow, cooked it well, drained off the liquid and served the tea as a vegetable.

The long Cape Breton winter, with snow on the ground and ice on the water, saw many larders growing empty. Oatmeal, costing £1 for 100 lb., barleymeal and bran would be purchased to keep hungry mouths filled. Food for the mind was a different matter. Judged by the day-book, the St Ann's community would not be considered great readers. " Welsh Sermons ", at 2*s.* 8*d.*, was the apparent best-seller, the other books mentioned being only vaguely described as " one reading book ", or " two school books "—at 1*s.* each. In this conservative community, however, reading occupied a different role from that it enjoys today. The Bible provided an inexhaustible well of drama, poetry and spiritual inspiration. Such books as they had were not read once and then thrown away. Even when the reader had memorised whole sections of them, he would return, in his rare intervals of leisure, to the comfort of the written word. One of the few books that have survived since those days is a well-bound volume presented to Bunyan McLeod, the minister's son, when he was fourteen years old. It had been printed in New England in the year

1695, and its formidable title was " The Parable of the Ten Virgins ".

If the day-book gives little indication of the cultural pursuits of the people, it indicates plainly that they were a healthy community. I looked in vain for purchases of medicine, apart from simple remedies such as salts, castor oil and senna, at 3*d.* an ounce. Senna in particular was a potent cure-all. In the spring and autumn a modest quantity would be bought, sufficient to prepare the children for the changing season. It was a custom that died hard, and the dose of senna tea is still remembered, not always nostalgically, by descendants of the pioneers.

The *Margaret* had already sailed from St Ann's when the first entry was made in the pages of John Munro's day-book. With the departure of the *Highland Lass* in the spring of 1852, a few names disappear from the list of regular customers. But there is nothing to hint at the migration fever that had gripped the community.

It had its origin in a letter that came to St Ann's in the year 1848 from Donald McLeod, wandering son of the minister. He wrote from South Australia, where he was engaged in newspaper work, and the result of his qualified praise of the colony is to be seen in a letter that his father sent to friends near Pictou.

Spring had been slow in coming that year, he told them. " The scarcity of provision, which has for some time been bordering on famine, throughout the Island, renders it inconvenient for some to leave their families; and they must fish, or do something else to provide for their daily support, to keep them from starvation. There never was anything like this in Cape Breton.

" We have recently received a letter from our dear son in Australia. There is so much in commendation of the soil and climate that many people here, among our friends, would wish themselves settled near our Donald. And indeed, if myself had my selection of associates along with me, there would be nothing but the impractibleness of getting forward, thro' such a fearful distance, to prevent my own removal to it, even in this evening of my days. Our dear boy has not once suggested the idea of invitation to any of his friends; for he would think it but a certain offence to us at this desperate distance to venture a remark on the subject; but we can very easily learn from his Journal several and various advantages in that country, over this part of the world. And I have little doubt that some people will sooner or later emigrate from here to Australia."

The coincidence of famine with the letter from Donald McLeod set many minds stirring. Norman McLeod, now sixty-eight years old, took no active part in swaying the people's decision. His wife had been an invalid for several years, and he saw no chance of her surviving the rigours of travel.

Summer brought no material improvement. Blight ruined the potato crop, and unseasonable August rain caused rust to strike at the wheat. At the same time, an improvement in his wife's health made McLeod think more seriously of migrating.

" Although it is very unlikely that it will ever take place, yet I cannot shake myself from many stirring thoughts on the subject. I know without hesitation, that it is a far more favourable country than this, for youth and young families; if a cluster of friendly emigrants could gain the advantage of settling together near good sea-ports and fishing-grounds, with the advantages of agriculture and the salt water's refreshing breezes."

His mind was not yet made up, and inevitably religious arguments came to support those roused by the serious economic situation of his people. He felt that Providence may have directed his son's " random emigration " to the distant land of Australia.

Norman McLeod had hoped that in Cape Breton he would be able to set up a community with a single-minded devotion to God and to himself. His new meeting-house, with seats for 1,200, was filled, and the congregation at times overflowed into the passages and stairways. But there had been defaulters. " Sinners," he wrote, " are still among and around us." Would it not be possible to make a fresh start in the vast unoccupied regions of Australia?

" We enjoy more than ordinary rest from religious open opposition; yet this calm is little to be depended upon by my family or friends, if I were once laid in the grave. I would not choose this place for the fixed residence of any of my sincere adherants; if the Lord, in his good providence, would open for them a likely door of escape."

The door was already opening. Another letter from his son " with great caution and delicacy encouraged his weak and tender mother to the voyage ". The minister, however, showed scant knowledge of the difficulties that might lie ahead. " Had we nothing in view beyond our own family, our children's coasting craft might freely carry us forward for tho' the distance is long indeed, the direct course is over the mildest ocean in the world; for which reason it has long been termed ' the Pacific '. But all our best friends are desirous of either accompanying or following us, if providence seconds their views."

Fortunately, among these friends there were many practical men—John McKay and John Fraser, Duncan and Murdoch McKenzie. They were merchants, master mariners and capable farmers, men whose knowledge of the world and practical ability made them ideal partners in the great venture. The McGregors, master shipbuilders, who had also thrown in their lot with the migrants, laid down two ships, one of them to be built at St Ann's, the other—to the order of the McKenzie brothers—near Baddeck. Planning was carried out efficiently. Under the minister's direction, stores were prepared for the voyage. Potatoes, shredded and evaporated, were packed in birch-bark wrappers. Codfish were dried, boned and packed in the same way. With the addition of water, palatable food could be quickly prepared. For the first time, " dehydrated " food had been exported from Canada.

How, it may be wondered, were they able to execute their plans without outside aid when, a few years before, they had been in a serious plight through lack of food? The answer is that famine, not poverty, had caused the trouble. If local production failed, it was no easy matter to purchase and import more food during the long Cape Breton winter. The bad harvest of 1848 was relieved by supplies that came from the United States, after Norman McLeod's friends near Pictou had sent what they could spare. The following seasons were good. Their simple economy had suffered no shattering blow, but there was always the fear that blight, bad weather and other factors—scarcity of fish, for example—might once again bring them face to face with want.

And so Norman McLeod, with the harvest gathered and the *Margaret* ready to sail, preached his last sermon in Cape Breton. This was, indeed, a great occasion; the fervour of his preaching, the strength and sincerity of the seventy-one-year-old man who had ruled so autocratically for thirty years found a ready response in the assembly that gathered in the open air above Black Cove to hear him. " Suddenly, everyone wanted to go with him," an old man recalled in later years. More than half a century passed, and some of those who had heard him could still repeat the words with which he said farewell to so many of his people. One woman, remaining at St Ann's, nailed up the door of her house, saying that no other minister would pass through it now Norman McLeod had gone. The singing, the weeping, the prayers ended, and in a solemn silence the *Margaret* moved slowly down the bay towards the open sea, on her voyage to an unknown land.

A month earlier there had been a different ceremony at the McKenzie shipyards near Baddeck, when the *Highland Lass* took the water for the first time, curtseying gracefully to the cheering people and to the piper who, with " The Highland Laddie ", played her down to the sea. The ice came before she could leave, as had been planned, in December. She sailed for South Australia early in the following summer. Then the rest of the would-be emigrants awaited developments. After a long time, letters arrived. The long voyage was safely over, but no permanent home had been found in Australia. A party had gone to New Zealand " to spy out the land ". Finally came the news that a place had been found in that country where they could resume the community life that they knew and preferred: a warm land, with good soil and timber trees in abundance, facing a bay that teemed with fish.

Here, John Munro's day-book again takes up the story. In the year 1854 he bought and refitted the damaged brig

Gertrude, a sturdy ship well suited to the rigours of trading in the North Atlantic. Neat entries in the day-book, in the owner's hand, show that he could spare time from his duties as a politician to attend to his own business. After one voyage the discharge of cargo, extended over nine days, cost a total sum of £21 18*s.* 10*d.* Local men did the work, but it was casual employment, and few of them were engaged for the whole period. The rates of payment varied also. John Munro senior reckoned his own worth at £1 a day, his son received 10*s.* The general wage for the others was 3*s.* 6*d.*, but Hugh Munro " and horse " received 6*s.* 6*d.*, and Alex McLeod " and oxen " 7*s.* 6*d.*

The Cape Breton section of the day-book comes to an end in December 1855, more abruptly than it should, for a number of pages have been removed at some uncertain time. There is no clue, therefore, to the sudden decision that John Munro made to take the *Gertrude* and about 190 passengers to New Zealand. All we know is that he suffered political defeat in May 1856, and that he sailed in the following month.

But the day-book went with him. It resumes with an entry: "Whangarei, November 6, 1860 ", in Munro's ornate script; and carries a list of store dealings in the new land. Butter he now buys at 1*s.* 6*d.* a lb. After that, probably because he was a member of the House of Representatives as well as of the Provincial Council, the day-book fell into disuse. Munro died in 1879. In 1884 Donald Munro was recording in it items very different from those that had provided its original purpose. There are stock lists, a note that sixty lambs had been marked and 158 sheep shorn. There are tallies of fish that had been caught—970 in August, 1885, 31 dozen mullet on September 24, 1888. Many of these were smoked, and others were sold fresh. They found their markets in places as far distant as Wellington.

There is a brief note on September 14, 1888: " Pig to wild boar. Due January 4, 1889 ". And below it on the page: "January 5, Pig has five young ones ". The Munros had mastered their new and strange environment.

CHAPTER FOUR

THE SEARCH FOR THE PROMISED LAND

Even when Captain Hugh Anderson had left the sea and settled to a sedate existence as a ship's chandler in Auckland, he had a " quarter-deck voice " that would make those who heard it, including his son Edward, tremble and vow to mend their ways.

There was only one man, he once told his son in a moment of confidence, of whom he was afraid; and that was his father-in-law, Norman McLeod. Which goes to show that, in Nova Scotia as well as in other parts of the world, love could find a way.

Captain Anderson was not alone in his healthy respect for the Rev Norman. In the Anderson living-room there hung a portrait of the minister, painted shortly after his arrival in New Zealand. More than seventy years ago, when Edward Anderson was a small boy, it had a potent effect on him. " I might have taken a cake from the kitchen ", he told me, " and be playing in the living-room. Then I would feel the steely eyes of my grandfather's picture following me about like a conscience. I would go out and play somewhere else."

When I met Edward Anderson, the minister's only surviving grandchild, he was more than eighty years old; a courtly, soft-spoken business-man of the old school, to whom his code of ethics was as important as the acquisition of money; although he was successful at that, too. Tall and alert, with a fresh complexion and as straight as a young fir tree, Edward Anderson could now look with an easy detachment at his grandfather's formidable character. " A hard, strong man, he would never have been able to act today as he did then. But there is no doubt he was fitted to his environment."

In the late summer of 1850 a barque arrived at St Ann's

from Aberdeen to load timber. The sea froze early that autumn, and the ship was caught in the ice before she could make her departure. Her officers and crew accepted the hospitality of the little settlement.

Among the barque's officers was a young Aberdonian, Hugh Anderson. For him, at least, the winter did not pass slowly. He had met the minister's daughter, Margaret, and before long they fell in love.

But it was to be no straightforward romance. Already preparations were afoot for the journey to Australia. Norman McLeod, his daughter felt, had too much on his mind to look favourably on a plan for her marriage, particularly when the bridegroom was a seaman with no settled prospects. And so, with the help of a few friends, they made a plan.

One day Hugh Anderson disappeared from his ship. No one knew where he was, and a search proved fruitless. When the ship sailed in the spring, the captain took with him to Anderson's parents the report that their son was lost, and that he had probably fallen into a crevasse in the harbour ice. But the young man was being well cared for; and, shortly after his ship had left, he reappeared in the settlement. No inquiries were made, but the rumour spread that he had taken cover in a deserted cottage, and that Margaret and some of her friends had supplied him with food.

Young Anderson had friends among those who were preparing to leave for Australia. He approached the minister boldly, offering his help with the work of rigging the ship, and later as navigator on the voyage. He also mentioned that, with the father's consent, he was a suitor for Margaret's hand. According to the story, Anderson's first proposal carried more weight in gaining the minister's approval. But he may also have seen, behind the young Aberdonian's deference, a determination that was unlikely to falter.

When the *Margaret* sailed in October 1851 Hugh Anderson was one of her officers. He married Margaret McLeod after their arrival in New Zealand; and a little later they settled in Auckland. In later years Hugh told his son that, in spite of the adventures they had experienced together, he never felt that he was one of the McLeod family. This may have resulted, however, from his own natural reticence; and it did not damage his relationship with others who settled at Waipu. The Anderson home, presided over by the warm and graceful Margaret Anderson, was an hospitable refuge for any Nova Scotian Highlander who visited Auckland.

But even in the everyday atmosphere of the little town, the story goes, ghosts could arise from the far-distant past. One day Captain Anderson, going about his work, was hailed by a voice that he had not heard for many years. He looked over and saw his brother.

" Why didn't you tell us you were still alive, Hugh? We had all given you up for dead."

Hugh Anderson justified himself in the grand manner. " I preferred you to think I was dead," he replied, " rather than know that I had deserted my ship."

On the *Margaret*, as she headed out across the Atlantic and down past the Cape Verde Islands, there was an ordered discipline as smooth as would be found on any ship of the Royal Navy. Norman McLeod well understood the need for maintaining mental and physical activity. There was religious instruction for all, and schooling for the numerous children. With a large proportion of seamen on board, the running of the ship was efficient and not too burdensome. And McLeod himself took daily readings to check the officers' navigation.

They did not aim to break records. Although the majority of the *Margaret's* passengers were active, she also carried many who were old or delicate. The 164-day voyage was broken at Capetown, where vegetables, meat and fruit were taken on board to vary the diet, and where the passengers were able to refresh themselves with a week ashore.

For most of them, the routine on the *Margaret* was pleasant, and some wished that the voyage would never end. They knew that the hardships of pioneering, already too familiar, lay ahead once again. Their courage and capacity for endurance were still with them, but it was only human to wish that the times of stress could be postponed. Fair weather stayed with them all the way. Friendships became stronger as the ship drew steadily eastward towards Australia. A century later, descendants of the pioneers would still talk of the family that lived "next door" to them on the voyage from Nova Scotia.

The *Margaret* arrived in the harbour on the Spencer Gulf on Saturday, April 10, 1852. It was a bare, uninviting land, scorched by a blazing autumn drought. There were few signs of life, for Adelaide, the young capital of the state, lay many miles up the Torrens River. It was too late to disembark that afternoon. The next day, Sunday, was also spent on board. Norman McLeod, still the master of their destiny, held a service of thanksgiving for their safe arrival. It heartened them while they looked at the inhospitable coastline. The harbour was full of fish which would have provided a welcome change from their monotonous shipboard fare; but it was Sunday, and the minister would not allow any to be caught.

They did not wait long in Adelaide, for the minister's son, Donald McLeod, had left word that he had gone on to Melbourne; and South Australia seemed too firmly held by the squatters to give them the opportunity they required. There was still with them the tradition of farming on the Highland pattern. They were not interested in becoming pastoralists. Life for them meant the growing of crops, timber-working, fishing and the keeping of a few animals. South Australia, it was quickly seen, did not have the forested, secluded bays where such a life could be followed.

At the beginning of June, the *Margaret* was at Melbourne with most of her passengers, the grey-haired patriarchs, simple and wise, who had seen so much since they left Scotland half a century before; the mature men and women, thoughtful for their families, refusing to be hurried out of their set pace; the young men, Canadians rather than Scots, with the vigour of the New World in their manner. For many of them, young or old, Melbourne was their first sight of a bewildering and distasteful way of life. Gold had been discovered the previous year. The struggling town, with a population consisting to a large degree of time-expired convicts and others with conditional pardons, had begun to grow with an unbridled energy. In

1841 Melbourne's population was 11,000; ten years later it was still less than 25,000; by 1861 it had swollen to 191,000.

Tents in Canvastown, two miles from the shopping area in Collins Street, provided homes for the new arrivals. The *Margaret* was sold, and the men sought work or tried their luck at the gold-diggings of Ballarat and Bendigo. Money suddenly assumed a new importance for them. A bucket of water cost 2*s*. 6*d*., and even then had to be strained through muslin before they could drink it.

Gold was found by some of them, and later helped to buy several of the Waipu farms. The more prudent, however, capitalised on the gold rush by taking work as carpenters and tradesmen. For all of them it was an adventurous interlude, with elements of humour and tragedy.

At the diggings a commissioner had been appointed with whom the miners deposited their gold, receiving in return a receipt on the Treasury in Melbourne. It was a flimsy guarantee. The unscrupulous were quick to seize the chance that begged to be taken. Almost every digger had several of these receipts on his person. Before long the road from the diggings to Melbourne was infested with bushrangers who killed or robbed the unfortunate miners for the sake of their receipts, which were then presented to the Treasury for payment.

Norman McLeod himself encountered a band of these men, and handled the situation in characteristic fashion. He came upon them when he was lost in the bush, and was told that it was only his calling that had saved his life. Night was near, and the bushrangers gave him a place at their camp-fire. The minister, undaunted by his strange position, lectured them at length on the evil course their lives were taking. It was probably with relief that the robbers gave their captive his horse and set him on the road to Melbourne in the morning.

In the town itself there were insufficient police to protect the law-abiding, and death could come in many ways. Robbery with violence took place even at the doors of the Queen's Theatre. As one man wrote, " On getting up in the morning it was nothing new if you were told that a man had been found strangled in the gutter ". The gaol was overcrowded with prisoners. Sessions were held every month, and the law's retribution was severe. Out of sixty awaiting trial, thirty might be convicted, and sentences of between ten and thirty years' imprisonment were the most common.

But there was another enemy more dangerous than lawless man. Typhoid fever struck at the just and the unjust; three of Norman McLeod's six surviving sons died within a short period from the scourge that accompanied insanitary conditions. It was a severe blow to him, coming at a time when their plans seemed to have gone awry. He felt that this might be a judgment of God on him for bringing the people from Nova Scotia. Had he been over-presumptuous? Did he lean too strongly towards a wish for his people's material well-being? They were worrying questions, but in a little while his sturdy faith and confidence reasserted themselves.

One definite result, however, was a strengthening of his determination to move from the evil town. But where could they go? Victoria, distracted by gold-fever, was no more suitable than South Australia had been. The minister and his friends listened with increasing interest to reports of another land across the sea, the colony of New Zealand. Donald McLeod had mentioned it in letters to Hugh McKenzie, the schoolmaster, before they left Nova Scotia; and even then they had been attracted by what they had heard. In Adelaide there was much talk of New Zealand, for Sir George Grey had gone there as governor after holding a similar post in South Australia. The country, it seemed, was inhabited by a warlike race, but Grey was rapidly making friends with the Maoris.

The women said: "In Nova Scotia there was snow, in Australia snakes and in New Zealand the Maoris. They will cause us the least trouble." And so Norman McLeod, on behalf of his people, wrote to Sir George Grey early in 1853 asking whether the Governor would form a special settlement for them in the colony of New Zealand. He received a cordial reply, and before long plans were being made for still another move.

Meanwhile the *Highland Lass* had arrived at Adelaide with a full list of migrants. When they left Cape Breton, the owners had engaged a captain, for their own hands would be full with shipboard organisation. But the captain proved a drunkard. He was removed from his post and put ashore at Capetown. For the rest of the voyage Captain Murdoch McKenzie was in command.

Although the oceans of the south were new to them, navigation was not a problem to the Nova Scotian seamen. When the *Bredalbane* came later, however, the captain's chart was a small one, and the name " Auckland " extended across the narrow isthmus from the Waitemata Harbour on the east coast of New Zealand to the Manukau Harbour on the west. Accordingly, he approached the west coast, his mistake being discovered only when he reached land.

The party on the *Highland Lass* did not immediately join the earlier arrivals in Melbourne, but the McKenzies, before selling their ship, made several profitable voyages in her and regained personal contact with Norman McLeod and their other friends. They agreed completely with the minister that Australia was not the promised land. It would be better to see what New Zealand could offer them; and already Sir George Grey had suggested that there were several areas ideally suited to their needs. Although they did not know it then, the Governor was anxious to settle them—a closely integrated community—in some part of the colony where their presence would place the Maoris on the defensive, and perhaps bring about their neutrality in any war that might develop.

But what concerned the Nova Scotian Highlanders chiefly was the thought that, if they delayed much longer, nothing could prevent the young men, the life-blood of the migration, from drifting away. The colonists had been disappointed twice already. The earliest arrivals had established themselves temporarily in or near Melbourne. There was little point in uprooting themselves until it was certain that New Zealand could supply the home they wanted.

The McKenzies bought the *Gazelle*, a schooner that had already proved her ability to trade across the often stormy Tasman Sea; and it was from Adelaide that the first party sailed for Auckland on September 2, 1853. They arrived fifteen days later.

The schooner and her passengers did not cause any great stir on the busy water-front, or in the town that climbed a ragged hillside to the sky-line. She joined a fleet of vessels that included tall barques from London, Sydney and the New Hebrides; and, at the other end of the scale, tiny 10- or 15-tonners—*Odd Fellow, Phantom, Piako Lass*—that brought pork, potatoes, firewood and kauri gum from the islands and bays of the Hauraki Gulf. There was, however, one feature about her that aroused the interest of the local shipping reporter: the *Gazelle's* captain, Murdoch McKenzie, was accompanied by his wife and family, and women and children outnumbered men in the list of passengers. The names, too, were all of Highland origin.

When the next issue of the *New Zealander* appeared on September 21, it contained an announcement, at the foot of the column devoted to Shipping Intelligence, that " the schooner *Gazelle* has brought a number of immigrants who we trust will prove a valuable addition to the population. They are originally from the north of Scotland, had first emigrated to America, from thence to South Australia, where they remained but a year, and have been attracted to this country by its superior agricultural advantages for which it is becoming so deservedly famed."

It was, of course, an excellent opportunity for the newspaper to score at the expense of the sister colony across the Tasman, especially as so many temporary New Zealanders had been lured to Australia by the hope of winning fortune on the gold-fields. The point having been satisfactorily made, and local pride stimulated, the *Gazelle* and her passengers were allowed to fade gently into anonymity.

The schooner continued to trade with Australia, and the travellers settled down in rented houses in Albert Street while they waited for new arrivals and the end of negotiations for land. Captain Murdoch McKenzie combined trading with bringing more of the migrants to New Zealand. Before long Norman McLeod was in Auckland, preaching at St Andrew's Presbyterian Church. On Captain Duncan McKenzie fell the difficult task of establishing the migrants' right to land.

As the *Gazelle* sailed down the east coast of the long peninsula north of Auckland, on her first trip with the Nova Scotian Highlanders, knowledgeable eyes had been turned towards the land. Here was a beautiful coast-line, with forest filling the valleys and climbing the hills. There were deep bays from which the land rose not too steeply, reminding them of the country they had dwelt in for most of their lives. The sun was warm, and the air mild.

They decided immediately and definitely that they did not need to look further for a home than the area on the east coast near Whangarei. But, as Duncan McKenzie and his friends soon discovered, they were carrying out their negotiations at a difficult time. Provincial government was being established and, although Sir George Grey "spoke most warmly of his interest in our views and success, and even assured us that our application would be favourably entertained, and that a formal communication to that effect would be made", the power to make decisions was at that very time passing from his hands. And he himself left New Zealand in December 1853, before the settlers' problems had been resolved.

For six months Duncan McKenzie, and then the minister's son Donald, acted as spokesmen for the migrants in a tedious and thwarting series of exchanges with Grey's successor, Colonel Wynyard. Their side of the case could be simply expressed: they did not have enough capital to buy a block of land sufficiently large to serve those who were planning to follow them from Nova Scotia; they were, however, ready to pay ten shillings an acre—the recognised price—for the land they took up immediately, provided an adjacent block was held in reserve for later arrivals. It was with this proviso that the Government could not or would not agree.

It was only in February 1854 that Andrew Sinclair, the Colonial Secretary, told Donald McLeod that the land was not yet the property of the Crown, although every effort was being made to purchase it from the Maoris. In the same month Sinclair sent instructions to the Surveyor-General that "certain Highlanders" should be considered the first applicants for the land, and that contiguous areas should not at present be surveyed or offered to public competition. In that month, too, Duncan McKenzie and a party of his friends left by cutter for the north to establish the boundaries of the block they were claiming.

The first round had been won, but their difficulties were not yet over. James Busby, British Resident at the Bay of Islands before New Zealand became a colony, had already bought much of the land from the Maoris. His claims were disallowed, but he sturdily refused to give up the fight. In June 1855 he brought a case against Duncan McKenzie for trespass. McKenzie offered no evidence, but left it to Busby, with a host of Maori witnesses, to prove his claim. Busby failed then, and many times afterwards; but eventually the Government was forced to pay him compensation.

Not until 1858 was the land situation clarified, through the efforts of the Auckland Provincial Superintendent, John Williamson, and his able supporter, John Munro.

In that year, also, the Provincial Government entered energetically upon an ambitious migration scheme. Agents were appointed in Great Britain, Germany, Nova Scotia and Prince Edward Island. The emigration agent for Nova Scotia, Dr John Emsley, himself travelled to New Zealand on the *Ellen Lewis*. He settled at Otahuhu, near Auckland, for the good health of the Nova Scotian migrants made it unlikely that a doctor would prosper among them at Waipu.

By that year the passengers of five ships had reached New Zealand. Those who had sailed long before to Australia had completed the last stage of their journey across the Tasman. Some remained there, having adapted themselves to Australian ways. The gaps in the ranks were filled sometimes in a romantic way, as in the story that Mrs Annie Finlayson, of Maungaturoto, told me when she was in her eighty-ninth year.

Her mother, Mary McBain, was born in South Uist, in the Outer Hebrides. When she was a young girl her family, feeling the restlessness that had spread from the mainland to their remote island home, decided to migrate to Australia. They made their way to Queenstown, from where the migrant ship was to sail; and there, before they had time to go on board, Mary and her elder brother, Lachlan McBain, were placed in quarantine suspected of smallpox.

There was no easy way out of the family's dilemma. The final decision, made with little time at their disposal, was that the rest of the family should go on as they had planned, and that Lachlan and Mary should follow later. But Lachlan died, and his young sister was left alone, with no knowledge of the English tongue, in a strange country.

What was she to do? Go back to the Hebrides, or seek her family? To her, Australia could not seem a very big country, bigger than South Uist, perhaps, or Ireland. She would go there and join her own people.

" At this time ", Mrs Finlayson explained, " the Nova Scotians were just after reaching Adelaide. A number of them went up to the gold-diggings, and among them was Ewen McInnes."

It was there that he came upon a young girl, who could still speak little but her native Gaelic. It was Mary McBain. Australia had proved bigger than she had thought, and separated by much more ocean than she had imagined from Scotland. But she had not despaired, and had found work as a dairymaid while she continued what must have seemed at times a hopeless search.

Ewen McInnes helped her to find her family, and then, when she was seventeen, married her. Mary McInnes, as she now was, set herself to learn English and, having a good intellect, she soon mastered it. She raised a family of sturdy sons and three daughters who were remarkable for their combination of strong character and feminine grace. At least two of her grandsons were given the name of Lachlan Bain, in memory of the deeply-loved brother whose death set her off on a strange but successful odyssey.

Mary McInnes brought to Waipu a lively and cheerful disposition that was not unduly oppressed either by the events of her youth or by the sober turn of mind of Ewen McInnes, who was one of Norman McLeod's most rigid followers. She brought with her, too, the old Gaelic songs that had been the heritage of her people for centuries, and continued to sing them.

It says much for her, and also for her husband, that her love of music and dancing passed on to her daughters, even though Ewen McInnes in his heart believed that the devil was in such pursuits.

And so, by 1860, the assembly was almost complete. The *Margaret* and *Highland Lass* had been followed by the *Gertrude*, the *Spray*, the *Bredalbane* and the *Ellen Lewis*. The migrants spilled out from Waipu, occupying land that was not too remote from the parent settlement. They did not allow themselves to become isolated. Their own small ships maintained contact with Auckland, where some of the migrants established themselves in the commercial field primarily as agents for their friends. They found a valuable ally, too, in John Logan Campbell, the father of Auckland, the Edinburgh doctor-turned-business-man who settled there in 1840 and was associated with the city until his death more than sixty years later. Sir John Logan Campbell sold the Nova Scotians land at Whangarei Heads, and presented them with an educational reserve at Waipu itself.

The Rev Norman McLeod was almost eighty years old when the last of the Nova Scotian ships arrived. But his prestige and power were as great as ever, and the latest migrants, or most of them, were still bound to him with a personal devotion that had, if anything, grown stronger during the nine years since the *Margaret* sailed from St Ann's. Among nearly 900 people, however, there were certain to be widely differing temperaments and opinions. As their horizons widened with their long travels, some of the people shook off the spell that Norman McLeod had cast on them. They remained loyal, but they became more objective. Others who came on later ships had had little contact with the minister. Particularly was this the case with many of the passengers on the *Bredalbane*. With them, cheerfulness could amount to frivolity and still escape moral censure.

Archie Bishop, whose mother travelled on the *Bredalbane* as a young girl, is a firm believer in the theory that there was more gaiety and humour in their lives than one would imagine from the Calvinist discipline that McLeod imposed on his followers.

The majority of the passengers on the *Bredalbane*, he explained, came from the island of Boularderie. Their minister, James Fraser, had been a strong opponent of Norman McLeod's doctrines, and they shared, in varying degrees, his views. But they also respected Norman McLeod's ability as a leader, and they could not ignore the first glowing reports that reached Nova Scotia from the settlers in New Zealand.

The *Bredalbane* was a cheerful ship. Archie Bishop remembers his mother telling him about the sea shanty that the sailors sang as the ship started on the long voyage on December 24, 1857:

> " Our ship's a blue-nose clipper; our skipper's a blue-nose too.
> Our cook's a blue-nose nigger, and we're a blue-nose crew!
> Heave hearty to the chorus, heave hearty as you can!
> For we are outward bound, with Nova Scotia men! "

Mrs Bishop remembered the song not so much for that reason as because the older girls, of whom she was one, used it as a lullaby on the voyage for the babies placed in their charge.

CHAPTER FIVE

HOME-MAKERS IN A NEW LAND

THE brave crest of the McKenzie Clan adorning the gate of the house in Donald Street, Whangarei, made me suspect that I had come to the right place. I knocked at the door and, after a short interval, it was opened by a tall woman, her hair not yet completely grey, who looked at me with an inquiring smile. Mrs Norman McKenzie, who was a schoolgirl in Nova Scotia before she sailed with her family on the *Ellen Lewis* in 1859, shook my hand softly and showed me to a comfortable chair in her sitting-room.

Introductions and explanations were made. Mrs McKenzie nodded her head. " I knew your grandmother well," she said in her quiet voice. " I was very fond of her."

I first met Mrs McKenzie on a Saturday afternoon in August 1951, a few days before her ninety-eighth birthday. She was planning to attend church the following evening, as there was to be a special service. She usually went in the morning, following a habit that had rarely been broken during her life.

Mrs McKenzie—Aunt Jessie to a wide circle of relatives and friends—was delighted to recall the events in which she had shared ninety years ago and more. She spoke of her first schooldays, under the gentle care of her father, which were interrupted by the five-month voyage from St Ann's to Auckland; of rumours of war with the Maoris that proved, fortunately, to have little effect on life in the districts where the Nova Scotians had settled; of the journey by cutter from Auckland to Whangarei, a prelude to the greatly-changed life that lay ahead of them.

At that time Whangarei, now a thriving town with a population of about 10,000, had one store and a few scattered houses. " We were met by a doctor," Mrs McKenzie said. " He gave my mother his horse to ride, and accompanied our party to Kauri, where my grandparents were already living. The rest of us walked, carrying our belongings. We were fortunate in having relatives with whom we could stay, for it was the middle of winter. And in their house, three months after our arrival, mother had another baby."

Kauri, one of the most attractive farming districts in the north, still bears signs of the heavy bush that covered it when the first settlers arrived. Not long before, the Government had bought the land from the Maoris for £550. Green fields are surrounded and broken by clumps of native bush, much of which has grown since the time of the pioneers. The stumps of the giant trees that Mrs McKenzie remembers have long since disappeared. But she still remembers, also, the endless hours of work that everyone shared while the farms were being carved out of the forest.

Within two years her father, a farmer now as well as a school-teacher, had his own house on his own land. His wife's brothers, expert at carpentry as well as at many other crafts, had helped to build it from pit-sawn timber felled nearby. An expert at building chimneys came from Waipu to give his help.

Only five years after their arrival, however, Hugh McKenzie died; and his widow, with a young family, was left to look after the property. Jessie McKenzie, as the eldest child, had her own responsibilities. They were heavy for a girl of fourteen, but not so heavy that they robbed her of her zest for life. Her eyes twinkled as she described one important part of her weekly routine.

" At first I used to walk to Whangarei with butter and eggs for sale or barter. Then we bought a horse, and that seemed too good to believe. But when, after a few years, we became the owners of a buggy, life seemed just too easy."

The simple social activities of the young district are what Mrs McKenzie finds most pleasure in recalling: the building of a hall, where Norman McLeod, by that time over eighty years old, preached to his people. " He gave us all a good dressing-down," she added, " but was most friendly again afterwards." The hall was used also for dances and as a schoolhouse.

Kauri weathered the difficult early years well. Fowls were kept and crops grown, but the men soon discovered that the rich soil would grow grass all the year round; and cattle were thenceforward their chief source of income. Today, on pleasant farms owned by descendants of the pioneers—the McLennans, for example—you will find native trees being planted on the boundaries of fields and nursed into vigorous growth by men whose fathers spent long hours felling, milling and burning the bush that had covered the land.

I chose Mrs McKenzie deliberately to open this chapter on the first years in New Zealand. For, whatever the men might be doing, wherever their work might take them, the role of the women was established and accepted as a matter of course. They were the home-makers, the ones who stayed at home; the mistresses of domestic routine, the producers and builders of families.

The men might be anywhere: trading in tropic seas, working in bush camps, building wharves or harvesting at Auckland, constructing roads and bridges in the far interior of the North Island; even shearing sheep on Australian stations. But the women's life followed a pattern that in its essentials varied little, whether they were at Waipu or any of the sister-settlements. Their days were full, but they had compensations that made up for the lack of labour-saving devices or modern cooking methods. The first and most important difference between then and now was that woman, the most sociable of God's creatures, was rarely denied the boon of companionship with others of her own sex and similar interests, in work that had as its objective the family's and the community's benefit.

A home was primarily part of the larger community, not a unit on its own, presided over in solitary state by one woman. A deep and healthy satisfaction came from working, often in the open air, with other women on a multitude of simple but essential tasks.

There, as elsewhere, the woman was often a better " man " than her husband. Her strength, her humour, her courage were the rock on which many a home stood securely.

And so the Nova Scotian women are given pride of place.

They knew that the burden of pioneering, the improvisation, the lack of medical facilities, the problems of raising a family in a new land would affect them more than the men. They accepted their responsibilities cheerfully. And they found that their unspectacular life had its own reward.

But before we grow too serious, it is necessary to remember that character shows itself in many ways; and that there was nothing stereotyped about the personality of the Nova Scotians, whether men or women. Fortitude, even when combined with patient resignation, is a worthy quality, and it can show itself in many ways. As in the case of the woman who lived not far from Whangarei. One of her sons, it seemed, had fallen into evil habits. He worked hard during the day, but in the evening was accustomed to saddle his horse and, with a set of boon companions, gallop furiously over to the nearest hotel. After a few hours, he would gallop home even more recklessly.

The woman shook her head over this, and would sometimes be heard to say that her son would surely break his neck through drink.

One night, when the revellers were roaring home, his horse put its foot in a hole, fell and threw the rider. His neck was indeed broken.

One of his brothers was deputed to tell the sad news to his mother. Reluctantly he agreed, and went into the room where the woman was sitting at her sewing.

" Have you heard the news, Mother? " he asked.

" No," she replied.

" Well," he went on, " you were right. A—— has broken his neck."

" How did it happen? " she asked. " Did he fall off, or was it that his horse fell? "

" His horse fell and he was thrown, Mother. Nothing could have saved him."

She thought for a moment or two, and then remarked, slowly: " Well, that's not so bad, then, after all."

Such Spartan women were not common. But there were many whose strength and mental power were coupled with a determination that stemmed from the necessity for survival.

Norman McLeod, when over eighty:
'An arrogant eye and a hard mouth'

The Western Highlands: The cradle

Whangarei Heads, New Zealand: The final home

Edward Anderson, only surviving grandson of Norman McLeod

Two survivors: Mrs Norman McKenzie and Mrs J. McRae, who sailed from Nova Scotia to New Zealand in the 1850s

J.A.S. Mackay, also known as 'Long Jim'

The Matheson home at Leigh forty years ago

Willie Kempt demonstrates a timberjack while Donald McLeod looks on

More than eighty years ago, two women carried the first plough over the hills to their home near the Waipu Caves, before a road had been made. John McLean's wife would walk to church, a distance of eight or ten miles, and on her return home on Monday would carry 50 lb. of flour in a pikau on her back.

But possibly a sense of humour, as well as the necessity for survival, governed the actions of Mrs Fenton during a boat voyage to Auckland.

It was an open boat, not very big, and crowded with settlers taking their produce for sale in the town about sixty miles away. Among them, in addition to Mrs Fenton, was a rather melancholy Scot nicknamed Corrady, from the Maori word for flax, which he used for tying up his trousers. Corrady had carefully stowed on board a wooden bucket, made in Waipu, full of good butter from his cows.

A wind sprang up as they sailed down the open coast. The sea became very rough and, in spite of the valiant efforts of the bailers, the water gained. Mrs Fenton was not daunted. She looked about. Corrady was busy being seasick, and did not notice her pick up his cherished bucket, tip the butter over the side and begin bailing furiously.

They arrived safely in port and prepared to land. And now Corrady, regaining an interest in life, found his bucket was empty. He complained bitterly. Mrs Fenton, quite unabashed, told him what she had done. His attempt to scold her was cut short when she said abruptly, with a cheerful laugh, "Well, Corrady, it was either your butter or yourself. Which was the better?"

Homesickness—for Nova Scotia rather than for Scotland—affected the men as well as the women. Many years after he had left Cape Breton, one lively man of ninety put down the newspaper he was reading in the evening and announced to his family: "I think I'll go home to Nova Scotia and see some of my old schoolmates."

The menfolk had wide interests, and soon adopted the ways of the new land. For the women, however, the milder climate of New Zealand, the imperceptible merging of the seasons, made Nova Scotia seem colourful in comparison. Many of them were, at first, sadly homesick.

It showed in little ways. Mrs Johanna McRae is four years younger than Mrs Norman McKenzie, but she has lived in New Zealand two years longer: since the *Bredalbane* arrived in 1858. She remembers her mother, the wife of McKenzie the Tanner, talking wistfully of the blueberries they used to gather from the Cape Breton hills. Many other references showed that Nova Scotia was still " home " to them. There was beauty in the New Zealand bush that came so close to their home, and through which she made her way, on dark and muddy tracks, to Hugh McKenzie's school. But there was a brooding, melancholy quality about this new forest, a seeming menace in the close-packed undergrowth through which no animals moved.

Mrs McRae experienced something of the dangers of isolation that faced the early settlers. When she was only a few years old, she was badly burned. The nearest doctor was at Whangarei, which was connected with Waipu only by rough tracks over the hills and through the swamps. It was on a twenty-mile walk that her father set out for help, although he must have felt the errand was hopeless. He found the doctor, who went off immediately on his horse, leaving the father to follow as quickly as he could on foot. Even the doctor must have thought his treatment gave only a slender hope of recovery, for when he again visited the household a few years later, he said he had not expected to see the little girl again.

By that time, Johanna was showing some of the sprightliness that was to be her distinguishing quality for ninety years. Periodically in its early days the settlement would be short of flour. The local harvest would have ended, and bad weather might have delayed the boat from Auckland for as long as a month. Corn, ripening in their garden, was a valuable substitute, but after a few weeks it became monotonous for the young girl. With a child's logic, she went to the garden, stripped the cobs and threw them into the river.

In spite of differences in temperament and behaviour, the

majority of the early Nova Scotian women had in common a quiet strength, an undemonstrative manner that usually succeeded in hiding their emotions. They were relaxed and easy to meet; one felt that they were on good terms with themselves.

As I recall her now, my own grandmother was a typical representative of her generation. She was born in New Zealand, but her speech had the soft, lilting inflexion that marks those who spoke Gaelic before they learned English. When she was old, confined to a chair through a fall, she could still draw people to her and refresh them with her own calm delight in life. She never raised her voice; she would speak and then listen, her eyes alert and interested.

She had strong, beautiful hands. Whether they were holding a book or, as was more often the case, busy with knitting, they fascinated, and in some strange way passed on to others something of their own sureness and control.

She had an interest in people that was far removed from inquisitiveness or a gossip's ill-mannered prying. Effortlessly she could recall the intricacies of family relationships, going back through several generations and following with ease the ramifications of a complicated family tree.

When she was over eighty, it was still impossible to forget that my grandmother had once been young. At an unexpected compliment she would blush like a girl, dropping her head modestly and with a charming lack of affectation. Having known them herself, she was quick to sense signs of restlessness among her grandchildren as they sat with her in church and the sermon dragged on interminably. Peppermints would be produced from her neat black purse and passed secretly to the transgressors.

In her old age she enjoyed most of all simple pleasures: a quiet talk with old friends, the gathering of her family around her, long walks on her own, provided they had a definite objective. She cherished her independence, but did not allow it to cut her off from the rest of the world.

The house where she spent her childhood stood in a secluded valley through which ran the Pohuenui River, quickly renamed the North River after another stream in Cape Breton. Bush, in a green mass, came down to the water's edge. The track to Waipu Centre led over low hills and past areas that looked fertile, but where only tea-tree and scrub grew. This was the gumland, sour, badly-drained country from which the forests had died away centuries before. It was to defeat the efforts of many farmers. But Ewen McInnes, her father, had some good land which he, his friends and family set about clearing with energy and enthusiasm.

Food was never short, even if it included few luxuries. In the autumn, fish were caught, dried and salted for the winter. Curds, or " gru " as they were called in Gaelic, made a good meal when eaten with home-grown potatoes. Near the house was a peach-grove where the fruit, untouched by brown rot or other disease, ripened in abundance.

There was not much time for growing flowers, and indeed there was enough beauty about them for their absence to go unnoticed. Ewen, the practical man, had a saying that the best flower he had seen grew on a potato plant.

Mellow autumn days gave the girls their first outdoor task. " When my sister and I were small," Mrs Annie Finlayson, another of Ewen's daughters, told me, " we were sent out to gather the heads of flowering clover. What beautiful work it was! I still remember the sweet smell of the clover, and how big the heads seemed to be. Later, father would take the seed and sow it. On rich new soil, it seemed to grow better than it does today."

As the girls grew older, they entered more fully into the routine of a busy house. Endless hours hoeing the crops; butter- and cheese-making, housework, washing and scrubbing. Two tubs stood under a willow tree down by the river. As soon as the tubs were set up there would come a flood to wash them away. But they never went far.

In the McInnes household, as in most others in Waipu, Sunday was bound by a host of restrictions. Potatoes for dinner after church were prepared on the preceding day, and water for household use was poured into tubs. The children earned a rebuke if they were caught going down to the stream for a drink. "There was God's sweet water running," Mrs Finlayson said, "and we could not touch it."

She remembers, too, one of her brothers running up with some eggs that he had found in the hay-barn on a Sunday. He was ordered to take them back again, but Father remembered where they were! In one way, at least, the children's ingenuity brought results. The peaches became ripe on Sunday as well as on other days of the week. They would eat them off the branches, thus overcoming the ordinance against picking fruit on the Sabbath.

There was a four-mile walk to church. "At one time the congregation stood to pray and sat for singing," Mrs Finlayson said. "Then the order was reversed. But one old man refused to change with the times, and sturdily followed the way of his fathers."

As dictator of fashions for Sunday, as well as moral guide, the Rev Norman McLeod expected that the women should be simply and modestly clad for church. Fate seemed to conspire with him in impressing this on the people. One young woman, shortly after her marriage, set out for church in a gay new bonnet. Her courage faltered, however, and before going in she hid her hat in the tea-tree outside the church. When the service was over, she went to reclaim it; but discovered, to her everlasting sorrow, that the pigs, straying in the Sabbath quiet, had devoured the bright ornaments.

The North River district is probably less visited today than when the McInnes family was young. The main road to Whangarei from the south is some miles away now; but in the 1860s, and for many years afterwards, the McInnes home stood on the direct route north for the restless wanderers, the soldiers discharged from the Maori wars, the men who were hoping to make a living on the northern gum-fields. They would often stop for a meal, and occasionally offer to do some work. They seemed to know that, although Ewen McInnes was very stern, he was also a fair man. And as for his wife Mary, she had a tender heart for the homeless and the unfortunate. Perhaps she remembered her own wanderings in Australia before she met her husband.

Apart from the changing parade past their door, variety came to their life in many ways. Regularly the women would collect their spinning-wheels, made by Fraser the miller, and converge on someone's house for a " frolic ". The whole day was occupied carding and spinning wool. There was plenty of conversation, and the woman of the house took pleasure in cooking for and entertaining her helpers. When planting time came round, all the neighbours, down to the small children, would gather to plant potatoes, corn and other vegetables. All through the fine spring weather the work continued, until every garden was full.

There were few holidays. Picnics at the beach would again be community affairs, taken at a time when there was no urgent work on hand. But dancing was the favourite pastime. Even Ewen McInnes' suspicions of the dangerous enticements of music could not keep his sons and daughters from dancing. The polka, the schottische and reels were favourites when they were young. And they danced wherever there was a floor large enough for the party to proceed. Many a dance took place on a nearby road-bridge, when the moon was bright, the sky clear and no other place was available.

Music, or its lack, was never a problem. Steps were improvised, and so was the music. If someone had a fiddle, that suited well. And if there was no fiddle, a tuneful whistler was just as good.

" We had several bards," Mrs Finlayson explained, " who could make up words to the old tunes. They were in Gaelic, a language well suited to their droll humour; for the words usually referred to some well-known character in the district." Nor had the old custom of lilting been allowed to die. The dancers, in chorus, would follow the tune to which they danced, sometimes improvising words as they went along.

And so the days of their youth slipped by. The girls married and moved away to homes of their own. The boys became famous as bush-workers in a community that produced more than its share of outstanding axe-men. They took with them, wherever they went, memories that were to remain fresh until the end of their lives.

On my first visit to Waipu for many years, Mr D. R. McKay offered to show me the farm to which my grandmother had gone as a young married woman. We passed the land which Norman McLeod had taken up, and which was then, ironically enough, occupied by an Irish Catholic. The narrow road followed the valley inland, climbed the shoulder of a jutting spur and then turned towards a saddle in the low range. To its left was the remote upland valley where my grandmother's home had been.

We stopped to look across the valley. Below us was a choked and reedy swamp, with a steadily rising hill behind it, newly cultivated and sown in grass. Behind that again there was a tangle of tall gorse and tea-tree, with splashes of lighter colour where the native trees—rimu, kauri, totara and tanekaha—were fighting back. A track crossed the hill from the high ground, running through an interlocking maze of hills and valleys to the sea. Along that track the children had gone to the Cove School, six miles of steady walking; and, said Mr McKay, they were never late.

I met the farmer who had bought the land some thirty years before. No road went near the site of the old homestead. His own comfortable house had been built in a more convenient spot. He stopped work to show me the way.

"You'll find a bridge across the swampy gully. Climb the hill across the new grass until you reach that high gorse. In there, you will see a young totara tree growing near where the old house was. There is a plough lying somewhere in the scrub, but not many other signs that a house was once there. They used good iron for the plough; it is very old, but, when I saw it last, still in working order."

The plough, I knew, would be one of the old McMillan brand, specially made for the Nova Scotians by the blacksmith who, in a different land, had helped to build the *Margaret* for her voyage to Australia.

Next day I climbed the hill. A century before, it had been green with forest trees. Ninety years before, it had shimmered magically as the wind moved the tall wheat that covered it. Then gradually, as my grandfather's interests took him elsewhere, the gorse and scrub had taken charge, until once again, with a new owner, the hill was ploughed, harrowed and sown in grass. But still, across its face, the hollow old track could be seen.

I reached the wall of gorse that marked the limit of improvement, and looked in vain for that totara tree the farmer had mentioned. Perhaps, I thought, the gorse—ten feet high and more—had hidden it. I plunged in at random, along a casual track made by cattle that found shelter and rough grazing in the gorse. Bush-lawyer clawed at me, and mounds of blackberry spilled over on the track. The ground fell away to the head of a small gully, where a clear spring broke, even at midsummer, from an outcrop of rock. Here, young forest trees had established themselves, and gorse and blackberry could not grow in their shade. It was a refreshing spot after the glare of the open hillside.

From this spring my grandmother had carried the water used in her home, climbing the steep slope down which I had just come. At that time there had been neither gorse nor bush. Fowls had scuffled in the dust, and farther down-stream the cattle had also drunk from the spring. But the well-worn track had long since disappeared, and there was no indication that this had once been the centre of a busy farm. I pushed through the gorse in a different direction, and came suddenly upon an open space with the totara tree in full view. Beside it there was a small mound of rubble, all that remained of the chimney and fireplace, a mound that would soon be completely hidden by weeds. The stillness was almost complete. Gorse-pods cracked in the sunshine, and a fantail watched with a beady, inquisitive eye.

A melancholy sight? I did not think so. There were no ghosts here to lay cold hands on the heart. It would have been different, perhaps, if even a few rotting planks, a broken piece of china or some other link with the days long past had been in sight.

My grandmother had been happy here. She was busy with her children, her domestic duties, and she had a deep affection for her husband's parents, who, and naturally so, lived as part of the family in their old age. She was sorry to leave the ordered and peaceful routine of the farm for the livelier air of Waipu Centre. But when the break was made, it was a clean one. No ghosts, but a host of memories, most of them cheerful.

CHAPTER SIX

FARMS AND FAMILIES IN THE OLD TRADITION

THE dog-leg fence that distinguished many of the Nova Scotian Highlanders' farms in the early days could be taken as a symbol of their attitude to farming. It was one of the features of their life on Cape Breton Island that survived the migration to New Zealand. Its chief function was to keep animals out of the cultivated ground, rather than to keep cattle within a field.

It was practical, simple and rather careless. It would not have satisfied the careful and orderly farmer of today. For the Scottish Highlander, however, farming was not the beginning and end of life, but a necessary accompaniment to survival. And their first descendants in New Zealand had seen no reason for modifying their point of view. The dog-leg fence, not particularly beautiful, but with the virtues of simplicity and cheapness, continued to be built.

Living near the bush, the farmer found all his materials close at hand. First, crossed stakes were driven into the ground, at right angles to the direction the fence would take. Then a longer stake was placed longitudinally, with one end resting on the cross, and the other firmly set in the earth. Other sharpened stakes, at the builder's discretion, were crossed and placed in position until the fence began to bristle fearsomely in all directions. There was one important requirement: the sticks must be set so that, if an animal happened to lean against the fence, it would not collapse. Rather, the weight of the beast would drive the sticks more firmly into the ground or wedge them more strongly against one another.

Outside the fence, the farmer's life was a battle against nature and his stubborn animals. His cattle were at home in the bush. Quite often they fattened there as well as they would have done on good pasture, for the sub-tropical forest offered shelter and a variety of nourishing food. Well enough, indeed, to gain a high price when they were shipped to Auckland. Losses of stock were high, but they had never been anything else either in Scotland or in Nova Scotia.

Milking the cows could be an eventful business. The operation was always carried out in the open field, and eventually, with quiet treatment, the cows would become domesticated enough. Heifers were three years old at least before they had their first calf and joined the herd. The direct approach was used for breaking them in. The skittish young animals, fresh from the unfettered life of the bush, were cornered and then secured by a rope around their horns. This was then attached to a tree, and the battle ended with the animal, not always gracefully, allowing the milker to approach. One especially active heifer is still remembered on the McKay farm. Roped to a tree, it charged madly at the man and the bucket, chasing him round and round the tree until brought to a strangled halt by the shortened rope.

Even though incomes may not have been high, life was less restricted and more varied than it is today. There was no careful selection of high-producing cattle, for their value was not very much greater than that of the meanest " scrub ". There were no expensive manures to make two blades of grass grow where none had grown before; but the soil still had much of its natural fertility, and there were no blights to neutralise their efforts. The farmer could afford a casual approach to his work. He sowed his wheat in the ashes left when the bush was burned. Sometimes it was hoed in, but even if left untouched it would germinate and grow. The hordes of sparrows and other imported birds had not then reached their bush farms to add another worry to the farmer's life.

One of their chief sources of income came almost by chance. A mattress, stuffed with grass for the voyage from Cape Breton, was emptied out near one of the houses. The seed grew and the grass flourished. Soon it had spread to all the farms in the district. At this time, and for many years after, there was a demand throughout New Zealand for grass-seed to sow the thousands of acres that were being brought into production from bush and tussock. Waipu brown top, as the new grass was called, became the most popular and successful. It was wiry and durable, of no great food value, but it stood up to drought and cold or wet weather. Brown top provided a steady income for many landowners. The grass was cut and stacked, and then thrashed for seed, some of the stacks yielding up to two tons.

Another casual importation was gorse. Captain Jacob, mate on the *Gazelle* and later master for many years of the Melanesian Mission schooner *Southern Cross*, was a farmer at Waipu both before and after his long period in the Western Pacific. To him goes the credit of introducing gorse to the district. At that time it was judged by its staid British habits, and considered a valuable plant for shelter and forage. Captain Jacob did not dream that, once it was acclimatised, without the check of cold winters, it would riot over thousands of New Zealand acres. At first, it needed coaxing to make it grow at all, and neighbours who helped themselves to seedlings from Captain Jacob's farm congratulated themselves when the frail plants began to thrive.

No one was greatly alarmed when the gorse began to spread. A determined party of men, assisted by fire, could put the enemy to temporary flight. In any case, the land was not expected to carry a great number of cattle. Too many would have been an embarrassment, for there was a limit to the capacity of their market. What could not be sold to feed the small town of Auckland had value only for their hides and tallow after boiling down.

Until refrigeration opened up markets on the other side of the world, the Nova Scotian migrants lived a self-sufficient life, in which the sale of farm produce played a comparatively small part. The casual rules that governed farming gradually became more strict, and breaches of them provided incidents that enlivened the community's quiet days. In one of these, Captain Jacob, " the only foreigner in Waipu ", played a firm part. By this time, the dog-leg fences had been replaced by more permanent structures, and land rights were clearly recognised by most of the residents. It was against nature, however, to expect a complete change to come suddenly.

" Gow " Finlayson's sheep always had a tendency to wander, although the owner was certain to collect them before lambing or shearing time. For several years a number of them had found board and lodging on Captain Jacob's farm, trying his patience severely. Finally, he went out early and sheared his sheep, including those that belonged to Gow Finlayson, a few weeks before the accepted time. A little later Finlayson arrived looking for strays. The sheep, without their wool, were sorted out for him. He complained bitterly, but Captain Jacob's only reply was: " Well, Gow, I grazed them for the year, so I thought I should shear them too."

The wandering sheep of Gow Finlayson were the cause, according to tradition, of the first court case to be heard in Waipu. He lived up Finlayson's Brook, a beautiful little valley that runs off the Braigh; but I am not certain whether he or Alex Finlayson, who also lived in the valley but on the other side of the road, gave it its present name. Alex and Gow Finlayson, who were not related, were separated from each other by widely differing temperaments and, in later years at all events, took no pleasure in meeting socially. Again, it was Gow Finlayson's sheep that were responsible for this unneighbourly position.

Growing weary of feeding the sheep, Alex Finlayson took the unprecedented step of sending them down to the pound. Gow was not pleased.

" That means I have to go down and drive them up," he said, " and also pay one shilling poundage."

"That is so," said Alex gravely.

The journey down to the pound did nothing to improve Gow's temper. He was a big man, and, as his Gaelic nickname showed, belonged to a family of blacksmiths. The hot sun shone, the sheep still showed a tendency to wander, and by the time he reached Alex's farm on his way home he was ready to explode into violence. He stopped to chide his neighbour again. A clean-shaven man himself, the sight of Alex's fine big beard, of which he was justifiably proud, proved too great a temptation. He spoke strongly on the subject of ingratitude and, to emphasise the point, tugged with equal strength at Alex's beard.

It was unusual for such cases to come before a court, but by now Waipu was beginning to accept the methods of control practised in the rest of the colony. The decisive evidence in the case was " Exhibit A "—the handful of hair that had once flourished on Alex Finlayson's chin.

When Ian McKay showed me the deeds for Mountfield Farm, where he has a thriving dairy herd, and told me what he knew of its early days, he might have been discussing a farm in a different land. The deed, signed by Governor Thomas Gore Browne on March 5, 1857, granted to Alex McKay a total of 189 acres, including nine acres for road reserves, at a cost of £90 sterling.

Alex was one of four brothers who came from Nova Scotia by way of Australia. They had a complete family understanding; for, when circumstances made it necessary for the others to come to New Zealand, Alex, who remained for a few years on the Victorian gold-fields, had the more favourable chance of gaining money. It was natural, therefore, that the money he made should be used in buying land for the other members of the family.

Even if they are judged only by numbers, the McKays were—and are—a remarkable family. Head of what might easily be called a new clan was Donald McKay, who was born in Ross-shire in 1753. In 1819 he turned his thoughts to migration, and accordingly sent his son John, better known as Ian Ruadh, to Nova Scotia to see what that land offered. Ian Ruadh was impressed. In the following year the rest of the family crossed the Atlantic. Ian Ruadh had been a student for the ministry and later a schoolmaster in Scotland. He now developed other qualities as well. One of the leaders of the migration to Australia and New Zealand, he died in 1885, a few months before his hundredth birthday. He was a lover of good horses. When he was nearly eighty, Norman McLeod had cause to censure him for riding too fast to church.

Ian Ruadh had four brothers and one sister who came to New Zealand, and all except one married. There were Duncan Ban, Roderick Seann (Senior), Roderick Og (Junior), Angus and Mrs Roderick Campbell. Eighty years later, two members of the family, Frank and E. C. McKay, decided to draw up a list of Donald McKay's descendants. It was a tremendous task. Everyone knew the number was great—at one time there were over thirty Mrs McKays on the Waipu telephone exchange alone—but no one was more surprised than the originators of the scheme when it was proved that there were over 800 descendants. One sister of Ian Ruadh, Mrs McCharles, had stayed in Nova Scotia, and another, Mrs Finlayson, in Scotland.

They used all the possible variations in spelling the name McKay, they invented new nicknames, but still—especially to "foreigners"—the McKays of Waipu are a bewildering enigma. With the foreigners could be classed the teachers who began to arrive at schools in the Nova Scotian settlements when education became free and compulsory. Before then, and often afterwards, the teachers were themselves Nova Scotians, familiar with Gaelic and the mysteries of family nicknames.

It was J. C. McKay, also known as Johnny Jack, who told me the story of his kinsman Fahy Rory Og and his first day at school. His official name would have been Farquhar, or Frank McKay, the "Rory Og" indicating that he was descended from Roderick McKay, Junior; but he was rarely known as that except on the most formal occasions.

When Fahy, a precocious child, was five, off he went to school, and duly came home again in the afternoon.

"How did you get on, Fahy?" his father asked.

"Well enough," the boy answered. "But our teacher cannot spell."

"How is that?" asked the father, somewhat surprised.

"He asked me my name, and I told him, but he didn't write it down."

"What did you tell him?" his father said, beginning to suspect what had happened.

"Fahy Rory Og," the boy said. "The teacher looked at me and asked how I spelt it. And so I had to spell it for him. But even then he couldn't write it down in his book."

"How did you spell it?" the father inquired grimly.

The slow drawl, the comic inflexion with which Johnny Jack gave the boy's answer cannot be set down on paper.

"Why," he replied with a twinkle, "that was easy. I said, very slowly, 'F, a, Ahy-ahy-ahy McKay!'"

And so we return to Mountfield, where Ian McKay, Johnny Jack's son and a former member of the staff of Massey Agricultural College, is now applying scientific methods to pasture control and to the building-up of his herd; methods that would have caused his ancestors to shake their heads in astonishment. Ian is sometimes known as Ian Johnny Jack which, being translated, means "John John John".

Behind his house is a steep hill, now deep in gorse. Ian is still considering the best way of bringing it into pasture. "Eighty years ago and more," he told me, "they were growing wheat on that hill. I think they must have harvested it with a pair of scissors."

Perhaps because they could be cleared more cleanly and easily than the wetter, heavier valley flats, perhaps because they were warm and faced the sun, many steep hillsides carried cereal crops in the early days. The methods of harvesting were as simple as they had been in the Highlands a century before. Sometimes it was done with a sickle, which cut too short for the wheat to be stooked. A scythe was more efficient. A harvesting "frolic" would make quick work of a wheat-field, with the scythes moving steadily through the crop and the gleaners following behind.

Necessity caused unusual methods at times. The story is told of one housewife who discovered that she had to provide a meal for visitors when there was no flour in the house. She went out to the wheat-field, gathered a few heads, winnowed them, ground the wheat in a handmill and was able to produce delicious scones for tea that same day.

The handmill, a regular feature of every home at one time, is rarely seen now, even as a museum piece. Its decline began when the settlers built a mill on what is still called the Millbrook. The mill was a marvel of ingenious construction. There was no metal in it, from the water-wheel and dam to the roof. All the farmers for miles around would bring their wheat in, the miller usually keeping one-eighth as his payment. Alex McKenzie of Limestone Hill recalls that one of the most expensive parts of the mill was the silk used for grading the meal into fine quality, seconds and thirds. The silk cost £5.

But the miller had other sources of income as well. When I sat down to lunch with Alex McKenzie in the kitchen of his old home, I remarked on the sturdy and handsome table.

Alex smiled under his white moustache. " It is a very old table," he said, " and it cost 12*s*. 6*d*. when I was a small boy. We supplied the timber, and the miller turned the legs."

Although it has been altered and enlarged since it was built about ninety years ago, the McKenzie homestead is one of the few houses that preserve authentically the atmosphere of the pioneering days. Alex McKenzie, a vigorous and stalwart man of over eighty, greets visitors with the natural dignity and friendliness that befit a former chieftain of the Caledonian Society. The old kitchen is now a living-room, but its huge open fireplace stlll has the crane, hung with an assortment of pots, that was made of iron brought from Nova Scotia. Dominating one side of the room is the chimney, built from massive blocks of the limestone that gave the farm its name. A staircase hangs on the opposite wall. It led to a small attic bedroom, where the young McKenzies slept securely.

Alex McKenzie has many treasures, most of them intimately connected with the life of the family: Maori curios that are a reminder of the large native population the district supported before it was devastated by tribal raids in the early nineteenth century; a set of bagpipes that sounded on the Crimea, and which he still gives an airing at times; photographs of thoroughbred horses that made the McKenzie name well known in the show ring many years ago.

Most of the old houses have gone. Many decayed because their timber was not selected for its durability, and with them disappeared some examples of outstanding craftsmanship. The timber was pit-sawn and smoothly finished. The joists were morticed into place, and the outer boards fitted so skilfully that nails were unnecessary. The houses were roofed with shingles cut from totara blocks 18 inches deep. Alex showed me the implement used—a " frou ", a simple piece of steel sharpened along one side and tapped with a hammer on the other, the handle being at right angles to the blade. Splitting shingles was one of the many ways in which the boys filled the winter evenings. " Frou " is an old English word that remained current in America long after it had become obsolete in Britain.

For convenience, the first houses were built near streams. Later, when tanks came into use, those that had survived fire and decay were hauled by bullock teams to more suitable sites. Their identity disappeared as more rooms were added; and often their timber was used in barns and sheds.

" The open door " was no figure of speech in those early days. One man, describing the home in which he spent his boyhood seventy years ago, said the doors might as well never have been there, for they were never closed. The high kitchen with its raftered roof was hung with hams, dried fish, onions and corn-cobs. Oats and wheat were stored in sheds, a week's supply being ground at a time. With plenty of land and the cordial help of neighbours, five acres of potatoes were planted each year with the plough. Cabbages were grown in great quantities. If there was a glut, they were fed to the cattle.

No warning of visits was given or expected. At the time of the jubilee celebrations fifty years ago, a house near Whangarei had twenty-eight visitors—Waipu-bound—who stayed the night. In the morning an extra one who had arrived after everyone else had gone to bed came to light. His presence was announced when he slouched into the kitchen from some corner of the house, looking for a cup of tea—or a mug of whisky—before breakfast.

There are few signs today of the period that came slowly to an end with the development of refrigeration. Here and there you will see a shed with mossy shingled roof and broken walls; or rails of black tea-tree still strong after ninety years of service. If you know where to look, you can see where the cattle were yarded before they were taken to the Auckland market. There are, too, in unexpected places, the remnants of stocks and slipways where boats were built; boats that served their communities well in the more leisurely days before transport had to be speeded up to keep abreast of the changes in farming methods.

It was, on the whole, a good and pleasant time. With no herds of cattle demanding attention night and morning, the men could go visiting for a day or two without feeling any sense of guilt. Pig-hunting and fishing had as much purpose behind them as tending the farm. And if work could be regarded as sport, so much the better.

Comparisons are difficult, and those still living who have experienced the old and the new ways hesitate to say which they prefer. An old woman remembered as " the happiest days of her life " the time when, as a little girl, she went out to a bush clearing to keep house—in a tent—for her pioneering father. Others think nostalgically of simple foods for which a healthy appetite was possibly the best sauce: the sun-dried fish, for example, grilled for Sunday night's tea, than which nothing tasted better.

It is in talk and reminiscence that the period chiefly lives today, in stories with the flavour of another world. The tale still told by those who knew the first settlers at the Whangarei Heads might have been set, with little alteration, in the Scottish Hebrides. Roman Catholic families lived there, too, men who were able to go fishing on the Sabbath without damaging their consciences. To the Presbyterians standing glumly on the shore, it usually seemed that results were particularly good on that day. They would watch the well-laden boats coming in to the beach, but could do nothing about it, even when the Irishmen offered teasingly to share their catch with those who were curbed by religious scruples.

At the Heads, too, there are memories of Captain McLeod's barn where the children played in the hay and where Norman McLeod, a sturdy and immaculate old man, preached when he visited the district. Usually, however, the people made the journey to Waipu, crossing to Marsden Point by boat and then walking or riding along the beach until they reached the Centre. It is remembered how, on one occasion, the boat capsized; and the women were kept afloat by the air that was caught under their gowns. And, in case it might be thought that life was over-solemn, there is the story of the merry party that one night climbed the craggy slopes of Mount Manaia, 2,000 feet high, and danced quadrilles on the narrow summit.

It was a good and pleasant time, judging by the memories that have remained alive until the present; but it had one major disadvantage. The farms, with their simple economy and few cash crops, could not support the large families that caused the population to grow so quickly. From the first years of the settlement it was necessary for the men to look elsewhere for work. Many of them found it in seasonal or casual employment, spending months at a time away from home. A large number became bushmen, returning to Waipu or their home for the New Year festivities, and then going away again until the following Christmas. Many of them stayed away permanently.

Okaihau, far to the north, was settled in this manner. More than eighty years ago, Alex McKenzie's uncle was one of a party putting the telegraph line through to the North Cape. They came to a northern valley that was practically in its virgin state, a warm valley suitable for farming. A number of the Waipu families sold their land and went there. For many years they worked under conditions that were even more difficult than those already experienced—" They might have stayed at home and done just as well," Alex says; but now Okaihau is one of the most productive parts of Northland.

But for the crowded generations, the most popular form of escape was through education. Schooling had never lost its importance with the Nova Scotian Highlanders. During the long Cape Breton winters there was time for the young to become formidable scholars in subjects that ranged from algebra to Greek. They brought their own teachers with them to New Zealand. Norman Matheson, with his skill in penmanship and in mathematics, laid the foundation of many a future sea captain's career. But for most of the young boys and girls in the early years of the settlement, school became of less importance than the immediate problem of breaking-in a farm.

Then there came another change. Education provided an outlet for the intelligent and ambitious youth to the larger world. Government scholarships brought large numbers of children to the grammar schools of Auckland. Many entered the public service. Before long Waipu and its sister-settlements were supplying more school-teachers in proportion to their population than any other part of New Zealand.

Temporarily handicapped by a leg injury, one young man of about twenty-three decided he would not waste his time. Quite unself-consciously he went back to school, sitting with lads a dozen years his junior at his little schoolroom desk.

Although the development of refrigeration ended what we now think of as " the good old days ", it also gave farming a more secure foundation. It was through the enterprise of men like J. A. S. Mackay, also known as Long Jim, that the change came to Waipu.

Very tall, amiable, with darting eyes, Long Jim wears usually on his round face a look of surprised but cheerful innocence. It is an expression that has misled many people, for Long Jim has a politician's brain, a talent for diplomacy, an ability to get things done that, in anyone less altruistic than himself, might have been classed as artfulness or cunning. At eighty-six, he still plays a good game of poker. In the larger battle of wits that we call life, the same qualities have not been lacking.

A farm-bred lad, he went to Taranaki on his honeymoon. For Mr Mackay, there is no sharp distinction between business and pleasure; and what was more natural than that, while in the nursery of New Zealand's infant dairy industry, he should visit some of the new butter factories operating there. What he saw impressed him, and on his return to Waipu the first steps were taken in a plan that was to transform the district.

The change did not come suddenly. The first shipment of frozen butter from New Zealand went to Britain in 1882; by 1894 there were eighty-two butter factories and forty-two cheese factories registered in the country. But it was not until about 1909, when good-quality butter was manufactured successfully from home-separated cream, that the industry began to look to a prosperous future.

At first, butter-making was a cumbersome business. All the milk was sent to creameries, and the cream, from which the butter was made, set in large pans. In Waipu and the other settlements where the discipline of Norman McLeod lingered after his death, milk could not be sent to the factory on Sundays. The farmers skimmed the cream themselves, and sent it with the next day's milk. For this reason they anticipated what was to be one of the dairy industry's most important advances—the discovery that good butter could be made from home-separated cream.

The milking machine, a power- or hand-propelled separator, made it possible for farmers to handle considerably larger herds. Instead of producing a variety of crops and fruits, they concentrated more and more on dairying, until butter was their chief source of income.

As in the rest of New Zealand, the farmer at Waipu and the other settlements found that he had one great advantage over his brothers in many other parts of the world: his cattle could graze in the fields all the year round, and it was unnecessary to grow tons of supplementary fodder for them. With the introduction of manures and improved methods of harvesting hay and ensilage, many of them discarded completely the use of the plough. The decision cut two ways. If corn and other crops were not to be grown for his herd, the farmer tended to overlook his own vegetable garden, and to rely on the shops for the bulk of his family's food. The dairy cow was a good servant but a bad master. There is no doubt that in many homes nutritional standards fell away while the farmer and his children spent long hours in the milking-shed or looking after the herd.

There are today some enthusiasts for "healthy living" among the descendants of the Nova Scotians, who urge a return to the simple fare of their forebears. One of these, a persuasive speaker, quoted as a warning the example of a family that he knew well. "First so-and-so became ill and died. A few months later a brother followed him. Within a few years scarcely any of that flourishing family were still alive. Too much strong tea, not enough home-grown vegetables—that was the trouble!" He shook his head sadly, and the rest of the group were morbidly impressed. Except for the man standing next to me, who told me in a whisper: "There is only one thing he hasn't mentioned; they were all about eighty years old when they died!"

It must be admitted, however, that there was much truth in the gospel he preached. When food could be bought easily, a farmer already working long hours would not take the same trouble to grow it. There had always been the "careful" ones in Waipu, as in any other community; like the man, for example, who, after unexpectedly spending a night at a neighbour's home, said to his friends later: "No wonder they are poor. The children all had an egg to their breakfast!" But for most of them, the growing and harvesting of their own staple foods was the chief material end of life. And, as long as the food lasted, there was no stinting of it.

Good roads, fast transport, improved machinery have now taken some of the drudgery from the farmer's life. There is time today for recreation—and even for gardening. The farmer and his family have realised, to some extent, that home-grown food is good for them as well as for their animals; and that time-saving tinned and processed foods do not have all the virtues.

But nothing will bring back the rather casual life that, in spite of their isolation, the early settlers definitely enjoyed. And the "characters" who were developed by the highly individual way of life will never return. Kenny Robb for many years lived in a whare next door to the cemetery. "I have plenty of good friends here," he used to say, "and they're all quiet."

Kenny kept fowls, which, like most of their kind, wandered far afield to lay their eggs and look for food. One particularly contrary bird persisted in making its nest on the tombstone of a man whom Kenny had never liked. He refused to eat its eggs.

Stories of such men have passed into the local folk-lore, but their kind will never come again. Some of them are remembered for their virtues or for their weaknesses; others for a chance saying that has retained its vividness.

Kenny had a friend, Alex, who had kept, in his English, all the imagery of Gaelic at its best. One day, on his return from fishing, he was explaining how he had lost his axe.

" I was cleaning a catch of hapuka fish down on the rocks," he said, " when up came a big shark—the dirty brute—looking for a meal. He came so close that I took a swing at him with my axe. There was a huge splash and eddy, and the next thing I saw was the shark swimming fast out to sea, with the axe-handle sticking up on his back, like a bloody cockatoo looking for land." A cockatoo, it should be explained, was the early term for a land-hungry farmer.

The hero of the following anecdote genuinely belongs to a time that has gone for ever. While on holiday in Auckland, an old man died suddenly. He was, of course, to be buried in Waipu; and one of his friends set out by steamer to carry through the sad but necessary task of bringing him back. The coffin was made and the melancholy freight deposited in the steamer's hold along with the rest of the cargo. On arrival at Waipu, its guardian was politely told what the transport charges were. He looked at the captain with an air of guarded triumph.

" That may be so," he said, " but I think it is not necessary. When I was looking through my poor friend's possessions, I found that he had bought a return ticket! "

Nicknames, as the story of the McKay family indicates, were a necessity in the Nova Scotian settlements if absolute confusion was to be avoided. Even with their use, ambiguity prevailed at times. The nicknames in general followed a broad classification, although there were exceptions. D. X. McLeod's second initial stood for no name but was purely a distinguishing mark, and William Aeneas Morrison Mackay was generally known as " Billum " !

Place-names were a fruitful source of inspiration. John McLean lived at the Birdgrove, and that became his unofficial surname. Others were Bridge, Cave, Tasmania and Omaha. " I am one of the Ferry boys," old Roderick McKay told me. He and his family had been born in the Ferry House, which still stands on the first farm taken up in the Waipu district. They were Roddy and Danny Ferry to everyone.

Occupations were drawn on heavily. There were families nicknamed Cooper, Miller (from Roderick Fraser), Tanner (from Murdoch McKenzie), Shoemaker and Mason. Donald McMillan was known as Gow Mhor, the Big Blacksmith; his children were Christopher and Mary Gow. Roderick Campbell, known as Buchan, comes into this class. He constantly read, quoted and practised the precepts of Dr Buchan, a medical man whose books had been famous in the Highlands a century before. His children were known, too, as Buchans.

Personal characteristics were seized on with a frankness that those concerned did not always relish. One man was known as " Slick "; another as " Perpendicular " because of his height. Angus McMillan became the Ricker, because he was as tall and straight as a young kauri—a " rika " in the Maori language. The nickname " Beg ", which means " little ", persisted even when its owner had grown to full stature. The Gaelic word for an ancestor's colouring—red, dark, fair, yellow-haired—remained with descendants who might well have lost the family characteristic. William McLeod was known as " Vinegar ". His farm at Kauri was called Vinegar Hill, and his children were distinguished by the same unusual name.

Chance remarks and anecdotes were pounced on as inspiration for more names. Donald McGregor went to Auckland and came home with a new suit. Someone said to him: " You look as smart as Levy "—a well-known Jew in Auckland at that time; and since then his descendants have been known as Levy. A formal suit bought by Murdoch McGregor gained for him the resounding nickname of " Governor ".

A small boy was taken to school for the first time. An elder pupil remarked: " You're no bigger than this ", and flicked his thumb and finger together. A new and durable nickname, " Flick ", was born.

A good name was not discarded lightly, although it might change in succeeding generations. Captain Duncan McKenzie, the Prince, had a son who was Tom Prince, " Tom " being a contraction of the Gaelic Tormod, or Norman. His grand-daughter became, by a natural process, Jessie Tom.

If the families had remained out of close contact with the rest of the world, there is no doubt that many nicknames would soon have become official surnames. Many are still in common use, but their bearers can also be identified by " foreigners " in more normal ways.

CHAPTER SEVEN

SEAMEN ON MANY OCEANS

WHEN Captain Duncan Matheson's father, Angus, was two years old, he left the Kyle of Lochalsh with his parents for Nova Scotia in the McLeod migration. The Mathesons were changing the scene of their operations, but their way of life was to remain much the same. They had been seamen and shipbuilders in Scotland, they continued on the same course for thirty years in Nova Scotia; and, when they sailed their own fast ship, the *Spray*, to New Zealand, their first object was to find a place where the Matheson vessels could be built to sail on new seas.

Within a month of her arrival in Auckland, the *Spray*, classed in the newspaper advertisements as " the fine, A1 Clipper Schooner ", was accepting cargo and passengers for Sydney, under the command of Captain Hugh Anderson. Within a few months her owners had discovered, half-way between Auckland and the main Waipu settlement, the little haven of Omaha, now known as Leigh.

When I went down to Leigh, Captain Duncan Matheson was waiting for me in his dinghy at the wharf, for there is still no access by road to his home, where he lives with his married son and a thriving family of grandchildren. Belying his eighty-two years, he pushed the dinghy away from the wharf steps and, with a smooth, apparently effortless stroke, sent his little boat across the bay. A handsome old man with a ruddy complexion, neat white moustache and a surprisingly deep voice, Duncan does the half-mile journey several times a day. In the morning he takes some of his grandchildren across to school, and then makes another trip with the cream. The afternoon sees the journey repeated.

Many Matheson farms are still scattered across the hills and valleys of Leigh, and on the beaches there are still boats—one of them more than seventy years old, that members of the family have built. Although, with the passing of sail, the slipways down which they would send schooners for the deep-sea trade have completely disappeared.

In recent years many of the family have gone away to school and university, to become business-men or school-teachers. But at intervals they still come back, for holidays and visits, to the quiet bay where they spent their childhood. Leigh has a firm hold on their hearts. I discovered why when we stood—Captain Duncan, two of his sons and myself—near the top of a 900-feet hill not far from Colin Matheson's farm. The view was magnificent. Northward, a beach of dazzling white sand curved past Mangawai to Bream Tail, with the peaks of the Whangarei Heads showing up sixty miles away. To the south were a myriad islands, a coast-line where land and water interlocked. Auckland city seemed far away, but there were her volcanic hills sharp on the horizon.

But the sea dominated the view, the immense Pacific Ocean stretching eastward as far as the eye could reach, dwarfing the islands so that Sail Rock, 400 feet high, looked like a wooden chip.

"We like to be near the sea," Colin Matheson said. "I remember once I was farming on the Northern Wairoa River. My neighbour's wife used to say that to her the river seemed a barrier. But to me it seemed an outlet."

And so the Mathesons farm their land happily enough, with the sound of the ocean in their ears and the cheering thought that, if they feel like it, they can always go fishing. Captain Duncan has the true seaman's attitude to the land. Although his sons are expert, he himself never learned to shear a sheep, and he does not feel that he has suffered for that reason. "And as for milking cows," he adds with a certain measure of pride, "we always looked on that as women's work."

When I asked him how long the Mathesons had been seamen in Scotland, it was obvious that the question had never occurred to him.

"Why," he replied thoughtfully, "they were weaned and raised on salt water. For generations they looked on the land as a convenient place to tie up their ships; but the sea has always been their home."

Knowing this, it is easier to place in its proper perspective the voyage of the *Spray*, a vessel of 107 tons, which brought its owners and ninety passengers half-way round the world to New Zealand in 1857. Surely one of the most remarkable voyages in the history of a sea-loving people, when it is considered that the *Spray* was no larger than an average coasting craft. She was built specially for the trip, and given a trial on the mail service between Halifax and Bermuda. She justified her owners' confidence. The passenger list was greater on her arrival than when she left St Ann's, for three babies were born during the voyage.

Duncan Matheson can remember no doubts having been held by his father or uncle on the *Spray's* ability, or fears at the length of the voyage. After what they had been accustomed to, he said, they considered it was like sailing to Eden. And, indeed, their early years at sea had been spent in the world's most turbulent waters. The Minch, where the Atlantic tides boil through behind the Hebrides, was no pleasure-pond; and after that they made their living in the North Atlantic, where fog and storm were a supreme test of seamanship. Their last work before leaving Nova Scotia was taking fish from the Newfoundland Banks to Halifax and other ports on the eastern seaboard.

But, Captain Matheson said, drawing on memories of his father's conversation, it was the climate that killed St Ann's for them. With six feet of ice in the bay, how could a sailor hope to make a satisfactory living?

And so Captain Angus and Captain Duncan Matheson, father and uncle of my old friend, set out with their Gaelic-speaking ship's company on the long voyage, accepting its hazards as a matter of course. There were incidents that, for less accomplished seamen, might have been serious.

During a southerly buster that drove her towards the coast of New South Wales, the *Spray* did not escape damage. The bowsprit snapped, in the words of a passenger, " like a pipe-shank at the cathead ". The wreckage, in the high seas, was crashing against the hull. Kenneth McKenzie, later known as Kenneth Omaha, who was a member of the crew, volunteered to be lowered over the side in the storm. At great risk, he succeeded in cutting away the gear that held the bowsprit, thus probably saving the ship. Kenneth, who became one of New Zealand's best-known seamen, will enter this story again in a later chapter.

Matheson's Bay, at Omaha, was beautiful, with forest down to the water's edge. Along the cliffs and over the headlands grew pohutukawa, covered with red blossom in the summer, and ideal for fashioning the frames of the ships they soon began to build. Less than three miles away, in Duncan's own recollection, was the kauri forest, supplying the best timber in the world for planking and for spars.

There, in vastly different circumstances, the Matheson's traditional pattern of life soon emerged. Timber was pit-sawn and brought down to a spot a little more than a mile away from Duncan's present home; and there the ships were built.

The brothers still spent much of their time at sea. "They would make a trading voyage to the Pacific Islands and then come home to build another ship." They had men working for them who were expert at their craft. One tradesman could split a match, held under his foot, with an adze; and even the most expert eye could not tell whether the deck of a new vessel had been finished off with an adze or a plane. As their reputation spread, they began to build, on contract for Auckland merchants, schooners and cutters that held a proud place in the local fleet. At that time Auckland was the centre of a thriving Island trade. Her businessmen had plantations and trading-stores in all parts of the South Pacific.

But still, Duncan recalls, his father and uncle would yield to the call of the sea. His father would return with a few casual remarks about the places he had visited, and fearsome weapons of carved wood from the cannibal tribes of the New Hebrides and the Solomon Islands.

The Mathesons kept in close touch with their friends and relatives at Waipu. At first—for there were no roads—they walked the forty miles between the two settlements, taking with them presents of fish or perhaps some curious articles obtained during a Pacific voyage. Duncan's mother did not find the walk too long, when she could enjoy friendly conversation at the end of it.

Then they went on horse-back, riding along the white beaches, turning inland over narrow tracks and finally back to the beach and over the last headlands to Waipu. The journey took about six hours.

" Sometimes we rode over to dances," Duncan said, " but usually just to talk."

Looking back, Duncan does not regret the days of his youth. " We could sail and row almost as soon as we could crawl," he said. " And now I see my grandchildren are the same." They went fishing in waters that were famous for their bounty. Crayfish could be taken in pots within the bay itself, and it was never necessary to go far for a boatload of fish.

They hung their fish out to dry on lines in the sun; they killed their own beef, a welcome change from the staple diet of fish; they grew their own vegetables. Wheat also, but it was often unsuitable for milling, for too much rain came at the ripening time.

Then, in 1882, there was a tragic event at Omaha. Captain Duncan had decided to build a fast schooner for the Island trade, and into its construction he put all his skill and knowledge. By then the most suitable kauri trees in their locality had been used. He combed the forests of the east coast for a tree that would make a worthy main-mast for his schooner, triumphantly named the *Three Cheers*.

He found it in a kauri bush at Waipu, not far from Alex McKenzie's home. The tree was felled carefully, a mast seventy-five feet in length cut from it, and the broad-bladed axes shaped its smooth roundness into eight sides. It was brought down to the sea in a two-wheeled wagon, drawn by three bullock teams. It cost £75—£1 a foot. Then it was towed by two dinghies, manned by the Matheson men and their elder children, the long forty miles down to Omaha.

But Duncan Matheson was not destined to enjoy a sight of his fine ship under sail. A careful workman, he preferred to carry out the rigging of the *Three Cheers* himself. The sheer-legs, fifty feet high, broke, the boom crashed down and killed him. The *Three Cheers* was the last sea-going vessel built by the Mathesons.

She gained a wide reputation for her speed and seaworthiness, winning the trading schooners' race at the Auckland Regatta, one of the grand sights of a colourful period. But she was not kind to her skippers.

In a copy of the *Sydney Daily Telegraph* dated November 19, 1892, I found a report of a tragic mission that the *Three Cheers*, now owned by the famous Mrs Forsythe, of Ralune, New Britain, made to one of the islands of the Bismarck Archipelago. About eighteen months before, a trader and his six servants had been massacred by savages on the island. The *Three Cheers*, commanded by an Italian, Captain Stalio, took the German Commissioner and a squad of native police to the scene of the tragedy. Captain Stalio volunteered to help arrest the murderers, who, armed with captured weapons, resisted strongly. In the exchange of shots, Captain Stalio was killed. The police shot down the natives, including the king and his son, who had taken refuge in their " idol " house. With the captain's body on board, the *Three Cheers* then returned to New Britain.

The graceful schooner, built in the peaceful little haven of Omaha, had taken part, innocently enough, in one of the numerous incidents that for many years disfigured the history of the South-west Pacific.

Duncan, the son of Angus, went to sea when the coastal trade was at its height, before it was stifled by road and rail competition. The timber industry in the north and at Mercury Bay, on the Coromandel Peninsula, was flourishing. Off Buffalo Beach there were often four overseas ships waiting to load milled timber. Among them, up to the boom where acres of kauri logs were held, Duncan's little vessel sailed busily. He loaded his logs " in the round ", by means of a manual windlass, for this was before the time of the internal-combustion engine. They were taken to Auckland and dumped on the mud-flat at Freeman's Bay, where the gas-works now stand.

There was cheerfulness and gaiety at Mercury Bay. A favourite recreation among the bushmen, and also with Duncan Matheson, was roller-skating; and the rink was something that could have been built only in a district where timber was produced and expended lavishly. The floor was made of scantling boards, six inches wide and two inches deep, each plank being set on its narrow edge.

Afterwards, for twenty-two years, Duncan made the run to the Little Barrier Island, a bird sanctuary off the coast at Omaha. He met many scientists, and from them learned that birds were not only for eating. He is pleased to see that the native pigeons, fat and unafraid, have now come back to the trees around his home. He does his best to encourage them.

McGregors, McLeods, Campbells, McDonalds and McKenzies—these and other families that came from Nova Scotia were rich in seamen and sea-going traditions. The minister's son, Donald McLeod, who spent his retirement at Waipu translating " The Ossian " from the Gaelic into English, was himself a sea-captain. He took a St Ann's-built vessel to Scotland from Nova Scotia and sold the cargo before he went to Australia to become a journalist.

The ships might have been smaller in those days, but the opportunities, as well as the responsibilities, were great; and an ambitious youth with ability and energy could be sure of gaining a command while he was young enough to enjoy it. At that time, too, a sea-captain in the normal course of events became part-owner of his ship, and then owner and possibly a merchant as well. The men from the north were quick to seize their chance.

On one occasion nine master mariners of the McKenzie family anchored their ships in Auckland Harbour at one time. They and their cousins, the McDonalds, formed almost a dynasty of sea-captains, and the story of their experiences can still stir the imagination.

It began with the two McKenzie brothers, Duncan Prince and Murdoch Captain; and their brother-in-law, Hector McDonald. Duncan, serene, stalwart and slightly aloof in bearing, gained his nickname, it is said, when he visited an

Irish port on a trading voyage from Cape Breton. Strolling in leisurely fashion along the pier, he was accosted by a member of the Royal family who had mistaken him for the Prince Consort. For Albert, like Haroun Al-Raschid, was accustomed to move incognito among the people so as to gain a better understanding of them. The name " Prince ", jokingly given him by his sailor friends, remained with him until his death, and then passed to his descendants.

Duncan and Murdoch were born leaders, with a high sense of duty. They represented their people in turn in the Provincial Council, Duncan first and then his brother. As one of the first men to purchase land in the Waipu district, Duncan also took the responsibility of maintaining communications by sea with Auckland. He built cutters—the *Flora McDonald*, the *Thistle* and the *Jessie*; while Murdoch traded as far afield as New York and China.

Murdoch was as fiery as Duncan was serene. It took a quiet, land-loving man of Waipu to score off Captain Murdoch when he had given up sea-trading and had settled again at Waipu.

The Captain, so the story goes, had some urgent business in Auckland, and invited this man to accompany him and work his passage. The land-lubber demurred, and made the excuse that he had no good coat to wear on this visit to civilisation.

"Wear my pilot's jacket," Murdoch answered. (It was never a coat in Waipu; in the same way, potatoes were cooked in their jackets, not in their skins.)

Murdoch had his way, and off they went down the river. It was probably an open boat, not more than twenty feet in length; and crossing the bar at the river-mouth was a ticklish business. The Captain, a very good seaman and a very vigorous swearer, took exception to his companion's efforts with the jib in the bow.

" Get to hell out of it, you —— fool," he roared, and the poor man wished more than ever that he had stayed on dry land. But all the same, the germ of an idea was born.

They reached Auckland without further incident, and returned safely home. Some weeks later, the Captain inquired after his jacket, tactfully hinting that it should be returned.

His former companion looked at him very blandly. "Do you remember what you said to me when we were crossing the bar? Well, as you told me, I took your jacket to hell, and it was burned!"

For once, Captain Murdoch was left speechless.

It was inevitable that there should be tragedies on the deceptively innocent coast that lay between Waipu and Auckland. Rough easterly weather could come up quickly. The little vessels, unable to attempt the shifting, sandy bar of the Waipu River in such conditions, were forced to run for shelter under the headlands at the northern end of the bay. Nor was this manœuvre always safe. Poor visibility, heavy seas that rose quickly, were hazards that could not be escaped.

On the night of March 29, 1868, the *Thistle* arrived off Bream Bay with sixteen passengers and a full cargo for Waipu. With darkness, a moderate south-easterly had developed into a roaring gale. The weather was thick and heavy with rain. To run for Whangarei in such conditions was impossible. Captain Duncan McKenzie's only alternative was to attempt to beat his way past the cruel rocks of Bream Head, directly to the north.

He tacked to the north-east and then to the south-east, with reefed mainsail and staysail. Before five o'clock in the morning he turned to the north again, but the gale had defeated him. In complete darkness, at twenty minutes past five, the *Thistle* struck about a mile inside Bream Head.

Kenneth and Norman McDonald jumped ashore, and a rope was secured through the crashing breakers. Three passengers —Hugh Sutherland, Alex McLeod and Robert Campbell— stationed themselves along the rope to help the others ashore. Their task was almost finished when a huge wave swept McLeod and a twelve-year-old girl, Joanna Mitchelson, away. They were both drowned.

Kenneth McDonald, his leg crushed between the ship and the rock, lay exposed to the weather for more than twenty-four hours before help, summoned from Whangarei, could reach him.

In all the chapters of tragedy, none struck more severely at Duncan Prince than the loss of his eldest son, Captain Kenneth McKenzie. Kenneth had commanded his father's schooner, the *Jessie*, and later took charge of the barque *Caberfeidh*, trading to America. He missed a voyage through illness, but, recovering before she returned, bought the schooner *William and Julia*, in which he made several voyages to the Pacific. He then bought the *Rona*, and sailed her successfully until the last voyage. Coming up the west coast in thick and stormy weather, he was unable to find the entrance to the Kaipara Harbour. Before the storm moderated, his schooner was carried into the breakers, where it capsized and came ashore bottom up.

Of Captain Kenneth, who was then in his thirty-eighth year, a fellow seaman said: " He was the finest man I knew, one of nature's noblemen. New vessels can be built, and those lost can perhaps be improved upon; but men of Captain McKenzie's character and worth cannot be replaced." When Captain Duncan heard of his son's death, he fainted; and did not speak for three days.

Where the sea took one man, several more came forward. Highly skilled and confident, they had the ability to do spectacular things in a matter-of-fact way. There was Colin McDonald, for example, who came down the Northern Wairoa River with a load of timber for Australia. He reached the bar at the entrance to the Kaipara—a graveyard of ships—and discovered six other vessels waiting inside. The signal showed that the bar was considered unworkable, but Colin took his ship out. When he returned to the Kaipara about a fortnight later with a load of coal, the signal was again adverse. He sailed in, and found the six ships still waiting for the bar to become more favourable.

Colin had a cousin, John Captain McKenzie, master of a barque that traded frequently to Auckland. John was famous for his seamanship; and one day, in a moment of exhilaration, he brought his ship in under sail and berthed her unassisted against the outer tee of the wharf. It was a manœuvre that called for sound judgment, and eventually word of it reached Colin.

The wharf was different in design from the massive concrete structures of the present day. In addition to the outer tee, there were berths projecting at right angles to its main length, a fact that Colin knew well. At the time he was master of the *Robin Hood*, the last brig to trade between Australia and New Zealand. On her next visit to Auckland, the *Robin Hood*, also under sail and without assistance, came smoothly to the wharf to tie up, not at the outer tee, but at one of the inside berths nearer the shore. No comment was necessary. Every seaman knew that if John McKenzie had made an error, he could have continued safely up the harbour; but if Colin had been guilty of bad judgment, his ship would have crashed into the main body of the wharf.

Much of my information concerning the McKenzies came from Hector Clark; much also in a letter from Jessie McKenzie Douglas who, when ninety-four years old, sent to me from her home in Toowoomba, Queensland, her recollections of the great men of the clan to which she was so proud to belong. She had not forgotten Captain Duncan McKenzie, whom she last saw when she was a girl in Waipu.

" On the deck of his ship," she wrote, " looking out on an horizon of distant peaked islets, he was the chief and centre of his surroundings. . . . When the waves gathered to fall in thunder on the shores of the entrance to the Waipu River, that stately commanding figure stood at the helm; from his kindly, large, dark-blue eyes fear seemed forever banished. In a steady voice which could be clearly heard over the rush of waves he gave orders to his sailors in the responsible task of weathering the ship into safety."

Written many years later, these words still carry the echo of a young girl's admiration. And the Prince was worthy of it.

Hector McDonald, who taught Duncan and Murdoch McKenzie their seamanship in Scotland before marrying their sister, did not go to sea again after he settled at Waipu. But his sons included three sea-captains. One of them, Duncan, was lost when his fore-and-aft schooner *Acadia* disappeared without trace after leaving Napier for Mercury Bay in the year

1880. But the other two sons, Colin and Murdoch, had long and honourable careers.

Colin McDonald did not go to sea until he was nearly twenty, for his father's farm made the first call on his time. This fact was to influence his career greatly. He became a sailor who also knew and loved horses. And horses played an important part in his life at sea for many years.

His first voyage was under Captain Jacob in the Melanesian Mission schooner *Southern Cross*. During the next few years, as he rose in rank, he became wise in the ways of men as well as in the ways of animals. When he was about ninety years old, looking back on sixty-two years at sea, forty of them as a captain, he could speak as follows: " It is all wrong to think that sailors are animals that have to be treated as such to maintain discipline. In the old sailing ship days I encouraged my men to respect me rather than fear me; and the result was that I never had the slightest trouble with them. I sailed with the roughest types, but when they learned my methods they were the staunchest fellows, and never wanted to leave the ships that I commanded."

A skipper who never swore at a sailor, and never logged one for failing to fulfil his orders would be rare enough at any time. But Captain Colin McDonald had his own ways of running a ship. One of his commands was the *Euryalus*, which took the second Australian contingent to the South African War. Seasickness played havoc with many of the troops who came from the inland districts of Australia. Becoming concerned, Captain Colin ordered soup to be provided for them. A few days later he stopped on his rounds to ask a weak and hollow-eyed soldier what he thought of the soup. " It's very good," came the answer, " but I can't afford to buy any more."

The Captain's expression did not change, but, knowing that one of his cooks had been battening on the men, he decided on the best form of retaliation. A notice was posted for the troops stating that, through a mistake by the cook, they had been charged for soup which should have been issued free. If they applied to the cook, however, he would be happy to refund their money.

The soldiers were Australians, and by this time were recovering from their seasickness. They made sure by their claims that the cook did not gain from his attempt at profiteering. He could not refuse whatever they asked, and reached South Africa a sadder and poorer man.

These were the stories that drifted back to Waipu and the other Nova Scotian settlements. They were rarely told in letters from the central characters. They came from other seamen; or perhaps, when one of them was home from the sea for a while, he would relax in the family circle and tell of the events that made up his life.

Thus they learned at Waipu that Hector McDonald's son Colin had, under the flag of the Alexander Currie Line, entered the flourishing horse trade between Australia and India. They may have been told, too, that Colin was establishing a reputation for bringing his valuable charges through the tropics with few losses; and also that, on his suggestion, doorways had been cut in the side of his ship through which the horses could be loaded and unloaded with speed and comfort.

During the First World War his ship carried thousands of remounts to the battlefields of France and Mesopotamia. He recalled one voyage which seemed as if it would never end. Colin and his horses had been diverted from the Mediterranean to Aden, through the sun-stricken Red Sea. From there, after delays and indecision that made both crew and horses suffer, they went to the head of the Persian Gulf, where at last, at a forlorn outpost, he found an army officer prepared to take delivery of the horses. Fretful with the heat and the monotony of his life, the officer was more terse than he might have been in different circumstances.

"How many horses lost?" he barked.

"None," replied the imperturbable Colin in his soft Highland voice.

The army man glared his disbelief. "And how many days will you need to unload?"

"An hour or two should be enough, as long as you bring sufficient barges alongside," Colin replied.

To the officer, with visions of the horses being lifted by slings and laboriously lowered on to lighters, this seemed an additional affront from a man who was obviously goading him to distraction. This time, he expressed his disbelief vigorously in words that were more colourful than polite.

Captain Colin did not raise his voice, but he disliked swearing, especially when it did not seem necessary. "You will send out the barges, and your horses will be unloaded as I have said. But you will leave my ship immediately."

The barges came out. The horses were unloaded as quickly as the transports could be brought alongside. When the work was done, the surprised officer came on board and apologised handsomely.

Colin McDonald retired to live in Melbourne when he was well over seventy, but he still acted as inspector for the British India Line on all their ships leaving for India. When his third war came, although he was approaching ninety, he again offered his services in any capacity; and he did not remain inactive.

The exploits of Colin's young brother, Murdoch, brought a taste of adventure, and of tragedy, to the people of Waipu. First, there was the story of the *Fortunatus*, which caught fire and sank when under his command in the Indian Ocean; the fortnight in open boats while he and the crew sailed to Mauritius; and then, capping the story splendidly, the verdict at the inquiry conducted by naval officers, when Captain McDonald was commended for upholding the best traditions of British seamanship.

Tragedy ended Captain Murdoch's life in 1926, shortly before he was due to retire. For many years he had commanded the *Klang*, a handsome vessel running between Singapore and Penang. A few hours after they had left Singapore, one of his officers came hurrying up to him on the bridge. A Malayan had run amok and had already killed or wounded several of the native passengers on the crowded foredeck.

"Take over the bridge," Captain Murdoch told him, and then he went forward to deal with the trouble in the best way he knew—bare-handed. But Murdoch, big and vigorous though he was, failed to realise that age had slowed him down.

He grappled with the demented native, but suffered a wound from which he died not long after. A pistol, which he had disdained to draw, was discovered in his pocket.

On one of his last voyages, Captain McDonald had as a passenger Sir Harry Lauder; and this is how the famous comedian described him in his autobiography, " Roamin' in the Gloamin' ":

" From Port Swetenham we sailed along the coast to Singapore in a lovely steamer called the *Klang*. The captain of the ship was a splendid Highlander by the name of McDonald who courteously welcomed every individual passenger as he stepped off the gangway on to the deck. He had such a pronounced accent that I asked him what part of the Rob Roy territory he hailed from. 'Alas and alack, Sir Harry', he answered, 'I have never seen the dear land of my fathers and of my dreams. I was born in New Zealand. All my life has been spent in these tropical seas. But soon I hope to retire and the first thing I shall do will be to go "home" to Scotland and see the hills and streams and villages my father and mother loved so tenderly.'

" These words were spoken in the soft, warm accents of the true Highlander and I could scarcely believe that the speaker had not been brought up in Callander or Balquhidder. He astonished me still further by telling me that he had the full Gaelic, and though my knowledge of the language is small he was overjoyed when I said a few Gaelic words to him, and he answered me volubly in the same tongue. In his cabin he had a set of bagpipes and he and I played many a tune on them during the passage. Some months afterward I was shocked beyond measure to read in a New Zealand paper that Captain McDonald had been brutally murdered.

" I tell you this story as another example of the extraordinary way love of country is embedded strong in the hearts of Scottish descent, even in cases where they have never set eyes on the 'Land of Brown Heath and Shaggy Wood'.

" There is a lump in my throat and a tear in my eye ", Sir Harry ended characteristically, " as I write this story of the captain of the s.s. *Klang*. I cannot help it, and I am not ashamed of it. The emotion springs from that ineffable, intangible but tremendously real and eternally vibrant thing called Scottish sentiment."

Through several generations families at Waipu, the Whangarei Heads and Leigh have produced master-mariners and engineers in numbers that defy cataloguing. Secluded though their homes might be, the people of the Nova Scotian settlements had the world brought to their doorsteps. In another way, too, they were reminded that they were part of a larger family. Those who remained in the parent settlements of Cape Breton Island also turned to the sea for a livelihood. It was no rare event for a kinsman, speaking perhaps with a Canadian accent, to bring his ship to Auckland and to call on his New Zealand relatives.

Letters would follow, and the old ties would be renewed.

CHAPTER EIGHT

AN INTERLUDE WITH THE BLACKBIRDERS

THE sinking sun, taking a backward glance at Lang's Beach, stains the breaking waves with a reddish hue. Out beyond the bay, the craggy heights of Manaia, the split volcanic peak of the Hen Island, still catch its full light. The waves break and surge, break and surge with a rhythm that never grows monotonous. The foam, drained of colour, shows pale against the darkening sea. Along the beach, gannets—those clean gulls built for swift flight—take their last sweeping turn above the sand and water.

As we walked along through the sober evening, my friend said suddenly: " Can you imagine the rum-runners coming ashore here? For that is what they did, you know. They would sail down from New Caledonia and, if conditions were favourable, land their cargo at the Cove, as this beach was called in those days. If it was wiser to keep away, either because of the weather or because the revenue cutter was about, they could take it ashore at Leigh or at the Whangarei Heads, or on Rangitoto Island, near the entrance to Auckland Harbour."

Captain Kenneth McKenzie, known as Kenneth Omaha, to distinguish him from the many other McKenzies to whom he was not related, carried the art of smuggling to its highest level. He brought to it an artist's delight. One feels that, even if it had not produced money, smuggling would still have been the occupation dearest to his heart. It was Kenneth who, at the risk of his life, had gone over the side of the *Spray* on her voyage to New Zealand to cut away a broken bowsprit. He settled down to no quiet existence in the colony. The blood of his marauding ancestors ran strongly in his veins. He found in the islands of the Pacific the natural outlet for his energy and his non-conforming spirit of adventure. It was dampened, but not quenched, when his son Willie, with six other members of his crew, was captured and eaten by the Solomon Islanders.

The Highlander's conception of moral values that had ruled a generation or two earlier found an enthusiastic recruit in Kenneth McKenzie. Scrupulously honest in his dealings with friends, the Highlander regarded anything that belonged to his enemies as natural plunder. Nor, in the years following Culloden, was personal morality in question if a man deluded that impersonal and largely obnoxious thing, the Government, by turning smuggler. Patriotism, and the paying of taxes, were not linked then. The smuggler's clients reaped the benefit, and he himself had a reasonable source of income.

Standards changed, but the old ways had not completely disappeared when Kenneth Omaha came on the scene. Many heads were shaken disapprovingly, but even those of the Nova Scotians who did not agree with his activities on moral grounds would not have considered giving him away to the authorities.

There are two stories, told to me by a friend of Kenneth's son, Captain George McKenzie, that show how greatly the world has changed since Kenneth's swift and dainty schooner brought her cargoes to New Zealand.

When he was a small boy, George accompanied his father on a trading voyage to the New Hebrides. They drew into a bay, where another schooner lay at anchor. A lean and rakish schooner, George observed, built for speed and quick handling in the treacherous waters of the Coral Sea. While George stayed on board, his father ordered a boat out and was rowed across to the other vessel. The boy noticed, with surprise and horror, that the body of a native was hanging in the rigging.

His father stayed there for three days, most of the time below in the captain's cabin. But in the cool of the morning, and occasionally in the evening, George would see him pacing up and down the deck, deep in conversation with another man, heavily bearded and tall. Finally Kenneth returned, and the McKenzie vessel sailed away.

In answer to his son's inquiries, Kenneth McKenzie explained that he had been visiting his former associate Captain Donald

McLeod, a member of the crew of the *Spray*, whose family (unrelated to that of the Reverend Norman), had gone from St Ann's to the Whangarei Heads. Donald, he added, owned many trading-stations in the New Hebrides. One of these had been raided and destroyed by a party of natives who were offended at some of McLeod's actions. The native had been killed and, as a warning to others, left hanging in the rigging.

A full lifetime separates this story from the next. George McKenzie proved as great a seaman as his father. Under his command the famous topsail schooner *Huia* set records for crossings of the Tasman that stand to this day. He brought his ship from Sydney to the Kaipara Heads in four days six hours, logging at times up to sixteen knots. One dark night, storming towards the Sydney Heads at over fourteen knots, he overtook and nearly collided with a passenger steamer running from Newcastle. Captain McKenzie, in the few seconds allowed him, threw his schooner aback and by superb handling prevented a collision when no more than fifteen feet separated the two ships.

When my friend visited him towards the end of his life, George McKenzie had given up active seafaring for maritime business, with an office overlooking the busy Auckland Harbour. He owned several ships. When they were tied up through a long strike, he continued to pay his captains and their crews their usual wages, although the general practice was to dismiss them at such a time. He had bought an island in the Hauraki Gulf, and there he planned to spend his retirement farming and growing a few vegetables, and perhaps doing some fishing. His companions, he hoped, would be some of his old sea-going friends who had no home of their own. But it proved a sailor's dream. No one, except himself, wanted to settle on the island; and, he added sadly, "When I get there myself, I shall probably be too old and too weak to use a spade." As he suspected, the island never became his home.

The sea was becoming big business, directed from an office desk with little room for sentiment or romance. At this time George McKenzie found pleasure in looking back on his father's career and his good-humoured encounters with the revenue agents. Kenneth McKenzie's character was outrageous in many respects, but he brought a Gaelic charm and zest to everything he did.

He laid his plans well. At the Cove, cattle were often collected for shipment to Auckland. And Captain Kenneth made use of this fact with the skill of a good general.

A few cases of liquor had been brought ashore at low tide; but, before they could be hidden safely elsewhere, the revenue cutter's approach was signalled. The cases were buried below high-water mark. The sea would not rise quickly enough to hide the tell-tale signs of digging. Kenneth called upon his reserves—a herd of cattle kept near at hand for this very purpose. They were driven along the beach, hiding any clues effectively. So well did they do it, in fact, that on one occasion after the foiled searchers had disappeared the buried treasure could not be discovered by its owners.

The battle of wits was keen, and fought in a gentlemanly style by both sides. The customs men arrived unexpectedly at Omaha one day with an authoritative " tip " that a search would yield results. They were met, very courteously, by Kenneth McKenzie on the beach. The officer in charge wasted no time. For all he knew, Kenneth's helpers might at this very moment be spiriting the cargo away. He assigned some of his assistants to probing the beach with gum-spears and beating the bushes, and himself accompanied Captain McKenzie to his house, where he declined the customary hospitality.

" I hope you don't mind me looking about," he said.

" Go right ahead," said Captain McKenzie cordially.

The officer began to search room by room, tapping walls and inspecting cupboards. But when he attempted to push one door open, he was halted by sudden screams from inside.

" My two daughters," Kenneth explained. " That is their bedroom. They are probably afraid that you will take them away to jail. But don't let it concern you. You must do your duty."

Kenneth himself gave the door a push, and the screaming grew louder. " They are rather nervous," he said apologetically. " Help me to force the door open."

With the screams ringing in his ears, and his chivalry coming to the fore, the officer shook his head firmly.

"Don't bother, Captain McKenzie," he said. "We'll go away now."

And off they went.

Some months later, the Captain and the customs officer met on the Auckland water-front.

"Well, Captain, you beat me that time. How did it happen?"

Captain McKenzie smiled. "My daughters were in that room, but so were many other valuable articles. In fact, there was only sufficient floor-space left for them to stand up. They had, as you can imagine, been well-trained!"

Needless to say, the smuggled goods from New Caledonia went to wider markets than the Nova Scotian settlements offered. According to their historian, N. R. McKenzie, whisky was in fairly general but frugal use among the early arrivals at Waipu and the other districts. Most of it came through the regular channels, although there were the inveterate Scots who preferred the product of stills that existed at key points in the various districts.

With the Highlanders of a century or more ago, strong drink had not been classed among the sins of the flesh, and was not necessarily associated with riotous living. When the minister called on his parishioners, he would be offered, not a cup of tea, but a taste of whisky. Norman McLeod was one of the first, and the most vehement opponents of the national drink. He had good reason from his early experiences in Scotland to link intemperance with soft living, soft thinking and lack of strong religious principles. His opinions were strengthened by what he saw of the grog-shops in Pictou, where sailors from overseas ships spent their money in what was considered the time-honoured fashion.

If he could have had his way, Norman McLeod would have banished whisky from his domain. A number of his followers approved of his precepts and carried them out; but with the majority of the migrants, strong drink, in its proper place, did not bring with it a sense of sin. Prohibition and total abstinence had not become the live issues that they would be in later years. And so, at weddings, funerals and other social events, whisky usually held its traditional place. N. R. McKenzie again reports that it was rarely taken to excess. He had almost reached manhood before he saw a drunkard, and that was a visiting gum-digger.

In Captain Donald McLeod, born to a sober and industrious family, the blood of some forgotten, free-booting ancestor predominated. For a seaman, there was in the South Pacific in the 1860s a chance of finding adventure and wealth; but only for a man completely devoid of scruples. The islands and waters of the Coral Sea were outside the control of any responsible nation. For the adventurers who swarmed there from all parts of the world, sandalwood, a sweet-smelling timber of great value when sent to China, was the chief lure. But the natives, although they did not know its value, were unwilling to allow white men, who quickly showed themselves capable of every form of violence, to land on their islands and, with bullets and knives, exact from them their tribute of timber. In Sydney, one of the headquarters of the trade, there was a saying that every stick of sandalwood from the South Seas had blood on it.

The brutality of the sandalwood traders was countered in the only way that the natives knew. Every schooner that approached an island contained potential enemies, even though at times they might be saintly men like Bishop Patteson. They were ambushed and massacred, and the mounting spiral of violence provoked even more savage retaliation.

Once the sandalwood and bêche-de-mer—a succulent slug much favoured by the Chinese for soups—had been exhausted, the natives of the New Hebrides might have been allowed to slip back into the fitful feuding that had always marked their lives. But about this time a civil war had begun in America; and, paradoxically, a war that aimed at suppressing slavery in one part of the world was responsible for its introduction to another.

American cotton supplies were temporarily interrupted. It was discovered that the tropical belt from Fiji to Queensland was suitable for plantations. A source of man-power was at hand in the New Hebrides and Solomon Islands.

The methods employed to gain labourers were as diverse as the characters of the men engaged in the trade. Some were lured on board with promises that they did not understand, and which were in any case rarely honoured. Others were decoyed by blackbirders who disguised themselves as missionaries, clapped their startled victims into the hold and took them to Fiji, where they were sold direct to planters, or to Queensland, where a " contract " system allowed them to return eventually to their island homes; unless they had succumbed to white man's diseases.

Local pressure forced the appointment of Government agents on the Queensland schooners, but these men had an unenviable task. Considerable force of character would have been required for an agent to disagree with the rulings of a captain on whose goodwill his life depended. And so the blackbirders continued to raid the islands, heavily armed to counter the resistance that their previous actions had provoked.

Apart from missionaries and a few comparatively enlightened traders, the men who frequented the Coral Sea looked upon the natives as something less than human. They were dangerous and, unless they could be kept in check, the simplest thing was to shoot them. The only restraining factor was that a dead native immediately lost his value as an article of commerce.

But it still causes a shock to read the following report of an encounter with Donald McLeod in "John Cameron's Odyssey":

" After these skirmishes we sailed for Aurora. . . . Before we arrived at another settlement we sighted a two-masted schooner bound in the opposite direction. She hove to, indicating that she wished to communicate with us. Soon a boat came alongside to warn us that the men of their vessel, the *Meg Merrilies*, Captain McLeod, had shot a chief and two of his retainers on the other side of Aurora in retaliation for the murder of a white trader. 'Twould not be safe for us there, continued Captain McLeod, for the natives would certainly have revenge on the first whites who came."

This neighbourly warning having been reported, we can now turn back to the year 1867, when Donald McLeod seems to have first entered the labour traffic. He found his market in the French colony of New Caledonia, where conditions were even more lax than in Queensland. But McLeod was a more acute business-man than most of those who risked their necks for a living in the Coral Sea. He established a plantation at Havannah Harbour, on Efate Island; with the help of natives imported from other parts of the group, he cleared land on Tanna Island and grew cotton; he set up a station on Mallicollo for collecting bêche-de-mer, which was boiled, dried and sold in the Chinese market for £150 a ton.

His life as a trader was eventful. Off the Maskelynes, the *Donald McLean*, his schooner, was attacked boldly by a fleet of native canoes, which were beaten off only after sharp fighting.

Another event can best be described in the words of Commander Markham, of H.M.S. *Rosario*, who visited the New Hebrides in 1872:

" Two or three years ago, two men, one a Scotchman and the other an American, were left in charge of some land (on Efate Island). Having nothing else to do, they beguiled the time by constantly quarrelling and disputing, until at length they separated and lived in different huts, and then they amused themselves by innocently taking shots at one another, whenever a fair opportunity presented itself. Eventually one was killed, and the survivor, who had some two or three bullets in him, was about twelve months after taken to Brisbane and arraigned on a charge of murder, but was acquitted for want of sufficient evidence, no other white man living on the island, and the word of a black not being taken as evidence in a court of law."

Commander Markham, naturally enough, was rather prejudiced against McLeod, the " Scotchman " in his story, and perhaps presents the facts with more colour than absolute truth. There is no doubt, however, that McLeod, in self-defence, killed his companion, a drunken American named Trueman, while his station was being established at Havannah.

After these events, McLeod, to quote a contemporary observer, became a "pioneer French settler". His plantation and trading-station on Efate Island thrived and, since he was now under French protection, he was able to supply spirits and firearms to the natives without any fear of British retaliation. For, as the 1870s passed, the restrictive influence of the Royal Navy became greater.

McLeod can be regarded, with some justification, as one of the unwitting originators of the "condominium"—between Britain and France—that still attempts to rule the New Hebrides. In 1882 an Irishman named Higginson formed a French company in New Caledonia "to colonise the New Hebrides with Frenchmen, and to remove the native population to New Caledonia to work as slaves on their plantations and in their mines. . . . But," wrote J. G. Paton in 1885, "the natives refused to sell them any land. They then offered to buy out for £5000 Captain McLeod, an old labour trafficker, and to give him £1000 a year as the manager of their company, to remain on the piece of land on which he lived in Havannah Harbour. He accepted the offer, and now as their agent, having given the French a footing on the group in defiance of the natives, backed by the presence of two French men-of-war, he helps them to claim possession of the land by every means possible."

One of Donald McLeod's ships, the *Caledonian*, also known as the *Caledonien* and the *Ernestine*, flew three flags in the same year; flag-changing being a popular local occupation. The vessel became the subject of Colonial Office correspondence, and a proposed international agreement.

At the same time, too, harsh words were being written in the Australian newspapers concerning the way Donald McLeod was allowing the French to enter what might naturally be considered a British domain.

Captain Oliver, master of an Australian labour vessel, had discovered during a visit to Tanna Island that the inhabitants were anticipating French annexation. His letter to the *Town and Country Journal* contained these words:

"Your report says Captain McLeod is an Englishman by birth, but how long is it since he abandoned his national colours and placed himself under the protection of the French? And what was his reason? Simply this, as he has partly admitted, that the laws of France permit of trading in firearms and spirits, as his well-filled purse can amply testify. . . . I observe that Captain McLeod has purchased a vessel. Query: Will he once more change his flag from the 'tricolor' to the Union Jack? I think not. He will find his purse assume more plethoric proportions, whether recruiting or trading, in both of which he is an adept, under his present colours."

In spite of this forecast, Donald McLeod was to change his colours again. But before that happened there was an incident that perhaps gives a touch of humanity to a man who might have appeared singularly lacking in that quality.

"Donald McLeod was outlawed by the British," I was told, "and at that time could not ship on a British vessel. But he must have been growing homesick, as many Highlanders unaccountably do. Whatever the reason, a French ship one night lay off the Whangarei Heads, and a man was rowed ashore. It was Donald McLeod, minus an ear that he had lost in one of his ungodly escapades. From the beach he walked overland to the house where his relatives lived. What they talked about I do not know, but it is hard to see how they could have given him a very great welcome. He stayed for a few hours and then, that same night, returned to the ship and sailed back to New Caledonia. That was the last they ever saw of him."

But Captain McLeod was not finished yet. Under the pressure of public opinion, blackbirding gradually died out and more orthodox trading took its place. One reference in the report of a Government agent on the labour schooner *Foam*, in 1892, shows that this latter-day pirate, now wealthy and safely within the law, had changed to no great extent.

"While the *Foam* was recruiting off Aoha, Captain McLeod came in with the *Mary Anderson*, of Sydney, to load copra from his station there. Shortly afterwards the natives were so drunk I had to forbid recruiting. As the *Mary Anderson* hails from Sydney and Captain McLeod is an Englishman, I think he should be punished for supplying the natives with spirits."

Captain McLeod experienced much during the lifetime that started in the quiet settlement of St Ann's, Cape Breton Island. He saw the beginning of the blackbirding era, an ignoble, bloodstained period in the history of the Pacific, and he saw its end. His kinfolk and their friends who came to New Zealand from Nova Scotia were not proud of him. News of the more spectacular events in his career came back to his people, but they were rarely discussed. And when he died, some of them refused to inherit money that had been acquired in such a dubious way.

Yet Captain Donald McLeod should not be judged too harshly. He was unruly and unprincipled, but he lived among men on the outer edge of civilisation. Even in Sydney, its nearest outpost, standards were low. When the *Spray* had arrived there on her way to New Zealand, the remark of a Customs officer was remembered with horror by most of the passengers. Asked whether there was any news, he had said, "Nothing much—only that a dozen convicts were hung up to dry this morning." To the tough sailor Donald McLeod the remark may have seemed in no way out of the ordinary.

CHAPTER NINE

MEN OF THE FOREST AND THE SPORTS FIELD

A LONG hut, where twenty-five men slept in two tiers of bunks down each side, became Willie Kempt's second home when he was sixteen years old. He was to spend more time in it, and others like it, than anywhere else during the years of his young manhood.

At one end of the hut was a huge open fireplace, where the cook prepared hot meals, bread and tea for the men. Down the centre ran a long table. It was made of planks, except at its head, where there was a four-foot block of kauri timber on which the cook served his meals. The men collected their food, and then went to their seats.

In the morning the cook blew a shattering call on his bullock-horn, and the men hastened to their places. When five o'clock came round they would hear the same signal far out in the bush where they were working; and soon they would be satisfying the healthy hunger that comes from ten hours' strenuous work in the open air. If they were near the hut, they might come home for lunch. Otherwise a meal would be brought out to them. Their food had to be well-cooked and nourishing, and the bread well baked. Beef and potatoes three times a day were what they demanded and, traditionally, were given.

Hard physical work, as long as the hours were regular, never killed a man, in Willie Kempt's opinion. In the isolated bush camp, far from the temptations of civilisation, lights went out at nine in the evening, by which time many of the men were already in their bunks. When their evening meal was over, they would dry their clothes and sit smoking their pipes in the fireplace, playing cards perhaps, but usually talking quietly, as men do when their minds are at ease and their bodies pleasantly weary. On Saturdays they finished work a few

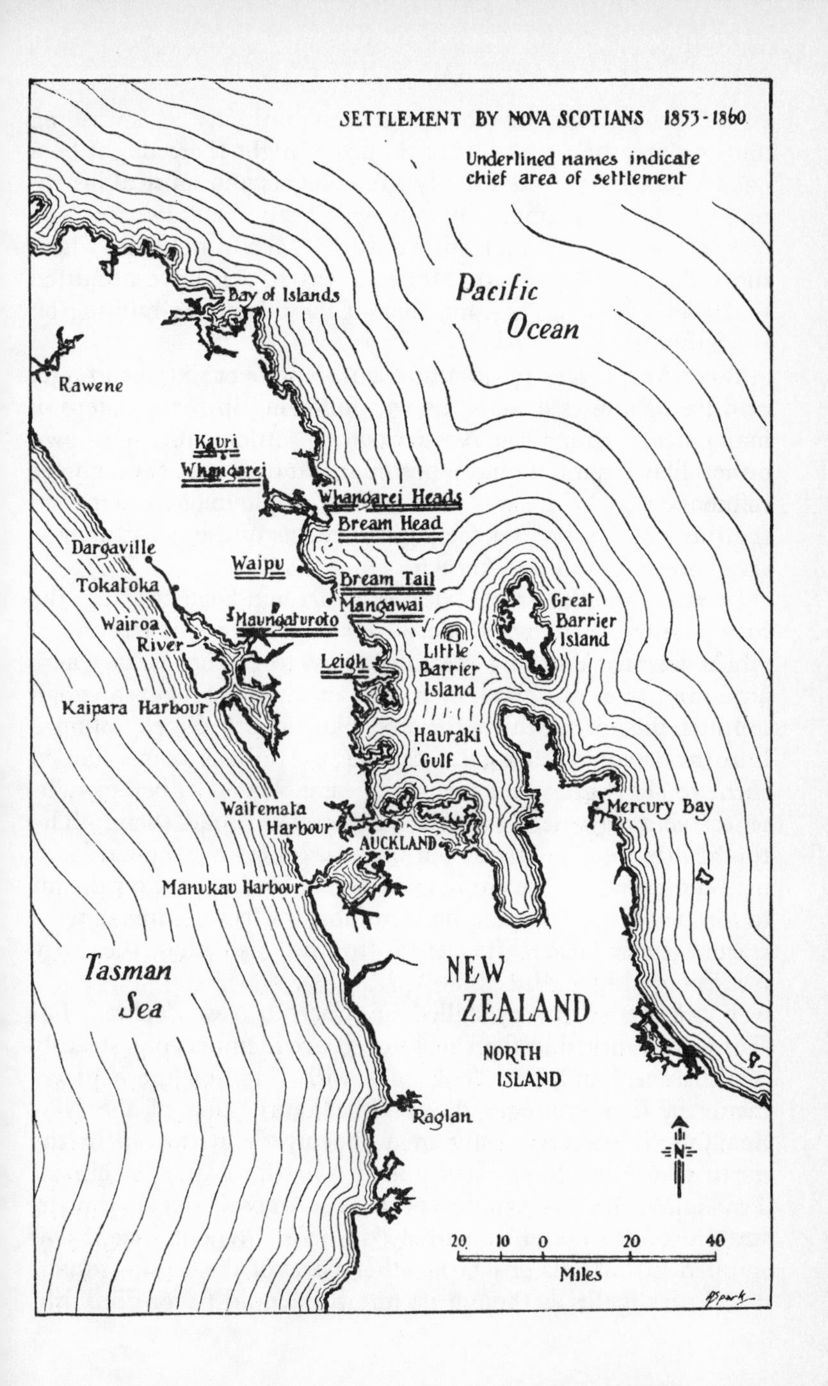
SETTLEMENT BY NOVA SCOTIANS 1853-1860
Underlined names indicate chief area of settlement
Pacific Ocean
Bay of Islands
Rawene
Kauri
Whangarei
Whangarei Heads
Bream Head
Dargaville
Waipu
Tokatoka
Bream Tail
Mangawai
Wairoa River
Maungaturoto
Great Barrier Island
Little Barrier Island
Leigh
Kaipara Harbour
Hauraki Gulf
Waitemata Harbour
AUCKLAND
Mercury Bay
Manukau Harbour
Tasman Sea
NEW ZEALAND
NORTH ISLAND
Raglan
N
20 10 0 20 40
Miles

hours early, giving time for the men to do their week's washing and to darn their socks. On Saturday night there might be a concert, for there were usually a few singers and musical instruments in every camp. Sunday was " all their own "; and most of the men spent it resting in bed. Men from homes where the influence of Norman McLeod was strong have admitted that they felt pangs of conscience if they went pig-hunting on the Sabbath.

When Willie Kempt became a bushman over sixty years ago, at fifteen shillings a week, he was following in the footsteps of many others from the Nova Scotian settlements. His own father had been a famous bushman, and it was through his influence that Willie was able to find employment when even the timber industry was feeling the effects of the worst depression New Zealand had known.

By that time the great stands of kauri had been cut from the easy country, although there were still tremendous reserves of virgin forest. Working steadily away from the areas where access by water was good, men with axes and cross-cut saws had toppled the trees, which towered like smooth Greek columns into the misty green roof of the bush. Bullock teams hauled them to the water, and then they were floated either to mills or to wharves where overseas vessels could load them. The round logs were squared with broad-axes for convenient loading, and grooves were cut in each side of the log to allow the air to circulate. By this method, millions of feet of timber were wasted every year. It seemed to the men that the huge forests could never be exhausted.

There are still many skilled bushmen in New Zealand, but those who worked in the kauri forests are members of a steadily diminishing band, who look back with pride on the achievements of their younger days. The kauri, king of the New Zealand forest, grew only in a sharply defined area in the north of the country. It supplied spars for Nelson's ships at Trafalgar. It was without peer as a smooth, clean timber, straight of grain and immensely durable. Where once it was shipped in millions of feet to other parts of the world, squandered prodigally as though its numbers could never diminish, it is now used, carefully, for boat-building and a few selected trades. National reserves where commercial cutting is not allowed give the visitor only a pale picture of the glory that has passed from the north.

Before the coming of the bulldozer and other mechanical aids, the kauri bushman had to possess great physical strength. Local inventions helped him. Logs that had once been painfully moved into position with wedges were, by the time Willie Kempt went to the forest, being handled with timberjacks. Small and compact, easily used by one man and capable of lifting tremendous weights, these implements found another use many years later—in rescue work during the air bombardment of Britain.

I had not seen a timberjack in action. Willie Kempt thought for a moment and then said: " " Cockatoo—Donald McLeod —has a small one. Come round and we'll show you."

We walked along the quiet Waipu road to where Cockatoo, a few years older than Willie Kempt, lived in retirement. At seventy-eight, Willie admits that he has shrunk by three and a half stone and one and a half inches since he was in his prime. But he is still an impressive figure, six feet one inch in height, with big capable hands and a long, easy stride that made me hurry to keep pace with him.

He rummaged in Cockatoo's shed and emerged with the jack, which weighed about fifty pounds. The two old men looked at it with affection. As he set it on the lawn, Willie said: " Once we used to lift the big ones—seventy-four pounds in weight—over our heads with one hand. And now I can scarcely lift this one at all! " He shook his head with a comic sadness.

The jack stood firmly on two steel points. As two projecting handles turned, a twin-pointed spear was forced upwards, biting into the timber and exerting great lifting power. They worked singly or in pairs. When the weight was taken by one jack, the other would spin down, its handles circling so fast that they defied the sight.

Out on the lawn, Willie Kempt, his eyes sparkling with enjoyment, his powerful hands deft and busy, demonstrated that he had not lost his skill. The jack-handles spun, he reached in, riding with the handle and bringing it to a stop. "When I had learned how to do this without breaking a knuckle," he said, "I thought I knew everything. But I soon discovered I was only starting to learn."

His first work in the bush was of a different kind. A dam had been built in the stream, with logs piling up in front of it and behind it. "As the pressure of water grew, leaks appeared. I was given the job of stopping the leaks. I picked 'bukau', which grows under the kauris, and threw it in the water above the dam. It sank and packed itself against the face of the dam, sealing off the leaks."

But that was no full-time job. A skidded road, made of small trees, had been built down from where the timber was being cut. Over this the thirty-foot catamaran—or "cat"—two young trees bolstered together and carrying a heavy log, were dragged by seven pairs of bullocks. The skids had to be greased, and this also became Willie Kempt's duty. In this and other ways he learned the routine of a bushman's life. He had to grow to his full strength before he was allowed to take on the crosscut sawing and other heavy work that qualified the expert bushman to earn his thirty shillings a week.

Whatever the hour of the day or night, the dam had to be tripped when it was ready. "Nearly always," Willie said, "rain was falling when they gave the word." At his first camp the dam was tripped by lantern-light. It was an unforgettable sight, the men, armed with timberjacks and long poles, working in the half-darkness to clear jams as the water came to help them.

He grew hard and fit. Without any training apart from his work, and weighing fourteen and a half stone, he won mile races at the New Year sports meetings. The bushman had to be quick-witted and alert. He was aware of likely dangers, and prepared for them. It was the unexpected that caused accidents. A log, lying on its side like a prehistoric monster, might break away before the cross-cut saw was through, and roll on a man. And the forest had other dangers that could not be foreseen.

"My mate Rory McAulay and I had just felled a kauri," Willie recalled, "and were standing near the stump for a breather. Up above us, but well clear, another kauri was brought down. Normally there would have been no danger; but as it fell, it struck a rata tree that forked like the wish-bone of a fowl, and sent it crashing towards us. I ran for cover under our tree, knowing that Rory would have seen what was happening. Before I could reach shelter, however, the rata came down, one huge limb on each side of me. I called to Rory, but he did not answer. He had run the wrong way and the tree killed him."

For many years, in forests throughout the north, Willie Kempt worked at his calling. So big were some of the logs that platforms were built before the men with their cross-cut saws could get to work. There would be two men on each end of the saw at times. The biggest tree he remembers cutting had a girth of twenty-seven feet, and would have supplied enough timber for two houses. Some were so large that they had to be blasted in half with explosive before they could go through the cutting benches of the mill.

In the bush itself, timber was needed for a host of purposes—for building dams, for making rails along which the timber trucks were hauled. Pit-sawing was back-breaking work. One man was in the pit under the log, and the other perched on top. Between them ran the ten-foot cross-cut saw. Even Willie, a proper enthusiast, admitted that pit-sawing six-by-four rails to lay a few miles of track was at times monotonous.

With up to forty men living and working together for six months or more at a time, and seeing no new faces during that period, it was surprising that there were not more fights. But a very real comradeship developed in the bush, probably because the men depended on and appreciated one another's qualities. Goodwill extended also to their employers. "Even though it might mean working longer hours," Willie said, "the men would often volunteer to take out a few extra logs. They knew the contractor was not making a fortune, in any case."

When they did occur, quarrels were usually settled quickly,

in the traditional way. " Two men who apparently had been unfriendly for a long time, happened to come to work with us. Finally, one evening, they came to blows. One of them knocked the other out with a beauty to the jaw. He became greatly alarmed, yelling for water and obviously afraid that he had killed the man. Someone brought a bucket of water which he splashed over his fallen opponent's head. The man sat up, blinked once or twice and shook himself. Then, rising to his feet, he hit his rival so hard that the fight was over for the night. So unnerved had the other become, that he did not even raise his fists to defend himself."

With little prospect of making a living on the land, most of the young men who did not go to sea or to the towns spent some part of their life in the bush. Danny Finlayson, who at eighty-eight keeps two riding horses shod so that he can adequately manage his farm near Whangarei, described to me the way in which his life's work started. With three mates he set off from Waipu across the hills towards the Kaipara Harbour. There, they knew, the Government was constructing a road through to the timber workings at Dargaville. It was a hot day for walking and, when they came to an isolated orchard where trees were bearing large, green fruit, the temptation was too great. These, they decided, would help to quench their thirst. They carried their booty for some distance before tasting them, speculating as they went on what the fruit might be. The young adventurers from Waipu had never seen quinces before, but the first taste of the luscious-looking, unripe fruit was sufficient to make them nurse their thirsts for the rest of the day.

The road, little more than a primitive track, was progressing slowly. The four friends approached the foreman, and named a price for making a section of the road; the contract was soon completed. Its end brought them their first money. Thus fortified, the party split up. Danny and a friend walked up to Tokatoka to the forest. He found work at thirty shillings a week, following the labouring bullock teams with a timberjack, axe and maul to keep the great logs moving on their way to the river.

During the years that followed, his path crossed that of many others from the Nova Scotian settlements. Having similar interests and background, they often teamed up and worked together. But while many, like Willie Kempt, preferred to work purely as bushmen, others found themselves attracted by the engineering problems that the building of dams afforded. Some of these called for skill of a high order. Danny helped with the building of one that was 150 feet long and twenty-one feet high.

The dams followed a pattern, varied according to the country in which they were located. Set in a solid frame of timber, the gate of the dam was pivoted at the top, with a trigger at the bottom to keep it closed. When the trigger was released with a block and tackle, the gate swung up, and the water surged through a flume that was heavily timbered underneath and at the sides. The logs made a spectacular sight as they were carried swiftly through the gate of the dam, but the strangest effect was obtained down-stream in the dry creek-bed. Here, at times, the logs seemed to gain a life of their own before the water had reached them.

Eventually Danny bought 1,000 acres of heavy bush at Purua, north of his old home. By now farming was developing a future. The good trees were cut and milled, one of the logs yielding over 16,000 feet of timber; the residue was burnt and the land sown down in pasture. A start had been made towards a prosperous farm.

New Year, the traditional time for Scots to gather together and celebrate, brought the Nova Scotians out of the bush and back to their homes. After months of clean and hard living they were, as Willie Kempt remarked with a reminiscent gleam in his eye, "fighting fit and ready for anything". The Caledonian sports at Waipu provided a suitable outlet for their energy. Tossing the caber, throwing the hammer, running and jumping events led to contests that are still remembered for their comic or Homeric qualities. Science had not then become paramount in athletics; stop-watches, tape-measures and running-shoes were not considered necessary for success. In fact, when Dan Neil McMillan, fresh from the bush, won the high jump, there was no way of measuring exactly the phenomenal height he cleared. An approximation was gained when one of the spectators, six feet two inches tall, walked under the bar without dislodging it.

McMillan was outstanding as a runner also, and in addition something of a humorist. One New Year's Day, when he was exceptionally fit, he lapped the field before winning the mile event, and amused the spectators by jumping backwards and forwards over a fence while he waited for the others to finish. But it was the tug-of-war that gave the weight and brawn of the Nova Scotian bushmen their greatest opportunity. Another McMillan, known as John Abe, was the anchor-man. His eighteen stone could have held a team of bullocks. When a contingent from Waipu attended an Oddfellows' picnic on an island in the Hauraki Gulf, their tug-of-war team could find no opponents from among the effete city folk.

The strength, agility and physical toughness that came with long hours in the bush proved of value in other ways. The standing jump, almost forgotten now as an athletic event, was popular with the Scots; and one of them, on holiday in Auckland, won a £5 wager from the licensee of his hotel when he jumped clear over a table in the upstairs bar. He was of a generous nature, however, and allowed the licensee, a cunning fellow, to make up his loss in bets with others who were prepared to wager that no one could do such an unlikely feat.

When this same physical fitness was combined with an enthusiasm for Rugby football, which has been described as the New Zealander's religion, some startling things happened. Especially was this the case with the Finlaysons of Maungaturoto, a family that supplied six brothers who made their mark in Rugby history. Their father Norman had been a bush contractor before he became a farmer. Horses were his sporting interest, and the stable that he built of sturdy pit-sawn timber is still standing. "He probably built it before he put up the house," one of his sons suggested.

Just why the football "bug" should have attacked his sons it is hard to say. The game was still in its infancy in the north when they were boys, although the exploits of the 1905 All Blacks in Britain had placed New Zealand firmly on the sporting map.

While he was still at primary school, in the isolated country district where his family lived, Jack Finlayson arranged matches by telegram with the Averys, another footballing family at a saw-milling settlement some miles away. He likes to think that this experience proved useful many years later, when he became president of the New Zealand Rugby Union.

When he and his twin brother Bain left school, the bush became not only the place where they earned their living but—and this was of equal importance to them—their training ground for football. The brothers, on one occasion, had taken a contract to clear a block of hill-country at £1 an acre. Early one morning they began to fell a huge rimu tree; one of them being left-handed, they could work together, chopping alternately. Bain slipped on one of the tree's projecting roots, and his axe caught Jack's hand. The victim's first thought was: "I won't be able to play on Saturday!" They would work in the bush in the morning, and then walk or ride many miles for the afternoon game.

When the First World War came, Jack, Bain and a third brother Tote, who had been christened Owen, gained places in the seven-a-side team that represented the Auckland Regiment in Egypt and won the brigade championship. Two of them were later in the champion side of the New Zealand Division. They came home after the war to find that the younger members of the family shared their enthusiasm; and to see Innes, a strapping lad, playing barefooted rather than go without his football.

Innes, better known as "Bunny", was fast as well as big. He began his Rugby career as a three-quarter, but later, having transferred to the forwards, he won a place in the All Blacks and renown as one of the greatest players the country has produced. Four of the brothers—Tote, Bain, Angus and Bunny—represented North Auckland on the same day. Angus later played for Auckland for many years, while Callum, another of the footballing Finlaysons, captained the province of Otago for two of the eight seasons during which he was a member of that doughty side.

The Finlayson brothers were among the last generation of the

Nova Scotian bush-workers, a generation that produced sportsmen who played hard, fast and clean. Many of today's footballers, living in a softer age, look for physical fitness in the training-shed rather than in their work. There are some who think that, for this reason, they are less capable than were their predecessors of absorbing the hard knocks that are part of Rugby. Jack Finlayson may have been thinking back to the days of his youth when, in an address to Rugby players, he remarked that no footballer could last a game out " unless he had muscle on his guts ". A terse phrase, not to be expected perhaps of a member of New Zealand's now extinct Legislative Council, but nevertheless very true.

In addition to its timber, the kauri offered another valuable source of income to the arrivals from Nova Scotia—a clear, amber-coloured gum that, even in the 1850s, was being exported to the varnish-makers of Britain and America. The kauri gum was something of a mystery. It was found on the beaches, deep in swamps, on scrub-covered hillsides where no kauris grew. It came to the homes of the Nova Scotians in the coal they bought from the mines near Whangarei.

It was clearly of great age. Had it been left after the ancient forests had been swept away by fire? They did not know but, along with other inhabitants of the north, they were ready to gather it when times were hard, or when extra money was needed to improve their farms.

The kauri, New Zealand's most magnificent forest tree, is also one of the few in the world that have survived unchanged from that prehistoric age when the earth was covered with lush tropical forest. Even in that company it would not have been disgraced, for it may grow 200 feet high, and the massive trunk often towers sixty feet into the air before the first branches spread out to form the characteristic umbrella-like top; branches that themselves contain as much timber as an average tree.

The Ice Age came, and the kauri forests retreated to their present limits, north of a line drawn across the North Island from near the Waikato Heads; and there for many centuries they flourished in a land that was their own almost exclusive domain. But, through those centuries, still long before New Zealand had been settled by man, the kauri was working out its own doom.

Having grown kauri trees for so long, the earth in many places became acid. Under the topsoil, as the rains washed deep, there formed an impermeable "pan" that ruined the drainage which was as necessary to the kauri as it is to a vegetable garden. The lordly kauri died, and young ones did not come to replace it. Instead, there grew scrub and a host of creeping plants that are now associated with the gum-lands. But the gum that had formed from long-vanished trees still remained.

To the Maoris it was commonplace. They used it for kindling fires, for making a tasty and everlasting chewing gum, and it also had a place in their tattooing ceremonies. Captain Cook, when he saw it on the beaches, conjectured that it came from the mangrove trees that infested the tidal estuaries of the north. French explorers surmised that it was of animal origin, rather like ambergris. By the middle of the nineteenth century, however, its identity and value were firmly established. For more than fifty years, thousands of men were to make a living digging for gum in the barren but strangely beautiful gum-land wastes.

The gum-digger was generally a wanderer, homeless except for a tent or the hut that he might build from slabs of timber or from tree-ferns. Among them were Dalmatians intent on earning money to buy land; runaway sailors, remittance men from Europe who numbered in their ranks even dukes' sons. The gum-land extended in belts through the Waipu district and other Nova Scotian settlements. One farm was sold, at the height of the boom in kauri gum, for £1,000 an acre—not for what it would grow, but for the gum that was known to lie under its surface.

Few of the Nova Scotians looked on gum-digging as a permanent occupation. In the early days, however, some of them earned as much as £1 a day—money that helped to establish them in their future careers. And schoolboys were able to help pay for their education by steady work during their holidays. When he was a boy, nearly seventy years ago, Archie Bishop went with his parents to a gum-field home. In a few years he had saved £200, a sum that set him up in business. Later, he collected as a hobby choice specimens of the gum that had given him a start in life. Gum that was as clear as fine glass, or richly coloured and cast in fantastic shapes; gum that held in it a long, eventful and almost forgotten chapter of the world's history. Not long ago Archie sent his collection to the McLeod Memorial Museum at St Ann's, Cape Breton. And there it attracts the interest, and at times the wild conjecture, of holiday visitors from many parts of the American continent.

"Kauri gum?" they have been known to say. "What is that? Can you eat it?"

And wondering idly where New Zealand might be—the home of kauri gum, and of the descendants of a band of Cape Breton men and women who crossed the world a century ago—they go on their untroubled way.

EPILOGUE

"THE LONG, LONG YEARS"

THE last day I spent at Waipu collecting material for this story seemed to take me nearer than any other to the times that have long since passed, and to the people who brought their rich but simple culture across the world from Scotland to Canada and New Zealand. For Mrs Willina Lang, whom I met that day, frail but indomitable as she approached her ninetieth year, seemed to evoke in her speech and manner the atmosphere of a period that ended long ago. Possibly because she has been blind for many years, she can paint in words a picture that is as clear to the listener as it is to her own inward eye. But in addition she is, all unconsciously, a poet, with the sharpened perceptions, the imagery, eloquence and passion that are given to few mortals.

A few days before I saw her, a young man had called at the house. He was, he explained, a member of the National Symphony Orchestra. On his way through Waipu he had stopped to examine the monument and, after reading the Gaelic inscription, had inquired whether there was anyone with whom he could speak in that language. A local resident had directed him to Mrs Lang's home.

The young man was diffident. He was not a Scot but, during several years at Edinburgh University, had studied Gaelic. He could read and write in that tongue but, through lack of opportunity, was no great conversationalist. Mrs Lang soon set him at his ease by asking whether he would like her to sing a Gaelic song. The one she had in mind, she said, had been written by a local bard, Alexander McDonald, for "Long Jim's mother's wedding". Long Jim, also known as Mr J. A. S. Mackay, is now eighty-six years old.

She sang the song in a high, clear voice, and the young man listened intently. When it was done he asked a favour. One of his travelling companions was able to write down music as it was sung. Could he introduce her to Mrs Lang? A few minutes later she sang the song again, with one of her listeners noting down the words and another the music of an unknown bard.

Like most of her generation, Mrs Lang is bi-lingual; but where others forgot their Gaelic when they left home, it is still as familiar to her as English.

When I went through to her room, Mrs Lang put down her knitting and turned her sightless eyes towards me. She clasped my arm, as if in that way to catch something of the personality of the visitor she had never seen. " He sounds just like his grandfather, Neil Ewen," she said to her daughter. " All that family had merry laughs."

She spoke of the young musician's visit and, prompted by her daughter Myra, sang a song for me too. " This," she said, " was written for the wedding of your grandfather's sister, Mary Campbell, and Norman McKenzie, son of the old Prince."

As she sang, she translated into English the words that were composed for the first time in 1874, and which had endured for a lifetime without being written down. Here is one verse:

" When I'll get you for myself
And we'll make a beginning
On the little green hill
Above the young growing grass.
You're the girl that I want,
The young brown lassie."

" He was a great poet," Mrs Lang said. " If someone asked him for a song, he would sit on the ground for a few minutes, and then come over with the words and music ready. Most of them would be remembered and sung at ceillidhs, or in the home to amuse the children."

The old lady smiled. " Do you know what a quaich is? Myra," she said to her daughter, " show him."

The quaich was a small drinking-cup, designed to hold a measure of whisky, and carved from wood. From its shape, it looked as if it would fit comfortably into the owner's pocket.

" There were lullabies of many kinds," she said, " but not many, as you can imagine, had the quaich for a subject. One evening, I remember, we were approaching old Jim McKenzie's house when we heard him singing this song, rather desperately, we thought."

She sang the words, and then translated them:

" Pass the bottle here;
Hand it round to all.
Hold the quaich steady;
Don't spill a drop! "

" Old Jim finished the song, and then started it again. What was going on? We entered the house, and discovered the cause of the trouble. Jim, a bachelor, had been left in charge of some little children, and this was the only lullaby he knew! "

Mrs Lang lay back on her couch. Her face changed swiftly as different memories came to life.

" The long, long years," she said softly, making the words an invocation, untouched by regret. " So many people, so many sad and happy things. Would you remember Mrs Mary McLeod, whose husband was drowned when the *Thistle* went ashore at the peak of the Heads? That was a tragedy, but she never complained; and she brought up her six children—the youngest three months old at the time, the eldest ten years—faithfully and well. They were a happy family, and there was only one thing we noticed. In the evening, while the children were playing in the kitchen, she would be busy carding and spinning. But when it came time for them to go to bed she would go up also. She could not bear to be alone.

" The McLeods lived next door to my father's house. The night had been very stormy, and the *Thistle* was expected from Auckland. Early that day Mary McLeod and her husband's sister, Mrs Mary McLean, went up on the hill with their knitting to watch for the ship. A few hours later a boy of seventeen arrived with the dreadful news. The *Thistle* had been wrecked. Alex McLeod and a young girl had been swept away by a great wave and drowned. They spoke to my father, Duncan Ian Ruadh:

" 'You, who are their friend, must go and tell his widow and sister.'

" The tears were running down my father's face. 'How can I do that?' he asked in agony.

" 'Somebody must,' they said, 'and you are their neighbour and friend.'

" Presently my father stopped his tears. He came back to the house, washed and dressed himself carefully, as if he was going to church. Then he went down the road and up to the hill where the two women waited with their knitting, their eyes fixed on the sea."

Until the end of her life, Mrs McLeod always had trouble with her English.

" Many of the old people were like that," Mrs Lang explained. " They thought in Gaelic, and tried to turn their thoughts into another language.

" One of Mary McLeod's sons sickened, and while he was ill, the wife of a neighbour would often bring some dainty to tempt his appetite. It was done quietly, but did not escape his mother's notice."

The son died, and Mrs Lang, then a young girl, walked back from the funeral within hearing distance of Mrs McLeod. The old lady was speaking about the neighbour who had done the kindly acts.

" Ah," she said, " that's a good, good woman." She paused to find the right words, and added with great emphasis: " The best woman—under the earth!"

After bidding Mrs Lang good-bye, I stopped at the cemetery that spreads over a low hill on the right bank of the Waipu River a few miles from the township. The stories that Mrs Lang had told me were still in my mind. Here, in this quiet country graveyard, rested many of those about whom she had spoken. The headstones gave the place of their birth: Assynt in Sutherlandshire, Lochalsh, Applecross, Skye and Harris; Baddeck, St Ann's, Boularderie, across the ocean in Nova Scotia.

Here they rested, in a place that must surely have been chosen by a man with the heart and mind of a poet. As I stood beside the old graves, my eye was drawn to the river, flowing smoothly and strongly between low banks. I followed its course as it swept down in a slow curve, past ragged, alien pines and sandhills covered with lupin.

Suddenly an old, half-remembered poem gained a new meaning. Half a mile away, the river forced an outlet through waves that rose and broke in foam on the sandy bar. Then, the brief, sharp struggle over, it lost itself in the blue waters of Bream Bay, and the ocean that stretched illimitably toward the rising sun.

GCSE Film Studies for WJEC

Jackie Newman
David Fairclough
Gerard Garvey
Julie Patrick

www.heinemann.co.uk
✓ Free online support
✓ Useful weblinks
✓ 24 hour online ordering

01865 888080

Heinemann is an imprint of Pearson Education Limited, a company incorporated in England and Wales, having its registered office at Edinburgh Gate, Harlow, Essex, CM20 2JE. Registered company number: 872828

www.heinemann.co.uk

Heinemann is a registered trademark of Pearson Education Ltd

First published 2008

14
10 9 8 7 6 5

British Library Cataloguing in Publication Data is available from the British Library on request.

ISBN 978 0 435368 10 4

Edited by Liz Cartmell
Designed by Tony Richardson
Typeset by HL Studios, Long Hanborough, Oxford
Original illustrations © Pearson Education Ltd, 2008
Illustrated by HL Studios
Cover design by Pete Stratton
Picture research by Liz Savery
Cover photo/illustration © The Ronald Grant Archive
Printed in UK by CPI

Websites
The websites used in this book were correct and up-to-date at the time of publication. It is essential for tutors to preview each website before using it in class so as to ensure that the URL is still accurate, relevant and appropriate. We suggest that tutors bookmark useful websites and consider enabling students to access them through the school/college intranet.

Acknowledgements

The author and publisher would like to thank the following individuals and organisations for permission to reproduce photographs:

20th Century Fox/Everett/Rex Features p99; 20th Century Fox /Marvel Entertainment/The Kobal Collection (**TKC**) p30(top); 20th Century Fox/Paramount/TKC p31(top left); p102(top); ibid Wallace, Merie W p31(top right); 78; 20th Century Fox/TKC p7(left), 9(bottom); 71(left); 20th Century Fox/TKC p7/Hayes, Kerry p30(bottom); 20th Century Fox/TKC/Morton, Merrick p16(right); 20th Century FoxWarners/TKC p75; 92; 108; A Band Apart/Miramax/TKC p199; Alamy p173; Alcon Entertainment/ TKC p187(top); Amblin/Universal/Warners/TKC p85; Aqil Kamran p174; Beijing New Picture/Elite Group/TKC p26; Bend It Films/ Film Council/TKC/Parry, Christine p5; Beyond/Everett/Rex Features p135(left); BuenaVist/Everett/Rex Features p66; Col Pics/Everett/ Rex Features p182(top); Dimension/Everett/Rex Features p19(left); Disney Enterprises/TKC p22; Dreamworks/ Everett/Rex Features p3(bottom left); Dreamworks/Paramount/ TKC p48; Dreamworks/Paramount/TKC/Aronowitz, Myles p100; Everett Collection/Rex Features p16(left); 102(bottom); 128; 132; 135(right); 142; Faizal Malek p194-5; Fox Searchlight/ TKC p125(right); Hollywood Pictures/TKC/Phillips, Ron p159; Horsepower Films/TKC p111; Horsepower Films/TKC/McEwan, Rob pxx; p95; Jim Sugar/Corbis p188; John Eder/Getty Images p113; Kathy deWitt/Alamy p198; KPA/HIP/TopFoto p63; Lions Gate/TKC p12; LucasFilm/20th Century Fox/TKCn p36; LucasFilm Ltd/Paramount/TKC p28; Matt Baron/BEI/Rex Features p162; MoviWorld/MK2/Miramax/TKC p140; p146; p149; p151; MGM/ Eon/TKC/Hamshere, Keith p54(left); New Line Cinema/TKC p196; New Line/TKC/James, David p200; Orion/TKC p21; Paramount/ Everett /Rex Features p14; p71(right); Paramount Pictures/TKC p38(left); 125(left); Paramount Pictures/TKC/Duhamel, Francois p32; p91; R.P.Productions/Runteam Ltd/TKC/ Ferrandis, Guy p19(right); Sipa Press/Rex Features p144; Stanley Kramer/United Artists/TKC p52; Tahirah Khatun p179; Tri-Star/TKC p38(right); Toho/TKC p67; TopFoto p7(right); Touchstone/Jerry Bruckheimer Inc/TKC p187(bottom); Touchstone/TKC p82; p89; Touchstone/ TKC/Masi, Frank p74; UGC/Studio Canal+/TKC p125(middle); ullsteinbild/TopFoto p31(bottom); United Artists/TKC p1; Universal/Everett/Rex Features p3(bottom right), p18; Universal/ TKC p9(top); p58; p60; Universal/TKC/Glass, Ben p117; Walt Disney Pictures/TKC p54(right); Walt Disney Pictures/TKC/Marks, Elliott p17; WBros/DC Comics/TKC p189; Warner Br/Everett/ Rex Features p182(bottom); Warner Bros/Legendary Pictures/TKC p173; Warner Bros/TKC/Barius, Claudette p3(top); Warner Bros/ TKC/Boland, Jasin p27; Zalika Mardenborough p177

Every effort has been made to contact copyright holders of material reproduced in this book. Any omissions will be rectified in subsequent printings if notice is given to the publishers.

Contents

The following additional case studies are available to download for free from the Heinemann website at www.heinemann.co.uk/Secondary/EnglishAndMedia/MediaStudies/:

- *Amelie*
- *Bend It Like Beckham*
- *The Devil's Backbone*
- *Goodbye Lenin!*
- *Ratcatcher*
- *Spirited Away*
- *Yasmin*
- *Whale Rider*

Introduction

Were you one of the thousands of fans who queued recently to watch the latest Harry Potter film in the first few days of its release? Did you enjoy talking about it with your friends? What kinds of things did you talk about? Perhaps the differences between the book and the film, or Harry's love interest? Or is James Bond more your thing? How do the latest films compare to the classic old Bond films?

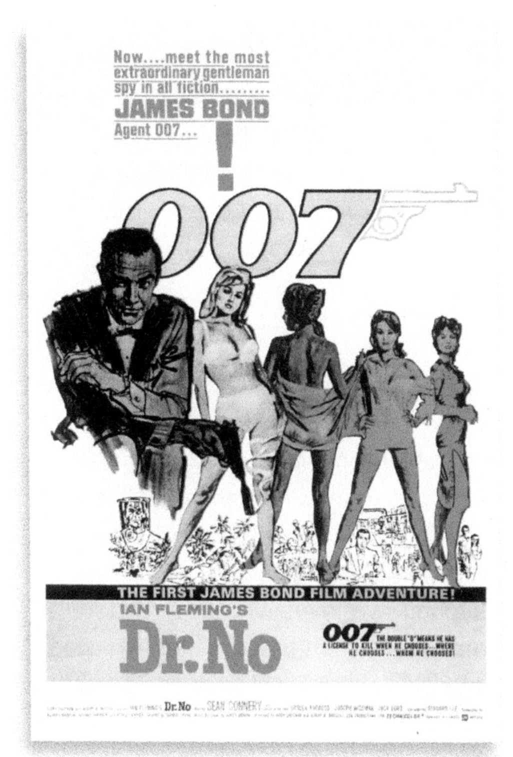

1 The first James Bond film

Whatever your taste, if you love watching and talking about films then this GCSE is perfect for you. During this course you will have the chance to study and discuss films that you already know a lot about: films made in Hollywood and in Britain. You will also have the opportunity to explore films which feature different people and places. You will learn more about how films are made and sold, and have the chance to experiment with the wide range of creative processes involved in making and marketing films.

This course has been designed to build upon your own experience of film, as consumer and creator, and to encourage you to investigate and develop your knowledge and understanding of the relationship between the film industry and film audiences. What is more, it can complement and deepen your understanding of other GCSE subjects such as English and Media Studies. It also provides a 'springboard' into A/S and A Level for those of you who may wish to take the subject to a higher examination level.

You will approach the course through three study areas. These areas are all connected and work together to give you a strong framework for studying and creating film:

- **the language of film:** the elements that create meaning within a film, and how they are organised in order to tell a story to their audience
- **film organisations:** the film companies which make, sell and screen the films we watch
- **film audiences:** the ways in which you respond to the films you watch and the issues raised by films made for a range of different groups of people.

How is the course organised and marked?

You will be expected to complete four linked pieces of coursework which will give you 50 per cent of your overall marks. Towards the end of the course you will complete two written examinations which will account for the other 50 per cent.

What do I have to do for my coursework?

Film exploration: industry (5 marks)

You will begin by exploring a film that you have particularly enjoyed and doing some brief research into how it was **produced**, **distributed** and **exhibited**. You will then complete a specially designed coversheet putting in a summary of all your research findings.

Key terms

Production: the various stages that a film has to go through before it is ready to be 'sold'

Distribution: the process by which a film is released

Exhibition: where and how films are screened

Textual (micro) analysis (20 marks)

After completing your first piece of research on your chosen film you will then think about the way in which that film's language is used to create certain meanings and how we respond to those meanings. As with any new area of study, getting used to understanding the ways in which, for example, lighting and sound can combine to create a particular kind of atmosphere in your chosen sequence takes time and practice. However, it is useful to remember that you automatically 'read' and understand these elements every time you watch a film.

Selling an idea – pitch and pre-production (30 marks)

These two linked pieces are designed to make you think carefully about the ways in which films are created and sold. You will have the chance to put forward your ideas for your own film. You will work on your own with a specific target audience in mind. Your first task will be to create a **pitch** for your film for potential **backers** who might help to fund *and* produce your film.

Key terms

Pitch: a short explanation of ideas for a film delivered to an agent or producer

Backers: the companies or individuals who fund a film's production

Log line: a one sentence summary

Pitch (10 marks)

Your sales pitch will be about 150 words long and should begin with a **log line**. In order to make any film it is important to have great ideas but you also need the necessary equipment and people who know how to use that equipment. You must also have an audience in mind for your film and places in which to show it when it's finished. In order to provide these things you require funding. Potential producers will need to be as sure as they can be that your film is going to be successful. So you will need to convince them that they are about to make a sound investment when they fund your film! Your pitch needs to convey a lot of information in a short time. Investors will need to be provided with a brief outline of the story and an indication of its genre. They will also want to know what kind of audience it appeals to, if it's like any other films, and what stars may be best suited to the main roles.

Pre-production (20 marks)

Once you have completed your sales pitch you will be able to choose *one* of the following pre-production options based on the film you have outlined in the pitch:

- Write a short script for the opening scene of the film (approx 500 words).
- Create a storyboard of approximately 20 frames for a key sequence for the film.
- Produce digitally a design for a front page and contents page for a new film magazine, featuring the new film.
- Produce a marketing campaign for the film (at least four items).

Production (35 marks)

This piece of coursework allows you to create a really polished film-based product using the appropriate format, codes and conventions. If you choose to make your own sequence for a film you may work in groups of *no more than four*. However, if you do work in a group you must be very clear about your role and responsibilities within the group. Your written analysis must also underline your specific contribution to the making of the film. All the other production options must be completed individually. These are the option choices:

- Create a short sequence of no more than 2 minutes for any section of a film.
- Produce a homepage and at least one linked page for a website which promotes a new film.
- Produce a poster campaign for a new film.
- Produce a press pack for a new film.
- Produce a feature about a new film for a film or school/college magazine.

Reflective analysis (10 marks)

When researching and creating your pre-production and production pieces your teacher will have asked you to note down what you have done, how your ideas changed and adapted as you developed your work, and what you have learnt creatively and practically. This final analysis will require you to reflect on what you have done and what you have learnt about the main study areas (film language, film organisations and film audiences) through your coursework.

What will the two written exams contain and will they be divided into Higher and Foundation tiers?

Both examinations are not tiered so you will all take exactly the same papers and have an equal chance of reaching the highest grades.

Exploring Film (1 hour 30 minutes)

Your first examination is called 'Exploring Film' and you will be expected to answer four questions about film genre. This will account for 30 per cent of your overall marks.

During the course you will have studied the concept of genre and its importance in terms of audience, film production and marketing. You will have looked especially closely at disaster films and all the questions set in this examination will focus upon this genre.

The knowledge and understanding you have gained through your practical coursework will also have helped you to explore the ways in which certain disaster films communicate to their audiences. You will have studied at least two disaster films in class and will have noticed and discussed the similarities between the films. You will also probably have seen several other disaster films and noticed that they have common patterns in terms of characters and narrative structures. However, most of us do not want to watch films that follow the same formula every time so you will also be aware of the differences between films which fit into the same genre.

The questions in Section 1 of the paper will relate to a sequence from a disaster film which will be shown three times at the start of the examination. It will usually take you about 20 minutes to watch and make notes on the sequence.

In Section 2 the questions will then broaden out in order to allow you to compare the sequence to the disaster films you have studied in class.

Section 3 will use print-based resource material which relates to the disaster film. You will be asked to study the resource and to identify typical features. You will need to analyse the layout, images and text used and comment on why or how they have been used. You will also need to consider carefully how this material appeals to its target audience.

Key terms

Codes and conventions: features that are repeated within genre films

In Section 4 you will have the chance to demonstrate your knowledge and understanding of genre in a creative way. Here the pre-production and production work you will have completed for your coursework will really help you. The questions in this section will give you the chance to show the importance of genre in terms of audience appeal and how it is used by the organisations which produce and market films.

NB the questions will allow you to demonstrate your understanding of genre. You may be asked to identify the typical features of the disaster film, for example, **codes and conventions**, camera techniques, characters, narrative structures and audience appeal.

Exploring Film Outside Hollywood (1 hour)

Your second exam will allow you to focus upon at least one film made outside Hollywood chosen from a set list. Two of these set films are covered in Section C of this book. The remaining eight case studies are available to download **for free** from the Heinemann website at tbc. You will have an hour in which to answer three compulsory questions. This will account for 20 per cent of your overall marks.

Section 1 of the paper will require you to describe and discuss the kinds of characters, narratives, themes and issues that have been explored in your chosen film.

In Section 2 you will have to focus carefully on an important sequence from your close study film and describe in detail the ways in which key themes and issues are represented. The work you have already done in the first part of your coursework, for example on mise-en-scène, camera movement and framing, editing and sound, will help to inform your answer. Your genre study will also help in terms of your understanding of how narratives are structured and the identification of specific character types and repeated ideas.

Section 3 gives you the chance to respond in a creative way to the film and to show your understanding of a range of the ways in which films are marketed and reviewed. You may, for example, be asked to write a review of your chosen film for a specific target audience, publication or media platform. Although this question invites you to think carefully about producers and audiences, your personal response to the themes, issues and performances within the film is really important. Remember, critics do not necessarily like the films they review *but* they always analyse the film's language and give clear reasons for their personal response.

How to use this book

This book is divided into four major sections:

A Film language

B Exploring film

C New horizons

D Coursework.

Each of these parts is divided into different chapters and/or case studies. There will be lots of Activity boxes containing questions for you to think about and discuss and practical tasks and research for you to do. These boxes will help you with lots of different areas of the course. You will notice they often have AO1, 2, 3 or 4 written at the top of the box: this is for you and your teacher and it highlights which of the four important assessment objectives contained in the specification are covered in the activities you are asked to do.

The assessment objectives you will be expected to cover include:

AO1	Demonstrate knowledge and understanding of how films communicate meanings, evoke personal responses and engage audiences.
AO2	Explore, respond to and reflect on a range of films and topics, including your own pre-production and production work, using key film concepts and appropriate terminology.
AO3	Demonstrate planning, research and presentational skills.
AO4	Use creative and technical skills to construct film products.

All the way through the book you will also see boxes entitled **Key terms**. These boxes will explain the meanings of really important words, or terms, that are used in the book. Remember though, if ever you don't understand what a word or question means you should ask your teacher who will make sure you are clear about the key term before moving on.

This book has been written by the people who helped to write the GCSE Film Studies specification and they will probably also have the job of setting and marking your examination papers and coursework. Every so often they will include a handy Examiner's tip for you; these will help you to make sure you have covered everything that you need to do in order to gain a good pass.

At the end of a particular section you will see a list of bullet points telling you what you should have learned. These Knowledge check boxes are a great way of checking that you have clearly understood each section. Again, make sure you ask your teacher if you feel there are knowledge areas that you can't yet tick!

Section A Film language

Chapter 1 How films communicate

In this chapter we will cover:

- the basic 'language' of film studies and how to put it into practice
- how we 'read' films rather than watch them
- what different devices film-makers use to help them tell a story.

Activity 1

AO2 – Explore, respond to and reflect on a range of films and topics

- Watch the opening of any film.
- What happens in the opening that draws you into the rest of the film?
- What visual aspects stand out?
- Is music used?
- How do you think this opening was supposed to make you feel?

Examiner's tip

The most essential aspect of your studies will be to gain an understanding of film language. Studying film is not simply a matter of watching a film and discussing why you thought it was good (although of course this is very important). In order to fully express a detailed knowledge about films and the way they work it is important to have a vocabulary in which you can discuss why, and how, a film tells its story. To gain the best marks you should understand film language and use it appropriately and often.

The opening of a film sets the scene for the story to come. In many ways, a film is like a book. Reading a film is just like reading a book but instead of making sense from written words, visual images and sound are combined together to construct the **narrative**.

Key terms

Narrative: a story, or account, of connected events (the term also refers to the way the story is told, i.e. narrative structure)

As a member of an audience you have an individual response to a film that you watch. However, the director of a film, like the writer of a book, will place clues along the way to help you piece together the different twists and turns of the story and draw you in to understanding the film from a certain viewpoint.

A writer wants you to feel unable to put down their book; the director wants you to feel that you can't turn away from the screen – the idea is the same, the techniques are different.

1 This still from The Perfect Storm (2000) *shows how expression and angle are used to create tension in the audience – this character has obviously seen something frightening, but have we seen it yet?*

Key terms

Genre: a type or category of film which has certain predictable codes and characteristics

A certain **genre** of book will have a recognisable style, through the words chosen, the types of plot and even the colours used on its front cover. And so film genres are recognisable, from the opening credits, the trailers and even the posters that precede their release.

Activity 2

AO1– Demonstrate knowledge and understanding of how films communicate

Exam preparation

- Look at these two film posters.
- Choose one and write a list of things in the poster that tell you what kind of film is being advertised.
- With a partner, discuss the similarities and differences between the two posters.

***2** An advertising poster for* The Ring (2002)

***3** An advertising poster for* Dante's Peak (1997)

The opening of a film is the most important part. It usually introduces the main characters and sets up a puzzle to be solved – a problem or a situation that in some way needs resolving. The opening of a film, like the opening of a book, has to grasp an audience's attention; make them want to find out more about these people or what is going to happen next. A film-maker therefore has to use all the technical tools they can, alongside a great story, to capture an audience's attention. Whether a film is sad, dramatic, frightening or funny, it will use the same techniques to create emotion and drama – it will just implement these techniques in different ways.

So one of the first elements of your Film Studies course has to be the study of how film-makers use technical film-making methods; what skills do they have and what devices do they use in order to tell a story and make audiences want to see their films? In Film and Media Studies we refer to this as **film language**.

> **Key terms**
> **Film language:** the ways in which a film communicates meaning to an audience

There are two sections to your studies of film language – **micro elements** and **macro elements**.

Micro elements are:

- cinematography – the use of the camera
- editing – the process of putting the shots together after filming
- sound – including music and sound effects
- mise-en-scène – the look and positioning of all the objects and characters in a shot
- lighting and colour – the level and direction of light and the colour palette used (often considered within mise-en-scène)

Macro elements are:

- genre – the features that fit a film into a certain type, e.g. disaster
- narrative – plot, viewpoint, the story and the way it is told
- representation – the way in which social groups and issues are presented in a film. Representation is a key aspect of Film Studies that crosses over between macro and micro film language.

So really we could say that macro elements of film language are the major aspects of how films tell stories and micro elements are the finer details.

Micro elements

The micro elements of film language can be observed in only a short sequence of shots and sometimes even in a still image. In Film Studies we separate the different aspects of micro film language for the purposes of analysis, but really they work together to communicate to an audience and portray the intentions of the director.

The visual aspects of micro film language are mise-en-scène and cinematography.

Mise-en-scène

Mise-en-scène includes:

- setting
- lighting and colour

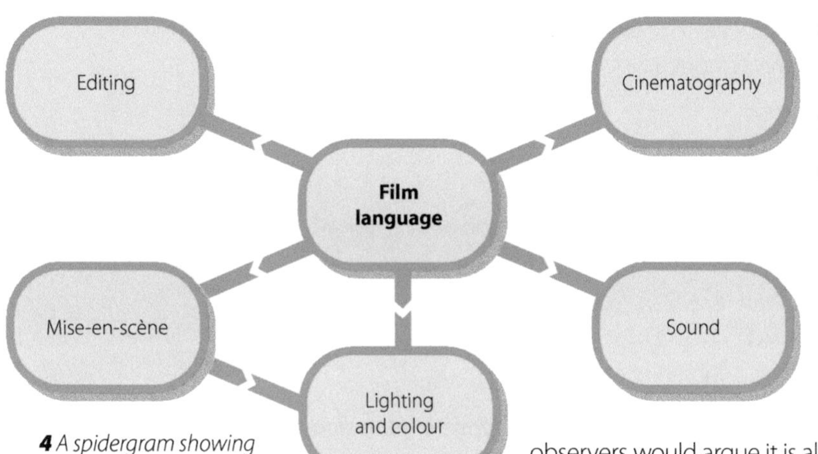

4 A spidergram showing the micro elements of film language

- positioning of characters within the frame
- body language
- costume.

All these elements work together to give audiences a good idea of where the film is set in terms of time and place. Depending on the genre of the film, how accurate the details of the mise-en-scène are will be of more or less importance, though some observers would argue it is always important to represent a place or time in history accurately. You may want to discuss this issue in class.

Mise-en-scène isn't just about creating a setting – it is also important for creating the mood; and this is where lighting and colour come in. The use of lighting can have a big effect on the atmosphere in a scene. Positioning lights onto characters or props brings our attention to them so we know they are significant to the narrative. Also shadows create places for characters to hide.

Activity 3

- What do you notice about the elements of mise-en-scène in this still from *Bend It Like Beckham* (2002)?
- List every detail of the image and also what each tells you about the time, place and circumstances in which the characters find themselves.

5 *A still from* Bend It Like Beckham *with Keira Knightley and Parminder Nagra*

Colour can connote various emotions and moods and is often used significantly in scenes, or even throughout a film. We also relate film genre to colour.

Activity 4

What colours would you connect to each of the genres below:

- horror
- science fiction
- action/adventure?

Why do you think this is?

AO2 – Explore, respond to and reflect on a range of films and topics

AO4 – Use creative and technical skills to construct film products

Coursework idea

- Design the home page for a website dedicated to one film genre. Make sure you consider all genre conventions, but especially the use of colour.

The relationship between colour and genre is often evident in the promotional film posters used to market new films. Film posters are an important way film-makers and cinemas advertise coming films. They will also use visual elements of film language to market the film – colour, lighting, positioning of characters are all significant on a film poster.

Cinematography

The use of the camera is also an important visual tool of the film-maker. In the early days of cinema, a single camera attached to a tripod recorded events so the set was always seen from one position in a long shot. Today new technology and techniques allow the film-maker to move the camera to different positions and use a wide variety of different shots. The camera can literally show us action and landscapes from a character's point of view; it can quickly reveal the reactions and emotions of characters and it can ensure we see the narrative clues necessary to piece the story together. Film is essentially a visual medium so the camera is used in many different ways to maintain audience interest and enjoyment. In Film Studies you will learn the terms for particular camera shots and types of camera movement and consider what effect these can create.

Sound

Alhough dialogue is still an important aspect of most films' narratives (because it moves the story on), we also focus on the use of music and sound effects in Film Studies. Sound was not included in films until the late 1920s but it was still important for creating an atmosphere in films and was created in cinemas by live musicians.

Nowadays we are well aware of the importance music and sound effects have on the impact of a film, and surround sound has greatly enhanced the pleasures received from action-packed films such as the action and disaster genres.

Activity 5

AO4 – Use creative and technical skills to construct film products

Look at these two film posters for films from different genres. Compare the similarities and differences, considering:

- layout
- positioning of characters
- colour and lighting
- style of text.

Coursework idea

- Create your own poster for a new disaster movie taking into account what you have learned.

6 *Independence Day (1996)*

7 *The Other Boleyn Girl (2008)*

Activity 6

AO1– Demonstrate knowledge and understanding of how films communicate

Describe the type of music that you might expect to hear during these scenes in films:

- A woman is walking down a deserted street at night, and we know a psychopath is on the loose.
- A speedboat chase.
- A soldier says goodbye to his sweetheart before leaving for battle.

Music in films often plays a crucial role in creating the appropriate atmosphere; horror films in particular seem to greatly benefit from the use of suspense-creating musical scores. The changing pace and volume in music can greatly affect the emotions of an audience and the style of music can make audiences scared, amused or very emotional. It can also be important when creating a cultural setting which is particularly evident in films like *Tsotsi* (2005) and *Whale Rider* (2002), where the music is relevant to the culture and the atmosphere.

Editing

Although it is just one element of film analysis, editing is probably the most important aspect of film creation. Some would say the editing process is where the film is actually made. This is because editing is where the film-maker sits down and connects all the camera shots together. At this stage they can decide:

- the order of scenes
- the pace of scenes
- which scenes they will include and discard.

When we look at editing there are two areas to concentrate on:

- the speed of editing (how long each shot lasts)
- the style of editing (how each shot is joined to the next).

Macro elements

Genre

Within your studies of macro elements of film language, genre refers to the categories into which we put films that share common aspects. This generally refers to the kinds of stories explored and the overall style of the film. So, for example, as soon as anyone mentions the 'horror' genre or a 'disaster movie', you will already be thinking about a film you have seen that you would place in that genre. It will have a particular kind of character in it, or be set in a particular place. And you will also be thinking about a typical story line that you associate with that genre.

Activity 7

AO1– Demonstrate knowledge and understanding of how films communicate

- Complete a table like the one below, adding three films that you can think of that fit into the genres listed.

Genre	Film 1	Film 2	Film 3
Disaster			
Romantic comedy			
Horror			

Key terms

Generic conventions: the various ways in which film language is typically used in particular genres

It is important for the industry and audiences to be able to categorise films, as audiences know what they like and the industry want to make sure they attract their target audience; so marketing devices such as film posters and trailers will follow appropriate **generic conventions**.

Examiner's tip

During the course you will look at various different kinds of films and discuss what genre they may fit into but you should remember that genre is not a fixed thing. Film styles change over time, as film-makers challenge audience expectations and try to make their films bigger and better than the one that came before. Also it is important to remember that genre as a term is used differently by audiences and the people making films, so what genre a film fits into is a debatable area.

However, it is also interesting to see how little certain aspects of genre can change over time. This first still is from *Earthquake* (1974) and the second is from *The Day After Tomorrow* (2004). Notice how the disaster genre still uses wide landscape shots – a generic convention still enjoyed by audiences.

***8** A still from* Earthquake *(1974)*

***9** A still from* The Day After Tomorrow *(2004)*

Narrative

Genre links very closely with narrative. The narrative of a film refers to the way the film tells the story. Initially a film is written in one form or other. It may have been specifically written for the cinema screen but it may also have been a book originally, or even based on a real-life event. This story will then need to be turned into a film. When we read we imagine sounds that are described and settings that are portrayed.

Activity 8

AO1– Demonstrate knowledge and understanding of how films communicate

- Below are two possible openings of films. Discuss in groups what genre you would fit them into and why.

  It is a dark, misty night. A young woman is walking home from a party. It is very quiet except for her humming of a tune she liked from the party. Soon we hear echoey footsteps behind her. After a while she hears them and they start to get quicker...

  A man in a white coat is dripping a bright coloured liquid into a test tube of clear fluid. It ferments and bubbles and the man quickly drinks it. As he does so he laughs dramatically and starts to choke, pulling a tortured facial expression...

Within your group you may have argued about what genre you would fit these films into. You may have thought they were both horror films, but equally the top film could have been a crime film and the second one a science fiction film.

This may be because you had limited information about the films but you should also be aware that films don't always fit neatly into one genre. And some genres share a number of characteristics.

Activity 9

AO4 – Use creative and technical skills to construct film products

Coursework idea

- Come up with your own 'film openings' in small groups. Discuss as a whole class whether or not they do or don't fit neatly into one genre.

Unlike an author, a film-maker has music that can help to create atmosphere and special effects that can create, for example, dramatic explosions; film is a medium that uses sound and image to create meaning so it is important that film-makers use these effectively in bringing stories to life.

However, the narrative doesn't simply refer to the story: it also refers to the way the film tells the story and how the audience understand that story. So when you are looking at a film's narrative you will consider things such as audience positioning. Do you sympathise with the main character? Are you given more information than they are so that you gain an understanding of events and characters not shared by the main character?

In disaster films, because the events of the narrative are so huge, we often follow one character or a small group of characters and how they deal with what happens to give us more detail. Without characters we knew well, we would find it difficult to get emotionally involved with the narrative of the overall disaster.

> **Key terms**
>
> **Narrative structure:** the way in which the narrative is ordered and organised within a film
>
> **Narrative voice-over:** the use of an unseen narrator to tell the audience parts of the film's story

It is also important to consider the **narrative structure** of a film. Stories in books and films aren't always told to us in the order of how things happen. The storyteller can move backwards and forwards in time and show us different aspects of events from different characters' points of view. Films use different techniques to show us they are moving to a different part of the story. Sometimes this can be done simply by using editing or colour but sometimes film-makers make audiences work harder to piece a story together.

Film-makers use other techniques to help us understand the story too. They might use a **narrative voice-over**, as in *Whale Rider*; or they can even use captions to tell us where the narrative is set in time or place.

Activity 10

In *The Day After Tomorrow* there is more than one story being told.

- Can you split the story up into the main narrative threads (the main storylines)?
- Why are all these elements important to our enjoyment of the film?

Representation

Representation refers to the way people are presented to us through the media. It refers to the image we are shown and the way we then interpret this image. Films communicate how characters in different situations behave and react but they also carry messages relating to things such as race and gender which we understand through repeated images in the media and from our own cultural and social background. You will probably notice how differently women are represented in disaster films from the 1970s to those in the 1990s and beyond, as the films reflect how women's roles have changed in society.

> **Key terms**
>
> **Denotation:** what we see and hear on the screen
>
> **Connotation:** the meanings which we may associate with what we see and hear on the screen

All films create meanings for audiences in different ways. Some of these meanings are directly expressed and others are implied. In Film and Media Studies we refer to these two methods as **denotation** and **connotation**.

Denotation refers to exactly what we see. So, for example, at the opening of *Independence Day* (1996) there are two distinctive groups of people represented – scientists and the military. The denotation of these characters would refer to:

- the body language
- the dialogue
- the actions of these characters.

Activity 11

10 *A still from* Crash *(2004)*

AO2 – Explore, respond to and reflect on a range of films and topics

- Watch the scene in the film *Crash* where Peter and Anthony are walking down the street, up to where they steal the car.
- How are they represented? What impression do you get of their characters?
- Do you think the director is trying to get across any messages?

The connotations of these representations would refer to how this creates meaning for the audience. However, we might not all see the same meanings within an image or film because, as individual members of an audience, we come from different backgrounds, have different beliefs and enjoy different things; so all members of an audience will not read a film or image in the same way.

Activity 12

AO2 – Explore, respond to and reflect on a range of films and topics

- Watch the opening sequence from *Independence Day*. Now copy and complete the table below to support your understanding of these key terms.

Scientists

Denotation	Connotation
Untidy clothes, all wearing different colours and patterns	*Unconcerned about appearance. Do not wish to fit in or follow rules by wearing a uniform.*
Excitable, moving quickly	
Quickly deciphering information from computers	
Range of people, i.e. men and women, different ages, ethnic backgrounds	
Sitting around in nightwear with no shoes on	
Humour – responses of senior scientist	

Activity 12 Continued

Military

Denotation	Connotation
Well-presented uniforms with medals	
Fast-paced walk around corridors	
Aggressive response of senior officer	
Short, sharp sentences	
White, male officers only	

Key terms

Stereotype: a simplified representation of a person or group of people, repeatedly used so it becomes seen as the norm

Some of these representations could be seen to be **stereotypical** and it is important that you always consider who is making the film and what messages are being conveyed. You will no doubt see a huge difference between many of the Hollywood films and the non-Hollywood films you study in preparation for the 'New Horizons' section of the exam, especially in reference to representation of people from different cultures.

Knowledge check

In this chapter you have had a brief introduction to the way film-makers communicate using the language of films. In order to discuss your knowledge and understanding of specific films you need to know how to accurately describe what you have seen.

Make sure that you are able to write a short definition of each of the following terms:

- macro elements
- micro elements
- cinematography
- editing
- sound
- mise-en-scène
- genre
- narrative
- representation.

Section A Film language

Chapter 2 Cinematography

In this chapter we will cover:

- how the camera can show the narrative from a particular point of view
- how atmosphere and emotions can be emphasised through the use of the camera
- the terminology used to describe camera shots and movement.

Key terms

Cinematography: cinematography refers to the recording of the moving image – a photographer takes *still* images, a cinematographer films *moving* images

Activity 13

AO2 – Explore, respond to and reflect a range of films and topics

- This image creates anticipation of the narrative. In groups, discuss why this is.
- What questions are left unanswered in this image?

11 *A still from* Indiana Jones and the Kingdom of the Crystal Skull *(2008)*

Though it is always important to be aware of how all the elements of film language work together to create meaning, it is still interesting to consider how each separate feature can communicate ideas and has its own set of conventions.

When studying cinematography, it is important to look at the choice of shot and camera movement. Shot duration (how long each shot lasts), movement and framing can tell us a lot about the characters and their actions. It determines whose point of view we see events from and draws our attention to clues about what might happen later in the narrative. When we talk about camera framing we are looking at what we can see within the frame of the cinema screen. Camera framing can draw our attention to emotions, bringing us very close to the action, or it can place us some distance away. Particular camera angles may create a particular feeling or impression.

In this chapter, we are going to consider how different uses of the camera do all these different things.

Camera shots

Long shot

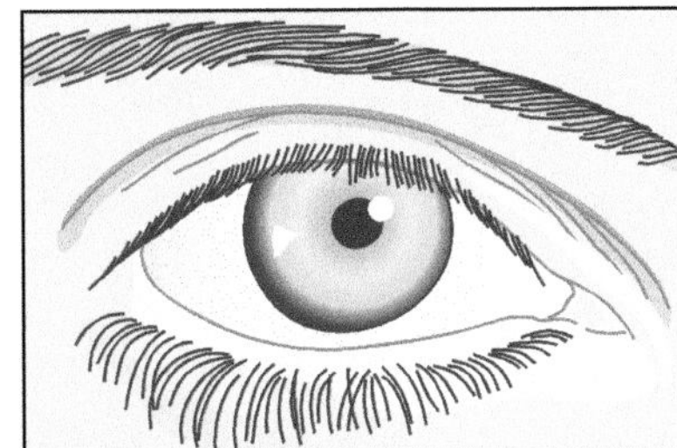
Extreme close-up

Mid-shot

Close-up

Point of view (POV) shot (long)

Low angle POV shot (mid)

High angle POV shot (mid)

12 *There are several different camera shots which can all be used to great effect*

Key terms

Close-up shot: when we are close up to a subject; the head and shoulders of a person to show that their facial expressions are important

Each camera shot can be described with a specific term, for example, a close-up, mid-shot or low angle shot; and generally these shots are chosen to enable audiences to understand events in a particular way.

A **close-up shot** is used if the director wants to focus our attention on one particular thing. This is often a character's facial expression. Close-ups emphasise a character's emotions as we generally read someone's feelings by looking into their eyes, or looking for reactions from their mouth movements. A close-up will ensure our attention is drawn just to one character's face so we will know if they are angry, frightened or even about to scream.

Activity 14

- Discuss what the director wants us to understand when we see these two close-ups.

13 *The face of terror* (Black Water, 2007)

14 *The look of love* (Romo and Juliet, 1996)

Key terms

Significant prop: an item in a scene that our attention is drawn to because it is going to become important later on in the film

Long shot: when the camera is a distance away from the subject so all of it is visible and maybe more of the setting and other people

Point of view (POV) shot: when we (the viewer) see exactly what the character is seeing

A close-up may draw our attention to someone's reaction to something that is happening; and this could be a significant clue to a development in the plot. Maybe this character has not played a very significant role in the film yet; this shot would suggest they are about to. In a similar way, a close-up can show us a **significant prop**. By focusing our attention on a knife on a table, or a letter left unopened, we are made aware that this object is going to be important at a later stage in the story.

An extreme close-up (XCU) shot focuses the audience's attention on even smaller details and these shots are often used more for artistic effect than due to generic conventions; though due to the tight framing of the shot, extreme close-ups give audiences a sense of discomfort so can be used to really get the audience close to the action and see things from the character's perspective. There is a good example of this in *The Mummy* (1999), where Rick is on the floor pinned down by ghostly soldiers who all have their spears poised just above his eye.

A **long shot** on the other hand shows us the whole of a character, thus drawing our attention to a person's costume and body language. A long shot may be needed to offer perspective. For example, in *The Day After Tomorrow*, we see a long, **point of view shot** of the wave approaching the library. This shot includes another main character, so why has the director focused our attention on the wave and not her? Because this is a disaster movie and the excitement and tension is created by what we, the audience, and Jake Gyllenhaal, are aware of but she is not.

Long shots often give us more background to look at, so setting becomes important to a scene as well as action. Sometimes this is because the setting is important to that character. For example, we often see long shots of Jack Sparrow on his ship in *Pirates of the Caribbean* (2003) because his pirate life is such an important part of his character.

15 *A long shot of Jack Sparrow in* Pirates of the Caribbean

A long shot is often combined with a wide angle to create a dramatic image of a setting. This is referred to as an establishing shot as it establishes a clear sense of place. If the director really wants us to take in the surroundings, they might pan the camera around as well. These shots are often used at the beginning of films, if the setting is particularly important to the genre. Crime films, for example, often have dark, city settings so the film might start with a long, wide shot of a cityscape.

Activity 15

AO1– Demonstrate knowledge and understanding of how films communicate
AO2 – Explore, respond to and reflect on a range of films and topics

- Watch the final sequence of *Revenge of the Sith* (2005).
- Why are so many long shots used in this sequence?
- Why does the setting seem so important to the action and outcome?

In the disaster movie, part of the pleasure for audiences is the spectacle of the dramatic action and the special effects used to create it, so long and wide shots are essential to an audience's enjoyment of these generic conventions.

***16** An example of a mid-shot from* Charlie Wilson's War *(2007)*

Key terms

Mid-shot: when we see the character from the waist up with a partial view of the setting in the background

A **mid-shot** allows us to see a person from the waist up and often this shot will be used so we can focus on the dialogue between two characters. A mid-shot allows us to gain some information about the setting as well, but not so much that it distracts us from listening to the conversation or considering what action is taking place.

Of course there are variations and the director doesn't have to measure how much of a character is showing but the three main shot types are:

- close-up
- long shot
- mid-shot.

The director's choice of shot can have a big impact on the way an audience reads the film.

Activity 16

AO1 – Demonstrate knowledge and understanding of how films communicate

AO2 – Explore, respond to and reflect on a range of films and topics

- Discuss with a partner how you think the director expects you to feel when you look at these two shots.
- What do you think you are expected to think about the strength of the characters in these situations?

17 *An example of a low angle shot from* Sin City *(2005)*

18 *An example of a high angle shot from* Oliver Twist *(2005)*

Key terms

Low angle shot: if the camera is placed below a subject looking up, it looks larger and more powerful

High angle shot: when a camera looks down on a person or object, it can look vulnerable

A **high angle shot** is when the camera points down towards the subject and a **low angle shot** is the opposite. If, as a member of the audience, you are placed higher up than a character, one of the simplest interpretations is that the director wanted them to look more vulnerable. We are placed in a stronger position than them. Conversely, if the camera is at a low angle, the character looks bigger, making them look important.

There might of course be other reasons within different genres for placing a camera in a particular way. For example, there is an excellent shot of Godzilla, where a close-up shot of a leg tilts up to a low angle shot of the rest of the powerful-looking creature. But a totally different way of using the same shot might appear in a romantic comedy. I am sure you have seen the classic point of view shot when a man has dropped to the floor for some reason and, when he looks up, the camera tilts to reveal the long leg of an attractive woman.

Examiner's tip

As you can see, it is really important when you are analysing aspects of film language such as cinematography, that you use your broader knowledge of film too. You have to also consider aspects of genre and narrative and how all the micro elements work alongside each other.

Also, when Spider-Man is whizzing through the city sky, swinging from building to building, the camera moves alongside him, sometimes above and sometimes below. This is not to show him as alternately vulnerable or powerful; it is to make the audience feel that they are alongside him, joining in with his adventures.

Key terms

Steadi-cam: a camera mounted on a harness attached to a cameraman, so the movement of the camera is smooth

Hand-held camera: the camera shots move in a disjointed way – the shots are unclear as the camera is held without support

Camera movement

A director of contemporary films can move the camera around in various ways to change an audience's experience of the images presented on screen. The difference in experience is clear when watching films made before the **steadi-cam** came into use and even earlier, when cameras were fixed in one spot and could not be moved at all.

However, sometimes a director might want the camera to move haphazardly, as this makes the audience feel that the action is somehow more real, partly because we associate the **hand-held camera** with the documentary genre. Action sequences and scenes where characters are running often use this technique as it makes the audience feel that they are running too.

Cameras can be placed on tracks (tracking shots), on cranes (crane shots), on trucks and even in helicopters (commonly used for bird's eye view shots). Films with lots of action will typically use a variety of these techniques.

Zooming in and out

Although it is not officially camera movement, as it only involves the lense moving, zooming in and out is also an important part of the way the camera brings us closer to the action or, when appropriate, takes us away from it. The camera will zoom in suddenly to emphasise a character's reaction to something, or to show us a place a character needs to get to in a hurry, so emphasising this is far away, but very important. Zooming out from something is often done when a character has reacted dramatically to an event, such as the loss of someone they care about.

19 *This still is a famous moment in the film* Platoon *(1986) where a soldier drops to his knees and the camera zooms away as he wails dramatically at the sky, emphasising the enormity of his pain by taking a small moment and giving it a larger context*

Activity 17

AO3 – Demonstrate planning, research and presentation skills

- Create a storyboard sequence for a disaster film, using as many of the camera angles and movements mentioned above as you can.
- You probably found it quite easy to use the camera angles and movements in this genre – why do you think this is?
- Compare your storyboard to others. Did you all come up with similar or different uses of the techniques?

Tilted frame, bird's eye view and framing

Other uses of the camera that are interesting to notice include the **tilted frame**; this is when the image you see is on an angle, so the camera is tilted. This is used to put the audience off balance – to show them something is not quite right. Horror sequences often use them as they emphasise the emotional state of the victim or even the mental state of the killer.

The **bird's eye view** shot (mentioned above) is when the camera looks straight down onto a setting or person, so you see it or them directly from above. This might be used to show we are watching someone but may well just show us a setting or landscape from a different perspective.

Key terms

Tilted frame: when the camera is tilted so as to put the image at an angle

Bird's eye view: when the camera looks down on settings or characters from high above

Key terms

Framing: the edges of the picture and what is contained within the space they surround

Framing refers to the edges of the picture – what has been deliberately placed in, or excluded from, the frame. This relates closely to camera angles but we often discuss the 'tight framing' of a sequence of shots, which would probably be used to describe a sequence of close-up and maybe mid-shots where little mise-en-scène is noticeable; our attention is focused on the characters, or where the frame seems to fit tightly around the characters, adding a discomfort to our viewing experience for some reason (it may be that the characters are in a small space or tricky situation).

Activity 18

AO1 – Demonstrate knowledge and understanding of how films communicate

- Watch the opening of *Rabbit-Proof Fence* (2002).
- Consider the effect of the bird's eye view shot.
- Why has the landscape been filmed in this way?

Examiner's tip

The best way to understand how to use camera shots is to analyse sequences from different genres and to practise with the camera yourself. Often students forget to draw storyboards using camera shots, so it is best to take actual photographs using your classmates as subjects. If you consider some of the things discussed in the chapter on genre, it is evident that certain genres will use cinematography in particular ways as part of the recognisable conventions of that genre, so think about your knowledge of generic conventions before embarking on storyboarding and filming.

Depth of field

Another technique used to distract our attention from background detail, or to make it very noticeable, is **depth of field**. This refers to the focus of the camera. Sometimes a director will want us to only focus our attention on certain subjects within a frame so they will arrange the shot so other elements are slightly out of focus or even blurred.

If the setting, colours or landscape are important and the director wants every detail to be sharp and intense, **deep focus** is used to give all elements in the frame equal focus even if they are further away. **Shallow focus** is the opposite effect and is commonly used for close-ups so our attention is focused on only one element of the scene.

Key terms

Depth of field: the elements within a frame which are highlighted by keeping them in sharp focus

Deep focus: where all elements in a frame are given equal focus

Shallow focus: where characters or objects in the foreground are in sharp focus with the background slightly blurred

20 *Notice how the background is still recognisable and the blurring connotes speed and confusion which corresponds with the worried facial expression of the character* (Enchanted, 2007)

However, the setting of a film, the colours and the landscape are often very important so in these cases the director will want every detail to be sharp and intense.

Activity 19

Task 1

- Watch the opening of:
  - a science-fiction film
  - a disaster movie
  - a crime thriller.
- Analyse and compare how each sequence uses camera angles and movement to draw audiences into the narrative of the films.
- How can you tell who the main characters are straight away?
- What props is your attention being drawn to?
- Are close-ups revealing reactions that are significant to events?

Task 2

- Storyboard your own short sequence from a disaster film using only photographs.
- Present the sequence to the class and they should try to guess:
  - who the main characters are and what their relationships are to each other
  - what is happening
  - what is going to happen after this sequence.

Knowledge check

In this chapter you have explored what is meant by 'cinematography' and the importance of camera shots and camera movement to your understanding of the meaning in films. Complete the following questions in order to check your understanding of the elements of cinematography.

1 Give examples of three commonly used camera shots and explain why the film-maker might use these shots in a film.

2 Name three camera movements. Give an example of each of these camera movements from films you have seen.

3 What is meant by the terms 'framing' and 'shallow focus'?

Section A Film language

Chapter 3

Mise-en-scène

In this chapter we will cover:

- how visual aspects within a frame create meaning for audiences
- how the positioning of characters and objects can give us clues to relationships and narrative development
- how lighting and colour can create atmosphere and meaning

In relation to the study of moving images, mise-en-scène translates as 'everything in the frame'. It is a French term which refers to:

21 *A still from* The Core

- lighting and colour
- setting
- props, costume, hair and make-up
- character positioning within the frame
- body language, expression and movement.

So when embarking on an analysis of mise-en-scène, there are lots of aspects you need to consider all at once. It is also important to notice how these elements work together to create particular kinds of meanings.

Activity 20

AO1 – Demonstrate knowledge and understanding of how films communicate

- The image above is a still from *The Core*, a disaster film from 2003. Look at the way the characters are positioned within the frame so all the important characters are visible and how different levels are created to add visual interest to an inactive scene.
- Jot down answers to the following questions and then compare notes with a partner.
  - Which characters do you think are the most important in this scene?
  - What gives you this impression?

Activity 20 Continued

- What do the props in the foreground and background tell you about what is happening?
- What typical elements of the disaster movie genre are evident in this frame?

- Now compare your answers to the ones below. Are there any points that you didn't notice? Did you spot things that we missed?

Answers

- *It is evident in this still that the group of men are having something explained to them. The man in the right hand side of the frame is holding a strange object and gesturing, as well as looking intently towards the group. All of the characters except one are looking towards the man with the object which also suggests he is explaining something to them. There is a man standing centre frame, away from the rest of the group, which suggests he may have a more central/important role in the narrative.*
- *The props include a blackboard and two desks with lots of paper on them. These are typical props of a classroom of some sort, which also suggests that the character explaining something is from an academic background, or some kind of expert.*
- *Often in disaster films there are scientific elements that need explaining, both to the characters and to the audiences, so this kind of scene is common.*

Lighting and colour

The use of lighting and colour probably impacts the most on other elements of mise-en-scène. A simple interior shot of a church can be made to seem threatening by flooding it with deep red light. Props such as statues and crucifixes become frightening and the Gothic horror genre is signalled.

Key terms

Symbolic: an image or object which has additional meaning or cultural significance

Colour

Often a director will have a clear sense of the way they want colour to work in a scene – as colour can have a big impact on our emotions and therefore on our understanding of a scene.

Colour can be used **symbolically** – what emotions do you think of if someone mentions the colour red? What does white make you think of? Your reactions to these questions may be influenced by your cultural background as different cultures have different associations with colours.

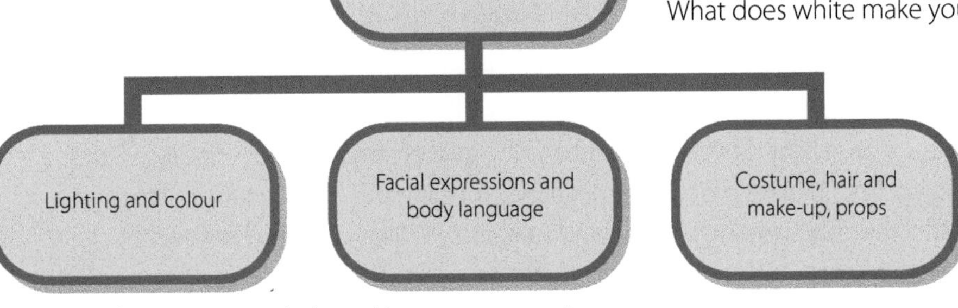

22 *Aspects of mise-en-scène which combine to create meaning*

Activity 21

AO1 – Demonstrate knowledge and understanding of how films communicate

- Look at Chapter 3 in the film *Hero* (2002).
- Notice how the colour changes in the scene each time the story is told from a different point of view.
- Why has the film-maker done this?
- Why do you think he has chosen those colours for the different scenes – do they seem to be significant to the action taking place?

23 *Colour is always important in creating atmosphere but some films actively use colour symbolically and artistically – as in this still from* Hero

Lighting

Lighting helps to convey mood or atmosphere. Often our attention is drawn to a particular object or gesture that is important within the film's storyline. The film-maker can also use shadows to hide elements of the scene and create suspense.

If a film is shot in a studio, lighting usually comes from three different kinds of lights:

- a back light
- a filler light
- a key light.

There are two distinct ways of describing lighting techniques – high key lighting and low key lighting.

High key lighting refers to a scene where lots of lights are included to create a colourful and/or bright environment. The key light is the main light used in a scene. This is a large light often placed at the front, by the cameras. This is because lighting a subject from behind has a particular effect; for example, it can create a silhouette or a distinctive glow coming from behind a character. Filler lights refer to the other lights used in a scene, and the director will want to ensure the filler lights 'fill' any gaps in the lighting, as otherwise shadows are created.

Key terms

High key lighting: bright lighting, when lots of artificial light is added to a scene

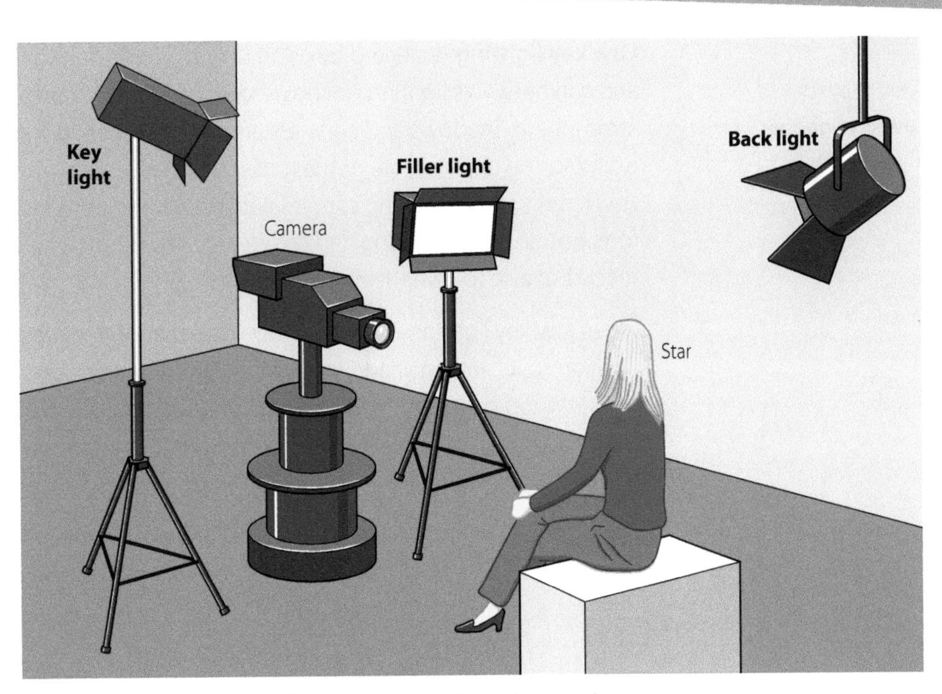

24 The three different kinds of light that are usually used in a studio

Activity 22

AO2 – Explore, respond to and reflect on a range of films and topics

- Watch the opening sequence of *The Matrix* (1999).
- What colours dominate?
- What mood is created?
- How do these colours impact on mood and atmosphere?
- How do these colours relate to the genre of the film?

25 A still from the opening of The Matrix

Key terms

Low key lighting: where fewer filler lights are used so shadows and pools of darkness are created

Low key lighting is created by using only key and back lights. This creates areas of light and darkness. This lighting will be used when a director wants to create a particular atmosphere. Shadows and darkness are often associated with particular genres, for example, the horror genre or the thriller, when a sense of mystery is part of the plot. Low lighting and flickering candles which create shadows can also be part of the romance genre. So lighting and colour are used for two main purposes – to set the mood but also to give the film a particular 'look'.

When low key lighting is used the key light might be moved away from its central position so it can cast shadows and light for particular effect. If you look at the still from *The Matrix* on page 27 you will notice the ways in which the light sources (computer screen, torches, window) all combine to direct our attention to the central character and what she is doing.

Often, as the characters can move in and of the light, changing emotions can be signalled and a sense of unease, or secrecy is communicated.

Activity 23

AO2 – Explore, respond to and reflect on a range of films and topics

- Watch the opening of *Raiders of the Lost Ark* (1981).
- What kind of lighting is being used?
- What does the lighting tell us about the setting?
- What is interesting about the way the main character is lit in this scene?

26 *A still from* Raiders of the Lost Ark

Setting

The set design or choice of location can be very important to a film. In disaster films, in westerns, in action films set in exotic places – the representation of the setting is part of the pleasure for audiences. Sometimes the setting plays an important part in a film's narrative. For example, in the film *Thelma and Louise* (1991), two women are trying to escape various aspects of their past as they travel through the American countryside. When they reach the Grand Canyon, the wide shots of the dramatic landscape seem to represent their quest for freedom. They seem small and powerless, dwarfed by the landscape but they also seem protected by the majestic environment that surrounds them.

Frequently, setting allows the film-maker to impress audiences with spectacular landscapes, massive crowds, huge spaceships and fantastic, futuristic worlds. Special effects are often used to maximum effect in set design and rather than employing vast numbers of extras, computer technology can now create artificial crowds.

Setting creates time and place. If set in a historical period, a certain amount of accuracy will be important to audiences. Obviously the authenticity is more important in some genres than in others. Costume dramas, for example, are set in a particular historical period and part of the audience's enjoyment of this genre is elaborate costuming and use of set. Therefore a certain amount of accuracy is important both to the film-makers and the audience.

Costume, props and make-up

In everyday life we often judge people on first impressions. These impressions are formed by what people wear, what they carry, their make-up and hair, and perhaps even their size or colour. In films, these things are important ways of telling us something about different characters. They can change throughout the film to show us that things are changing for characters within the narrative.

Costume

Costume simply refers to the 'clothes' worn by a character, so this could be the armour of Predator, a glamorous dress or the furry feet of a hobbit!

It can tell us what people do for a job, if they are rich or poor and even give us clues about what kind of person they are, for example, through the symbolic use of colour.

For some characters costume is essential both to the genre and the narrative. Spider-Man uses costume both to mask his identity and to work with his special powers. The X-Men put on 'uniforms' to show they are about to use their powers and work together as a team.

Costume works alongside setting to establish the historical setting of a film and aspects of individual characters within that place. Changes in costume might be used to tell us about personality changes but also about time passing. In films like *Titanic* (1997) and *The Towering Inferno* (1974) it portrays the original party atmosphere and glamour of some of the characters involved. However, when the disaster strikes and the characters are trying to survive, their costumes are torn and their make-up must show dirt, burns and injuries.

Activity 24

AO1 – Demonstrate knowledge and understanding of how films communicate

- Compare the two images below.
- Jean goes through a transformation in the films – changing from a 'good' character to a 'baddie'.
- Which do you think is the good and bad Jean?
- What brings you to these conclusions – costume, props, make-up, facial expressions?

27 *X-Men: The Last Stand* (2006)

28 *X-Men: The Last Stand*

In *Titanic*, Rose's costume is very important in showing her social class but also how restricted she feels. At the beginning of the film she moves stiffly and seems to hide behind her clothes and hat. As the film goes on, her clothes become less formal, although they are still appropriate for a woman of her social standing. She is even naked at one point, signifying how she is shedding her old life (not just her clothes!).

Activity 25

AO1 – Demonstrate knowledge and understanding of how films communicate

- You can see from the stills above how costume and even hairstyling can show different emotions and reveal aspects of the narrative.
- What image do you get of Rose from these stills?
- What do you think is happening?

29 *Rose in formal wear* (Titanic)

30 *Rose lets her hair down* (Titanic)

31 *Disaster has struck* (Titanic)

Examiner's tip

Film-makers use costume and make-up to show changes in situation for a character, so to get the best marks you should always be aware of this when you are analysing a clip or creating your own.

Make-up

When make-up is mentioned you may have instantly thought about glamorous women wearing make-up to look more attractive, but in films make-up is often used to make actors look grotesque, or much older than they are in real life. It can even transform them from one gender to another as in *White Chicks* (2004) or *Mrs Doubtfire* (1993).

Make-up can create characters from fantasy and aliens from different worlds. Of course, make-up is also used to create scars and injuries – essential in dramatic disaster movie sequences!

Character positioning within the frame

A character's position in the frame is significant for various reasons. If a character is in the foreground and in focus, then we can be sure that there is something very important about them. We may be listening to a character in the background but the character who is foregrounded grabs our attention.

Activity 26

AO2 – Explore, respond to and reflect on a range of films and topics

- These stills are from *World Trade Center* (2006). The characters are carefully positioned to show the most significant characters in the narrative.
- Who are the two main characters?
- What does the positioning of the characters in the frame tell you about their relationship with each other?
- Do you notice anything about focus?

32 *A still from* World Trade Center

33 *A still from* World Trade Center

Often the director will 'balance' the screen by carefully positioning characters within the frame. They may place them at different heights to show their various positions in terms of power and importance. Characters can be positioned to show their relationships with each other. For example, if an argument has taken place, characters may be positioned far apart. The classic western 'shoot-out' shot is still a commonly used image.

Body language, expression and movement

Body language tells us about the relationships between different characters on screen. The hero in an action or superhero film will have a strong stance. A weaker character might be fidgeting to show they are nervous. We are accustomed to reading elements of body language as signifiers of a person's status or emotional state so we look for these clues in films too.

Examiner's tip

Although we separate elements of mise-en-scène for analytical purposes, the different parts work together to create an overall effect; you should always consider all the different elements as part of one whole.

Activity 27

AO3 – Demonstrate knowledge and understanding of how films communicate

AO4 – Use creative and technical skills to construct film products

Coursework idea

- Design a storyboard for a sequence on a spaceship in a science fiction movie. Ensure you consider character positioning, set and lighting as a way of showing significant characters and aspects of the narrative.
- Design a film poster for a new superhero movie, ensuring your use of costuming and positioning of your characters shows a heroic stance and a clear sense of 'heroes and villains'.

Knowledge check

In this chapter you explored what is meant by the French term 'mise-en-scène'. You have covered the ways in which it closely links with genre conventions and gives the audience clues as to how the narrative is going to develop. You have explored the ways in which every element of a visual image can carry meaning; the position of elements within an image, colour and lighting, camera shots and movement all affect the way we interpret what we see.

Answer the following questions in order to check your understanding of this rather 'tricky' term 'mise-en-scène'.

1. Name the important aspects of mise-en-scène which combine to create meaning within a film's frame.
2. Give an example of the way in which a particular colour can be used in a frame in order to create meaning.
3. Explain what effect low key lighting has within a scene.
4. Describe the costume, make-up and body language of the villain in a film you have seen.

Section A Film language

Chapter 4 Representation

In this chapter we will cover:

- how we interpret the images of people and places we are presented with in films
- how different genres represent people and places
- the ways in which everything we see or hear on a cinema screen is created and constructed for our viewing and listening.

Representation is a key concept in Film and Media Studies as it refers to how the world is re-presented to us in the media. It is important for *everyone* to consider representation, not just students like you, as so much of how we understand the world today is seen through the 'eyes' of the media first. Think about how much of your knowledge is actually gained through personal experience. How much of it have you learned from films, television or your computers?

Activity 28

AO2 – Explore, respond and reflect on a range of films and topics

AO4 – Use creative and technical skills to construct film products

- Watch the opening sequence of *The Poseidon Adventure* (1972).
- We are being introduced to the various characters and immediately you can see clear character types – the passionate priest, the shy lonely man, the ex-cop and the loving old couple. These characters have particular functions within the narrative and clearly represent the types of people that the audience will be able to identify with or recognise.
- Why is it important to do this in a film?

Coursework idea

- Devise a list of main characters for a new idea for a disaster film and decide what function they would have in the film. Pitch your idea in a presentation, giving your film a name and creating a synopsis.

Our points of view about things are usually formed by a number of different factors: our parents, our friends and our cultural background. What we read or what we see shapes the way we view and understand the world. So when we watch a film, it is important to remember that the images shown of a place, or of a person, are all carefully selected and organised in order to communicate meaning and create a response from the audience. In film, representation is especially important because of the extra ways in which film can create meanings through the use of film language and through using well-known stars to play particular roles.

How people and groups are represented in film

The representation of 'groups' usually refers to categorising people by: ethnicity, different abilities, age, gender, nationality, region, religion, sexuality and social class.

People usually belong to a number of groups and each one will have some defining characteristics. Humans are naturally social animals and generally live in communities of some sort, either with friends or family, in cities, towns and villages. However, when they are placed in these categories in media forms, it is difficult not to stereotype. This is because it is difficult to show society is made up of lots of different types of people when you only have limited time or space.

Film genres such as disaster movies or adventure films often use stereotypical representations, possibly because audiences enjoy the spectacle and action and are not necessarily interested in complex characters.

Stereotyping

We all belong to different specific social groups. Teenagers are a social group defined by their age. People from Britain are a group identifiable by their nationality. You might now be thinking: 'Well, I'm not a typical teenager and I have nothing else in common with lots of British people other than the country I live in.' So... what is a typical teenager? How could we identify a British person without speaking to them if we were in a foreign country? When we say 'teenager', some people immediately think of a trouble-making, hoody-wearing 'chav'. The stereotypical Englishman abroad might conjure up a vision of a large, loud, beer drinker wearing an England shirt. Of course, you are nothing like the teenager described and neither are the majority of men who go abroad for their holidays. That is because these are **stereotypical representations** and stereotyping social groups is not unusual in media representations.

Key terms

Stereotypical representation: a simplistic way of representing people, places or social groups

Activity 29

AO2 – Explore, respond and reflect on a range of films and topics

Exam preparation

- *Bend It Like Beckham* offers some interesting representation issues for you to consider.
- How does this film represent Britain?
- What typical representations does it challenge?
- Which does it reinforce?
- In what ways can you relate to (or not) the feelings of any of the main characters?

We are all guilty of making assumptions about people from time to time, because of where they are from, what they look like, or what their religious beliefs are. Sometimes the media reinforces, or influences, some of our prejudices or beliefs through representations in the news, in films and on television. This is not necessarily done on purpose but when, for example, the newspapers run a number of stories on one theme (such as teenagers carrying weapons) it affects people's view of this group of people. We know that not all teenagers carry weapons, just as we know that not all Russians are spies (as in Bond films), but the repetition of a representation can alter our perception of groups of people.

Archetypes

Some representations of people are even passed down through myths, legends and fairy stories and these are referred to as **archetypes**. You may have heard a character referred to as an *archetypal villain*, suggesting they are instantly recognisable as an evil character by a particular culture or society.

Key terms

Archetype: an instantly recognisable representation of a character that has been in use for a very long time

34 *Darth Vader, one of the most archetypal villains in film history*

Action films in particular use clearly defined heroes and villains. It is usually easy to see the differences between the two. Heroes are nearly always strong and attractive; villains may be scarred or ugly. What message does this give us – that anyone who isn't beautiful is bad? Obviously this is an exaggeration but you may want to spend some time considering heroes and villains.

Activity 30

AO3 – Demonstrate planning, research and presentational skills

- Visit the website http://tamicowden.com/villains.htm and create a poster explaining and illustrating famous heroes and villains.
- Society and beliefs change throughout time and how people live in many places in the world is very different to how it was 50 years ago. This is why representations within the media change. Think about the representation of Native Americans in Hollywood westerns of the late 1940s and early 1950s. Why do you think these representations have changed in the last 50 years?

Exam preparation

- The disaster movie is a good genre to study when looking at representation. Because these films were so popular in the 1970s, it is interesting to compare the representation of age, gender, race and religion. We can also discover the differences in how people may have been presented in films made during periods in cinematic history.
- Compare the representations of characters in: *Twister* (1996) and *The Swarm* (1978), or *Earthquake* and *The Day After Tomorrow.*
- What do you notice about the way women are represented, or people from different social backgrounds? Are any of the main characters from different ethnic backgrounds? Why might this be different now to films made in the past?

Generic type

Key terms

Generic type: a certain personality or type of person seen repeatedly in a particular genre

Certain genres often contain characters that are only associated with that type of film. We come to expect these characters; they seem to 'fit' the style of the film and we can easily predict what their role will be within the narrative. These representations are referred to as **generic types**.

A good example is the action, or action/adventure film. *Pirates of the Caribbean* is, in many ways, a traditional swashbuckling adventure film – a genre that was very popular in the 1920s. Originally these adventures would contain many sword fights and athletic stunts. Men would leap on and off the pirate ship rigging, huge sea battles would rage and a beautiful female would be rescued by a handsome young sailor. The men always wore the trousers. Today, women's roles have changed and in *Pirates of the Caribbean* we see Keira Knightley wearing trousers, fighting alongside the men and playing a central, active role.

Examiner's tip

The best students will now be making links between genre, narrative and representation. Genre changes over time, not just because of technology or film-makers, but because of people's views. If a narrative changes the protagonist of a disaster movie from a man to a woman this may challenge representation and develop the genre.

As you study disaster films from different eras, you will, no doubt, notice the different representations of women here too. Men are often still seen as more heroic and strong but women may still be scientists as in *Twister*, or intelligent and brave, like Laura in *The Day After Tomorrow.*

Activity 31

AO2 – Explore, respond and reflect on a range of films and topics

- Compare the images of the two characters below.
- Even though one is a woman, in some ways these representations of 'the action hero' are very similar – how?
- Design a new action hero that challenges typical representations but could still work within the action genre.

35 *Lara Croft from* Tomb Raider *(2001)*

36 *Sylvester Stallone in* Rambo *(1982)*

Ideology

Key terms

Ideology: this refers to a group's, an individual's or a country's values and beliefs

When studying representation in films, it is also important to consider where the films you are watching are being made. Every country has its own **ideology**, which means its own values and beliefs. These beliefs will be evident in the country's laws, in the education system and within the media.

That is not to say that a film-maker will only make films that support the ideology of their country; they will not always support everything their government or the media says. We still have individual beliefs and values. But films made in different countries often have an identifiable 'look' and can reflect the values, beliefs and ideas that are common within that country. A film like *Tsotsi*, for example, which is made in South

Africa, reflects aspects of South African culture through the setting, music and issues with which it deals. This is something you will consider as part of your work on films made outside Hollywood.

Of course, all films from one country don't deal with the same themes and issues, or fit into the same genre, so there will always be a wide variety of films produced. In addition, it is not only representation that is interesting to consider about films made in countries other than America – even films made in the UK have different production values (you will look at this in more detail in later sections of the book).

Hollywood ideology

It is interesting that most cinema audiences in Britain watch films made in Hollywood, so nearly all the films we watch carry American ideological values. Consider *Independence Day* for example. The film portrays the whole world having to fight against aliens from another planet. However, it is an American scientist who cracks the code, and an American pilot who works out how to bring down the spaceships, and the whole event is tied into American Independence Day.

The representations of other countries are crude and simplistic. We see black children running barefoot through a poor village and immediately assume this is Africa. Of course this representation shows only one part of a huge continent but it is a stereotype western audiences will recognise.

Why do you think we accept these stereotypes and representations in this type of film?

Realism

Key terms

Realism: a believable representation of events

Social realism: a style of film-making that deals with social issues and uses particular techniques

Realism is an important issue which relates to representation. Film is essentially a realist medium. When you study a novel in English Literature you are asked to imagine characters and settings; even when they are described in detail we will all have a different picture in our head of what they look like. In a film they are presented to us as 'real'. Often, the techniques used by the film-maker, camera work and editing combine to help us forget we are watching a film. Nearly every Hollywood-style film has this quality – some of the films you will study from other countries may be quite different.

Because a film usually only lasts for about 90 minutes, and we only have a short time to get to know the characters, 'typing' is important for film-makers. However, we also expect to see, especially in specific genres, developed, complex characters rather than simplistic stereotypes. Even fantasy/science fiction films must have characters that we can associate with and sometimes these are even more likely to challenge stereotypes. For example, *Star Wars*, made in 1977, features a strong female character, Princess Leah. Likewise, *Alien*, made in 1979, featured Sigourney Weaver playing Ripley, the astronaut who has to save the world from a powerful, extra-terrestrial being. These kinds of representations were uncommon at the time and were seen as unconventional and challenging.

Social realist films attempt to reject stereotypical representations because this is a genre where complex characters and strong messages are very important. In fact, these films can even work against conventional representations to make points about our society and its assumptions. (If you choose *Ratcatcher* (1999), *Ghosts* (2006) or *Yasmin* (2004) for your close study films you will have a chance to learn more about **social realism**.)

Certainly Hollywood films cannot get away with as many stereotypes as they have in the past. Audiences are becoming increasingly critical and able to voice opinions through fan sites and blogs.

Activity 32

AO1 – Demonstrate knowledge and understanding of how films communicate

- Watch the opening of *The Devil's Backbone* (2001) and the opening of *Final Destination* (2000). Both of these films contain horror genre elements.
- What similarities and differences do you notice between the two films? Other than the language, are there other ways you can tell they are made in different countries?
- Use www.imdb.com (the Internet Movie Database) to carry out some production research into the two films. Who do you think the audiences are for these films? Are they different? Would both films be shown at multiplex cinemas?
- Why would the fact that these two films were made in different countries make them so differently viewed when they are similar in genre?

The audience and 'readings'

Key terms

Preferred reading: what the director wants you to see in a film

Negotiated reading: blending your own reading of a film with an understanding of what the director wants to say

Oppositional reading: disagreeing with the film's messages and values

When studying representation, you also need to consider the importance of the audience, the viewer of the film – you. Everyone has an individual response to a film. This response may be linked to many issues such as social and cultural background but you will still have your own tastes and viewpoints. In Film Studies a response to a film is described as a 'reading' and this can be a **preferred**, **negotiated** or **oppositional reading**.

If you agree with the *majority viewpoint* of the audience, or clearly understand the points the film-maker is getting across, you have a preferred reading of the film, as this is what the director wants you to see in the film. (Of course, not all film-makers will tell you their intentions and a film might be read on different levels, so this isn't always as simple as it sounds.)

If you agree with *some* of the film's representations and appreciate some of the points made, but not others, this is a negotiated reading.

And finally if you hate a film and all it stands for, you have an oppositional reading of the film.

What kind of readings is each of the characters making in the artwork overleaf?

37 *Preferred, negotiated and oppositional readings of a film*

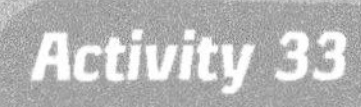

Activity 33

Exam preparation

- Representation is particularly significant to your studies on 'Films Made Outside Hollywood'. In this exam, you will be asked to consider how people and places are represented in the films you have watched. Here is a chance to practise the kinds of things you will be asked to do in the exam on one of the set films.

Whale Rider

- *Whale Rider* is set in a place called Whangara in New Zealand. The central character is a girl called Pai and the main theme is the clash between cultural values and social change.
- Watch the trailer of the film.
- What different things do you learn about the central character, Pai?
- How do you know the Maori traditions are important to the film?
- How do camera work and sound give you clues as to what the film is going to be about?

Knowledge check

In this chapter you have studied representation and you will have considered the number of different aspects involved. Representation is a complex issue and an emotive one, often causing many debates in the classroom. It draws on our experience of the world and re-presents it to us. It is always important to think about the choices film-makers have made and to think about how these influence different audiences.

Everything we see or hear on the cinema screen has been created or constructed for our experience. Answer the following questions in order to check your understanding.

1 What is a stereotype? Why does the use of stereotypes sometimes give us a negative view of a group of people, e.g. teenagers?

2 What is an archetype? Give an example of an archetypal character in a film you know.

3 Explain what is meant by a preferred, negotiated and oppositional reading of a film.

Section A Film language

Chapter 5

Narrative

In this chapter we will cover:

- the different ways a story can be told to audiences through the way it is structured
- how film-makers manipulate time to condense and lengthen moments in a narrative
- how audiences are placed so that they see the narrative from a particular point of view
- how narrative theory can be used to understand films.

Activity 34

AO2 – Explore, respond to and reflect on a range of films and topics

- Look at the opening and ending of the film *Titanic.*
- Who is narrating the story?
- Why do you think the director chose to use a narrator?
- What does this add to the film?
- The end of the film returns to the beginning but then adds a further conclusion to the narrative; why do you think this was included?

Narrative refers to the way the story of a film is told, as well as the story itself.

In your studies of narrative you will consider narrative structure. This refers to the order in which the action takes place. It is also important to consider where the audience is placed in relation to the narrative and whose eyes we see the story through. This isn't always the central character. We may observe the narrative subjectively and we may even see events through different characters' eyes at various points in the film.

During your studies you will also be linking films to some of the major theories associated with narrative; you will be able to decide if these theories relate to films you know and films you are studying.

Narrative structure

There are essentially three ways in which a narrative can be structured:

1 circular

2 episodic

3 linear.

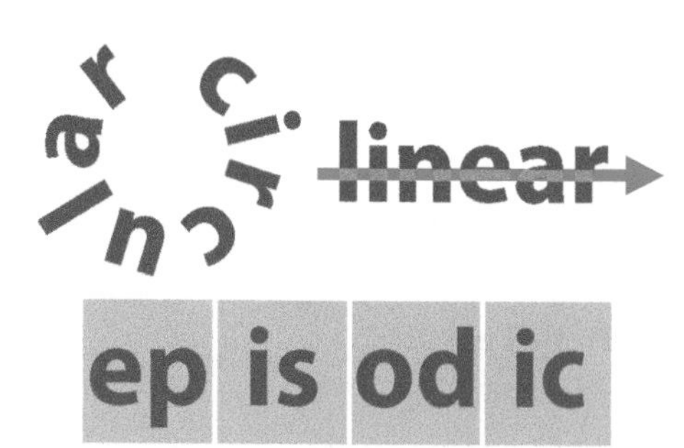

***38** Narratives can be circular, linear or episodic*

Circular

A circular narrative is a film that begins at the end. This might sound strange but, if you think about it, there are many films that start at the end and then use a series of **flashbacks**, or construct the whole narrative around one flashback, and then return to where the film began.

Road To Perdition (2002) begins with an image of a young boy standing on a beach, with an adult **voice-over** introducing the narrative. It is clear that the adult voice is the boy later on in life and then the narrative follows him through the action of the film. At the end of the film we return to the image of the boy and hear his adult voice narrating again, so the film has returned full circle to where it began.

Key terms

Flashback: when a film moves to a scene in the past that is relevant to the present

Voice-over: when a character from the film or an unknown voice gives us additional information about something that is happening, that the characters in the film cannot hear

Activity 35

- Write down the title of another film you have watched that has a circular narrative structure.
- Write a short paragraph explaining why you think the director chose to start and end at that particular point.

Episodic

However, not all narratives with flashbacks and voice-overs are circular. *Forrest Gump* (1994) has an interesting narrative structure because, although events unfold more or less in chronological order, rather than just seeing Forrest at the beginning and end of the film, we keep returning to him sitting on the bench telling his story. His life story is amazing; he has witnessed many historical events important to American culture. Therefore the narrative has more of an episodic structure which breaks up these events into more manageable narrative pieces.

The episodic narrative structure is directly comparable to how fictional books break up a story into chapters. Often these chapters follow on sequentially but sometimes different viewpoints or aspects of the story are told in different chapters and these interrupt or disrupt the chronological flow.

Linear

A linear narrative is the most simple and commonly used narrative structure; it refers to a story that is told in the order in which events happen – from beginning to end. These are sometimes referred to as 'cause and effect' narratives, as the consequences of one event have an effect on something else and things move along in this linear fashion.

That is not to say that linear narratives are boring. There can be many twists and turns in the plot within this structure and audiences may still have to work hard to find out what's going on. *The Sixth Sense* (1999), *The Matrix* and *Pan's Labyrinth* (2006) all create mystery and intrigue but yet follow linear narratives. Linear narratives are only simplistic in reference to time and place, not in terms of plot.

Activity 36

AO4 – Use creative and technical skills to construct film products

- Take a well-known story – it could be from a film or just a simple story you know people will recognise, as long as it has a linear narrative structure.
- Construct a new version of the story that is circular.
- Then try to create a version using an episodic structure.

Coursework idea

- Write these ideas as if you were going to pitch them to someone as an idea for a new film.

Narrative viewpoint

Key terms

Restricted narrative: a narrative that only allows us to know what the characters know

Omniscient narrative: a narrative which allows us to know more about the characters and their situations than they know themselves

As well as considering how the narrative is to be read by audiences, it is important to think about whose viewpoint they are being asked to see the story from. A narrator can tell us which character we are meant to feel most connected to and the camera can also add to this by showing us relationships or events from their point of view (even offering us point of view shots). If a director really wants us to feel part of the film's narrative, they can add to this feeling by giving us a **restricted narrative** viewpoint. In a restricted narrative the audience only get to know as much as the characters do. This way we are as puzzled as they are and have to work out what is going to happen as the story goes along, just as they do.

Other films give audiences a god-like perspective. In these films we see much more than the main characters. We see events that they don't and might be aware of others plotting against them. This is referred to as an **omniscient narrative**. Omniscient narratives create suspense rather than mystery because we know lots of aspects of the narrative; we are just left in suspense about how the main characters will find out.

Activity 37

AO3 – Demonstrate planning, research and presentational skills

- Try to think of two films you like, one with a restricted narrative and one with an omniscient narrative.
- Write a synopsis of each story and comment on why you think the audience has been put in this position to the narrative.

Some genres tend to use the same kind of narrative viewpoint as it fits with other generic conventions. For example, crime films often use a restricted narrative because working out the clues alongside the detective is part of the enjoyment of the genre. Disaster films, however, often put us in an omniscient position where we know more than the characters. We see the meteor or the giant wave before they do; we may learn more scientific knowledge than them and we see all the different characters with their different knowledge of events.

Narrative time and space

Key terms

Editing: the process of putting the shots together after filming has finished, using editing equipment which is generally based on computers

Ellipsis: the gaps in narrative time where unimportant events are missed out of the narrative

Editing is a micro element of film language but it is very important to the way a narrative is structured; during the editing process the order in which events are revealed to the audience is finally organised. In addition, it is in editing that the pace of certain scenes is decided through the amounts of cuts placed between shots. Time is manipulated quite a lot in films without us really thinking about it. It can be stretched so that a moment lasts much longer than it would in real life and it can be reduced so that all the uninteresting or irrelevant parts of a character's day are cut out.

We accept the gaps in narrative time (they are referred to as **ellipsis**). When a character is travelling from one end of the city to another, we do not see every detail of their journey. We don't see characters eating breakfast or brushing their teeth unless something is happening that is relevant to the narrative, because these are unnecessary details. Again we accept their omission as part of the film world rather than the real world.

Disaster films often stretch time so the build-up to the drama can last much longer than it would in reality. This increases the excitement and tension in the audience as they watch the different characters' reactions as time ticks away towards the climactic event.

Activity 38

AO2 – Explore, respond to and reflect on a range of films and topics

- When a film runs in real time it is generally used to give a sense of realism.
- Watch the scene in *World Trade Center*, where the towers have just collapsed on the policemen (Chapter 6).
- How long is the scene in complete darkness?
- How does this make you feel?
- How long is it before the scene changes and why is this?

A good example of this can be found in *The Day After Tomorrow* in the scene where the tidal wave hits New York. It takes just under 3 minutes of screen time from the wave hitting the Statue of Liberty to the point where it engulfs the library where the main characters are. During this scene we cut between various shots of the wave; some characters on a bus and Sam saving Laura as they manage to outrun the wave and escape into the library. We know that time has been stretched here but, as an audience of a disaster film, we accept this as a generic convention and enjoy the excitement.

Activity 39

Coursework idea

Film a simple sequence lasting about 1 to 2 minutes which uses a variety of different camera angles. Then experiment with editing to change the pace of the scene. Even something simple, such as a family discussion over a cup of tea, can be made tense or exciting depending on the way shots are edited.

Narrative theory

Several academics have applied theories to narrative structures. This means that they have compared stories, and the typical ways they are structured, and created ways of categorising them.

We use these theories in Film Studies to help us to understand how characters are used within films to create meanings for audiences and we examine common patterns of storytelling in different genres of film.

Vladimir Propp

One of the most well-known of these theorists is Vladimir Propp. Although his theories were originally written in the 1920s, and refer to Russian folk stories, they have since been used in reference to many modern films in Film Studies.

Propp referred to eight main character types. These are:

- the hero
- the false hero
- the princess
- the father (of the princess)
- the helper
- the villain
- the donor
- the dispatcher.

Obviously you can't take a theory from around 80 years ago about Russian stories and relate it directly to every film made. Having said that, if you take into account social change and the difference in form, it is surprising how accurately some of Propp's character types can be applied to many modern film narratives.

As an example, think about *War of the Worlds* (2005). The characters in this film could be categorised as:

- the hero = Ray
- the princess = Mary Ann
- the helper = Robbie
- the villain = the aliens
- the donor = Grandmother
- the dispatcher = Harlan.

See if you can come up with your own lists for another genre film.

39 *The characters Ray and Mary Ann from* War of the Worlds *(2005)*

Each of these character types has a specific role within the narrative. The dispatcher sends the hero on their 'quest' – the princess is the reward for the hero's endeavours. Sometimes, one character may take on more than one character function. For example, Lara Croft in *Tomb Raider* combines the roles of princess, hero and helper. The helper and the donor are similar as they both assist the hero in some way, but each role is slightly different. The donor gives the hero something to help them, whereas the helper helps them along the way. For example, Gandalf, in *Lord of the Rings* (2001), acts as dispatcher and donor.

You must also remember that a narrative can have several versions of these character types: there can be more than one villain in a narrative.

Key terms

Protagonist: the central character in a film

A fantasy film has been referred to here because it is often easy to observe Propp's character types in these films. The *Star Wars* films are often referred to in discussion of Propp. That is because these kinds of stories commonly have a main character that goes on a quest. However, many narratives from many genres have central **protagonists** who must achieve a goal by the end of the film and characters serve either to help, or prevent, them from reaching this goal.

You should also not presume the 'princess' has to be a woman. In modern terms the 'princess' could refer to a character who needs 'rescuing' or is the 'reward' and this is not always a woman in contemporary narratives. Here again, Lara Croft is a good example of a modern-day hero.

Activity 40

AO2 –Explore, respond to and reflect on a range of films and topics

Download at least three film images of Propp's character types from the Internet. In groups of three or four, create a poster using your images and label them, highlighting their typical characteristics.

Describe at least one character from different genre films which fit with Propp's theory of character types.

Suggestions include:

- *Back to the Future* (1985)
- *The Devil's Backbone*
- *The Bourne Identity* (2002).

Todorov

Todorov, a Bulgarian academic, devised a way of looking at narrative structures according to the different stages of the narrative:

1. The equilibrium – the state of balance in the narrative, where we get to know the characters and their situation.
2. The disruption – oppositional characters are introduced and the story moves forward.
3. The recognition (of the disruption) – where the story develops, different events and characters become involved and more drama occurs.
4. The attempts to repair the disruption – where there may be a twist or climactic point.
5. The new equilibrium – the problem is solved and harmony is resolved, though things may have changed.

Activity 41

AO2 – Explore, respond to and reflect on a range of films and topics

- The dramatic narratives of the disaster film are an ideal place to try to apply Todorov's theory, as well as giving you additional knowledge of the genre ready for your exam.
- Choose a film such as *Volcano* (1997), *Twister* or *Dante's Peak* and see if you can apply this theory to different stages of the narrative. Create your own chart like the one below which shows each stage of the narrative. Work in a small group in order to describe each stage of your chosen film.

Todorov's narrative stages	
Equilibrium	
Disruption	
Recognition of disruption	
Attempt to repair	
Reinstatement	

Activity 42

AO3 – Demonstrate planning, research and presentational skills

- Below are two other theorists who considered patterns in narrative structures. Use the Internet and textbooks to produce a worksheet on their theories.
  - **Levi-Strauss** devised a series of *binary oppositions* which he suggested were the basis of conflict in narratives.
  - **Barthes** suggested five narrative codes that can be related to films, including the code of enigma and the action code.

Knowledge check

In this chapter we have explored the different ways in which film stories are told. Although the theorists we discussed looked at the elements that narratives have in common, there is a great deal of variety to consider in the way that different films and genres decide to tell their stories. Complete the following questions in order to check your understanding of character functions and the way that films are structured.

1. Describe what is meant by circular narrative, linear narrative and episodic narrative? Give examples of films that have these types of narrative structure.
2. Why might a film-maker decide to use a narrator in a film?
3. Give an example of the hero, the helper and the villain in a film you know.
4. What do you understand by the term equilibrium? When are you most likely to find a state of equilibrium in mainstream films? What happens after this?

Section A Film language

Chapter 6

Genre

In this chapter we will cover:

- what the term genre means in Film Studies
- how we identify a film's genre
- the relationship between genre, industry and audiences
- the conventions associated with specific genres.

This chapter does not aim to identify every film as belonging to a specific genre. It is more important to appreciate that discussing the elements of a film in a systematic way opens it up for study. Section B of this book will allow you to focus closely on one specific genre – the disaster movie.

What do we mean by 'genre'?

Let's start with what we mean when we talk about a film's genre. The word 'genre' refers to a type or category. In your study of books or plays for English you will probably have encountered the concept of genre. When you listen to music you may have a favourite genre, for example, pop or rock or blues. Genre can be an important factor when choosing which film you want to watch. If it affects the audience's choice of film then clearly it will also affect the kinds of films that are produced – after all, film-makers need to 'sell' their films to as many people as possible!

Sometimes it only takes a few minutes to recognise the genre of a film from its particular look, sound or characters. Genre study has become a key way of looking at how films are made, analysed and received by audiences.

Activity 43

AO1 – Demonstrate knowledge and understanding of how films communicate

- In pairs, make a list of all the genres you can think of.
- Combine your list into a class list.
- Think of a film for each genre category.

There are a massive number of films which could be studied, so it is helpful to be able to break down the list into groups and consider them in smaller chunks. If we do this we can see what they have in common, how they differ, and what film language they share with themselves and films in general. This helps us to understand the films themselves, the meanings that are created and the reason for any genre's continued use or popularity.

How do we identify genre?

It should be clear from the activity above that you are all pretty good at identifying genre already, so let's take a step back and ask ourselves *how* we identify it. What kinds of things are we looking for? Are there any problems involved when trying to categorise certain films? We group films together according to various similarities, which include:

1. **setting** (location, historical time period), e.g. frontier towns in the wild west
2. **themes**, e.g. greed, law and order, corruption, building new lives, justice and freedom
3. **characters**, e.g. Cassidy, the former gunslinger who arrives in town looking to build a new life; Jake, the hard-hearted leader of the bandits; Marylou, the local teacher whose husband, the former sheriff, has been shot by Jake
4. **props or significant objects**, e.g. the sheriff's badge, Stetsons, guns, horses, the town clock
5. **narrative and plot**, e.g. small-town citizens are terrorised by bandits who steal their money and threaten women and children
6. **style**, e.g. wide shots which emphasise the landscape, majestic music, fast editing in gunfight sequences.

Obviously these examples are from the western and in many ways this is one of the easiest genres to identify. The task in Activity 44 may cause you a few more problems!

40 *Gary Cooper in* High Noon *(1952)*

Activity 44

AO1 – Demonstrate knowledge and understanding of how films communicate

AO3 – Demonstrate planning, research and presentational skills

- In pairs, look at the six areas described above – the common codes and characteristics of the western genre.
- Now think about the science fiction genre. Note down examples under each of the headings. For example: *setting – outer space.*
- Create a chart showing your ideas.

I don't think you will have found this as easy as the western.

This is where the fun begins because genre is 'a one size fits all' category which means that sometimes we ignore the bulges and squash everything in, regardless of how well it fits. For example, if we consider the science fiction genre, in general we expect it to be about the future and speculation about technology that does not yet exist. So which film is described below?

> *Set in the past, on the frontier, with good guys encountering bad, featuring a trade dispute and shoot outs as the evil corporation attempts to swallow up individual settlers and traders.*

A western? Yes, many typical elements are here but it's actually a description of *Star Wars*, the most famous of all science fiction films.

This is a very simplistic example of how genre study can work when we only look for the elements listed above. Very often, the point of genre study is to understand that genre is a general classification, and the more specific we make the entry qualification to a particular 'genre club', the fewer members we will find.

Activity 45

AO1 – Demonstrate knowledge and understanding of how films communicate

- Look carefully at the posters for *Pirates of the Caribbean* and *Die Another Day* (2002). What genres are suggested by the posters?
- Watch the opening sequence of *Die Another Day* (or any other Bond film). How quickly can you identify which genre it fits into? Which characteristics enable you to make that identification? Did you have any expectations before even watching the sequence? If so, why?
- Watch the opening sequence of *Pan's Labyrinth* or *The Devil's Backbone*. Can you easily identify its genre? Did you have any expectations before watching the sequence? If not, why?

Activity 45 Continued

41 *Poster for* Die Another Day

42 *Poster for* Pirates of the Caribbean

Identifying an action film seems relatively straightforward but even Bond contains, for example, elements of romance and the thriller. The second sequence is much harder to categorise, perhaps because it isn't the kind of film we see often so we don't view it with the same kinds of certainties that we have when watching Bond. Our expectations, our knowledge and understanding, our ability to predict what might come next is invariably based on our experience of similar films.

The relationship between genre, the audience and the film-maker

Genre is very important in terms of audience. Think about the ways in which the 'audience' uses genre:

- as an easy way to spot the kinds of film they like or dislike at the multiplex
- as a way of subconsciously responding to the short cuts and clues within its film language
- as a way of comparing one film with another.

Can you add to the list and think of any other ways in which the audience uses genre?

Genre is also important to the film-maker. Think about the ways that the film-maker uses it. Of course it is a simple and effective way of selling their films to a specific target audience; but how do they ensure that the popularity of a particular type of film is maintained or re-invigorated? We may be fans of a specific genre but few of us would want to see the same film over and over again.

Examiner's tip

It is important to remember that the study of genre is as much about noticing differences as it is about spotting similarities. After all, none of us wants to see the same film over and over again! Genres change over time and film-makers are constantly producing new and different mixtures of all the elements that go to make up film language.

So film-makers must constantly look for ways of bringing something new to an old genre. Think about the recent success of *Pirates of the Caribbean*. Pirate films, or 'the swashbuckler', were popular in the first half of the twentieth century with stars such as Douglas Fairbanks and Errol Flynn, but very few pirate films have been made during the past 50 years. What is it about the *Pirates of the Caribbean* formula that has made it so successful that two more follow-ups have been produced?

Most film-makers will want to 'put their own stamp' on whatever they do and this is how genres evolve and change. Sometimes they want to subvert the genre, surprising audiences and getting them to think by turning genre features upside down or inside out. Quentin Tarantino, for example, says he loves to 'bend and twist and stretch genre' in order to create something new or surprising for his audience.

During your course you will spend a good deal of time focusing on one particular genre – the disaster movie .You will have a chance to explore this genre in depth. You will also have the chance to explore the use of genre creatively within your coursework. You will look at films as both audience and film-maker and recognise the meanings that are created. You will have to 'recognise the signs', know where they are pointing and decide whether the audience actually went where the film-maker wanted them to go.

Through your studies you will:

- become even more familiar with some of the main genres, especially the disaster genre
- learn how they work
- explore the reasons for their popularity.

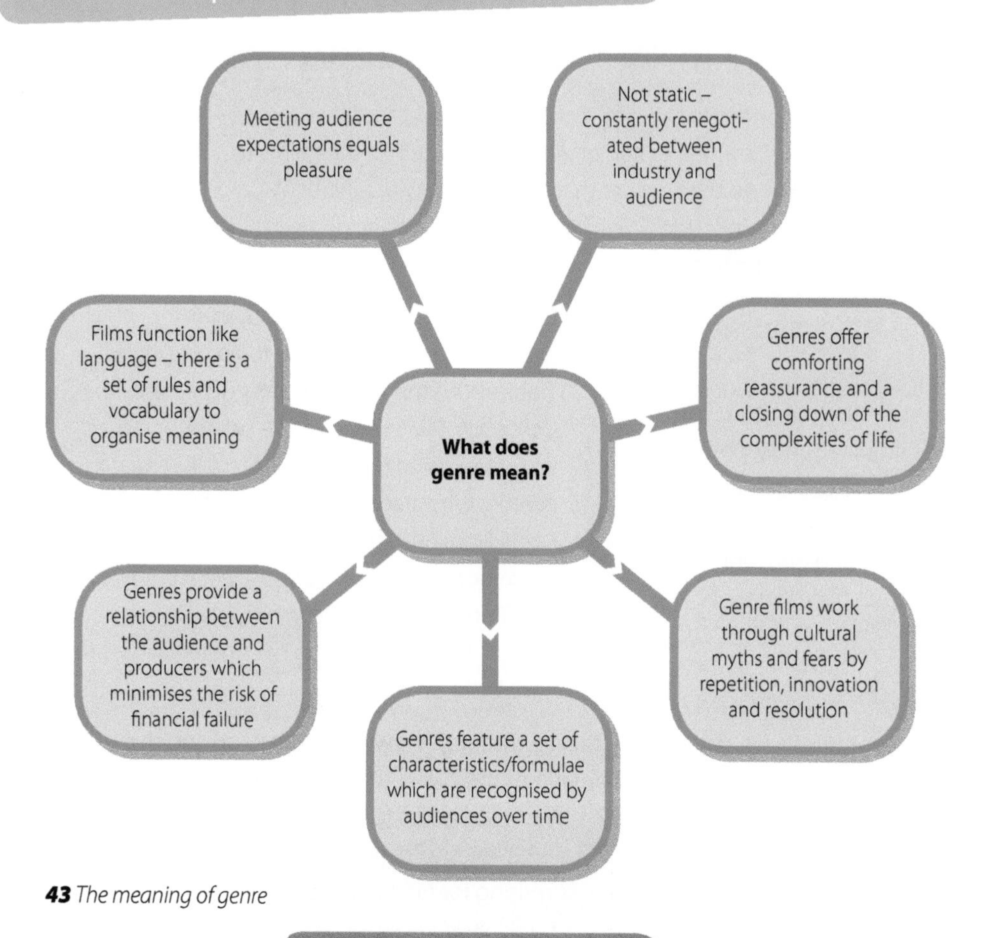

43 *The meaning of genre*

Knowledge check

In this chapter you have learned that genres are constantly changing and adapting, that genre characteristics allow audiences to classify films, and that films are often cross generic. You have also explored the importance of genre for producers and how some genres and films are easier to categorise than others.

Complete the questions below in order to check your understanding of the work you have covered.

1 List the five key ways in which we identify genre.

2 Describe a typical setting for a science fiction film.

3 Discuss three ways in which genre is used by an audience.

4 Why is genre important to the film-maker?

Section B Exploring film

Chapter 1 The disaster genre

In this chapter we will cover:

- genre
- defining genre
- defining the disaster movie.

1 Earthquake *(1974): the aftermath*

You are now starting out on Section B where we are going to look at:

- film language: how a mainstream Hollywood genre uses both micro and macro elements to create meaning and achieve its aims
- film organisations: you will explore the modern Hollywood system and how it manages production, distribution and exhibition
- audience: What is an audience? Who is an audience? How and why do we consume the films we do?

In this part of the course you will focus on one specific Hollywood genre – the disaster movie. This will involve two main themes, **film language** and **film business**. You will use the tools you have acquired in the film language part of the course to explore the boundaries of this genre and to increase your understanding of the films that fall within them. You will also look at the disaster movie as a product and at how and why Hollywood continues to revisit the genre in purely financial terms.

Key terms

Film language: the techniques used to create meaning in films

Film business: the commercial aspect of making films – production, distribution and exhibition

What is a disaster movie?

Act 1: a beginning...

To help us come up with a definition of the disaster movie, let's revisit the definition of a genre. A genre can be defined as a type or grouping of films with similar characteristics, themes or features that readily identify a film as being a member of that group.

So what might be the defining characteristic of a genre called 'the disaster movie'? That's right – the disaster! Of course this is only part of the answer.

Activity 1

AO2 – Explore, respond to and reflect on a range of films and topics

- What does the word 'disaster' mean? Have you ever experienced one? Swap stories with your classmates.
- As a group or a class try to agree on a definition for the word 'disaster'.
- Make a record of your results to compare it to what you learn later on.

Key terms

Hollywood: the name used to describe the mainstream American film industry

Audience: the people who watch films (often divided into sub-groups with similar characteristics)

Cinema of spectacle: films created to maximise the impact of the big screen and special effects

What do we mean by a 'disaster'? It is a frequently used word. Some people call running out of credit on their mobile phone a disaster. While this might be true on a personal level, both **Hollywood** and the **audience** are thinking in larger terms. The term 'disaster' refers to the big, or the massive, the kind of event that affects us all – usually with negative consequences (the drama). A disaster is an event that makes us all feel small, no matter who we are. To be in the presence of these events is to feel overwhelmed, often physically and almost always mentally.

This is where Hollywood comes in! There is a long tradition of what has been described as the **cinema of spectacle**, where the audience is attracted to the cinema to experience these events from a safe distance (but not so safe that we don't feel involved).

Examiner's tip

Always keep a note of any ideas and thoughts you have when reading, watching or listening. Especially if they are ideas about what you would do or how you would change something you have seen. These may be useful when you have to create things for yourself.

Activity 2

AO3 – Demonstrate planning, research and presentational skills

- List as many real disasters as you can think of. Compile a class list.
- How many have been made into disaster films?
- Which of the others (if any) would you make into a disaster movie?
- What is it about these events that interests people? You should start by talking about whether and why they interest you.

Act 2: the middle...

We are still on the trail of a definition of the disaster movie. What have we got so far? Probably something like:

> *A disaster movie is any movie with a disaster in it – where a disaster is any big, bad event that has a large-scale effect.*

It's a start! If you have thought up a list of disasters it might have included things like war, or even a crime wave. This is where we start to get more choosy. When we look at disaster movies we do not include all the things that might be disastrous. War belongs to the war genre and crime to the crime or thriller genre. So what kind of disasters are we talking about? The 'classic' disasters of the genre are natural disasters involving fire, wind, water, earth and plagues, using creatures of all sizes and descriptions. Sometimes

Examiner's tip

Always keep the different versions of any work you do. This rough work can be used to prove the work is yours and to show how you have developed it. Most importantly, if things don't go the way you'd hoped, we can look at these earlier versions for inspiration or clues as to what went wrong.

they happen 'by themselves', almost as if nature is bored, or perhaps fed up with humankind. Sometimes we are to blame, usually through those great human narrative providers – arrogance and ignorance. Of course, given Hollywood's inventiveness and appetite for ideas there will be, from time to time, other things that creep onto the list.

Activity 3

AO3 – Demonstrate planning, research and presentational skills

- List as many disaster movies as you can think of. Compile a class list.
- What features do you think they share?
- Compile your first list of disaster movie features.

2 *George Kennedy in* Airport '79 *(1979) – everything you need for a disaster movie!*

Act 3: an end...

Hopefully, in thinking about some of the films you have seen, your list gets beyond our first definition of 'a disaster movie is a movie with a disaster in it'. Whether the disaster comes at the start of the film or at the end, it will need to be there. Often the timing of this will be affected by the narrative (especially if it is a real event) or by financial or technological limitations. Even so we need the 'big bang', whether it is an eruption, a quake, an impact or an iceberg.

Yet without another vital ingredient, a disaster movie would just be a fireworks display and probably struggle to fill the 90 minutes of a feature film. We also need people. What really keeps audiences interested is how the disaster affects people. We might ask ourselves, 'How would I react?' Which of the characters do we hope will survive? Let's not forget the 'guilty pleasure' of hoping one of the cast will be 'killed off'.

So, if we combine the disaster and the characters, we might have a working definition of the disaster movie genre:

> *A disaster movie considers the effect on people of a large-scale catastrophe. This event will typically be a natural disaster or its like stimulated by the actions (or inactions) of mankind.*

Examiner's tip

The trick with this part of the course is not to memorise a definition to write out in the exam. The best candidates will remember the process and how defining a genre can be tricky. The examiner will be interested in how you argue for whatever definition you have settled upon.

Remember that this is a working definition so we are always going to find exceptions. In some films the disaster will fit our definition and yet the film will not fit the genre. In others the film will fit the disaster genre and yet the disaster itself may not fit our definition. Part of the fun of genre study is the argument about which films do or do not fit a genre. If you can have these discussions then the chances are you have got a good understanding of the theory.

We clearly need more detail than a simple definition. A definition is a good starting point and can serve as a guide. What we need to do is study some of the movies that best fit our definition and come up with some more specific features that the films have in common. We will deal with these in the next chapter.

Activity 4

AO2 – Explore, respond to and reflect on a range of films and topics

- Which films from your original list fit the definition? Which films don't?
- Discuss which films fit and don't fit – does it matter? Can you improve the definition and, if so, how?

Knowledge check

In this chapter you have extended your study of genre by focusing upon the disaster movie.

In order to test your knowledge and understanding of what you have covered so far, check you can provide definitions for the following terms:

- film business
- the disaster movie
- Hollywood
- audience
- cinema of spectacle

Section B Exploring film

Chapter 2 Codes and conventions

In this chapter we will cover:

- the disaster movie in more detail
- the codes and conventions of the disaster movie
- audience expectations
- stars
- remakes.

Examiner's tip

Whenever you watch something that is labelled as a specific genre, try to think about what puts it in that group. Is the label right or wrong? What characteristics does it have?

All genres have a menu of things that the audience expects to see played out in a film of the named genre. A list of these things can be referred to as the genre's **codes and conventions**. This list will always include a degree of flexibility. Some films may not include them all and some films may use them in very different ways. Yet if the film is to meet our expectations of the genre, then recognisable features must be present.

Key terms

Codes and conventions: the detailed 'rules' of the genre – the micro and macro aspects we come to expect when we hear a genre name

Activity 5

AO1 – Demonstrate knowledge and understanding of how films communicate

- What are the ingredients a film needs to be called a disaster movie? Make your own list of codes and conventions.
- As a group or a class, try to agree on a basic list of ingredients for a disaster movie. Refer to films you have seen to help with your decision.
- Keep a note of your list. Check films against it to test both the film and the list.

Case study: The Poseidon Adventure

What do we expect from the disaster movie?

3 The Poseidon Adventure – *our band of heroes*

The best way to start to get our list together is to look at a specific film. We are going to explore *The Poseidon Adventure* (produced by 20th Century Fox in 1972). Despite the fact that *Airport* came out two years earlier, *The Poseidon Adventure* is considered to have been responsible for putting the disaster movie on the map and establishing it as a true genre in its own right. It includes almost all of the codes and conventions that more recent disaster movies rely upon.

The structure of the story is a convention in itself; most disaster movies would have been a very straightforward pitch, the very definition of **high concept**. *The Poseidon Adventure* is no exception:

- luxury liner
- New Year's eve
- giant wave
- steaming too fast
- capsize
- small group trying to survive
- ship sinking
- will they make it?

Even this summary may be too detailed!

Key terms

High concept: a film based on a very basic narrative idea – it will often rely on special effects and celebrities to make the concept work

Case study: The Poseidon Adventure

Yet within that short summary is the first and most important convention of the disaster movie – the pairing of 'the big and the small'. The prime feature of the disaster film as we discussed in Chapter 1 is the disaster itself. This is what we can describe as 'the big'. What we describe as 'the small' are the individual characters involved. Usually this is a group of people who initially only have the disaster in common and they are brought together through their attempts to survive it.

Activity 6

Coursework idea

- Try to think of some disaster movies or blockbuster films and what their high concept pitch may have been.
- Write out a brief pitch for three or four of the films on your list. (Remember, a pitch is a short explanation of ideas for a film which you would deliver to an agent or producer.)
- Try to come up with a high concept for a new disaster movie.
- Write a pitch for it.

The disaster, or the 'big', in The Poseidon Adventure

The disaster in *The Poseidon Adventure* is the freak wave that capsizes the ship which is unstable because its unscrupulous owner is forcing the captain to steam too fast.

As the ship capsizes we are presented with all manner of 'world turned upside down destruction'. This culminates with the famous 'man crashes through the glass ceiling window which is now on the floor' shot. All this occurs roughly half an hour into the film. Why so soon? Where is the tension now that the 'big bang' has gone off? The answer is that, although the capsizing is the high point of destruction in *The Poseidon Adventure*, the real disaster is that the ship now begins to sink. Most other ship-based disaster movies follow a similar pattern. In the many films about the *Titanic*, the disaster can be seen as the collision with the iceberg; the rest of the film is again played out against a sinking backdrop. *The Poseidon Adventure* is different because the initial disaster is more spectacular than the inevitable sinking (which we do not actually see but are expected to assume).

Activity 7

Watch the capsize sequence in *The Poseidon Adventure* and analyse how film language has been used to create meaning. Helpful questions might be:

- What were the film-makers trying to achieve?
- What were the film-makers trying to say?
- How does what we see on screen reflect this?
- How were the four elements of film language used? Were any elements more crucial than the others?

Case study: The Poseidon Adventure

The 'small', or the survivors in The Poseidon Adventure

The Poseidon Adventure features a group of ten:

- a preacher (Gene Hackman)
- a cop (Ernest Borgnine) and wife (Stella Stevens)
- a pair of grandparents (Shelley Winters and Jack Albertson)
- a young brother (Eric Shea) and sister (Pamela Sue Martin)
- an older bachelor (Red Buttons)
- a young singer (Carol Lynley)
- a ship's waiter (Roddy McDowell).

Not only does this present a very varied group of characters 'to play with', it also increases the likelihood of wider audience identification – there could be someone on the list that might be us. This list of individuals and couples is the reason why the wave takes half an hour to capsize the ship. The initial part of the film takes some time to sketch out who these people are.

The narrative often relies upon **stock characters**, or even **stereotypes**, to make sure they are not total strangers. This is important; as an audience we will have more invested in a 'journey' with people we at least know something about. This is one of the reasons **stars**, or familiar actors, are cast so that the film can draw upon their personas as well. We may be thinking 'How will Ernie Borgnine cope?' as much as we are thinking 'What will Roddy do now?' We may (in slightly more ghoulish fashion) be wondering how, and when, our most or least favourite star will meet their end. This leads us into the other fairly consistent convention – that of the 'killing off', 'whittling down' or the 'falling by the wayside'.

Key terms

Stock characters and stereotypes: simple characters that are only very superficial and depend on our knowledge of clichés to recognise them

Stars: the most famous of actors – the kind of actors who audiences will pay to see in almost everything – actors with their own audience

Activity 8

AO4 – Use creative and technical skills to construct film products

- If *The Poseidon Adventure* were to be made today, which modern actors would play each of the ten main roles (you can suggest 'unknowns' in a few cases)?
- Discuss your choices as a group and the reasons for them.
- Draw up your own final cast list. For each choice explain why you have given them the part.
- How is your casting different, or similar, to the original?

Case study: The Poseidon Adventure

The 'killing off' in The Poseidon Adventure

Just like the song, we start *The Poseidon Adventure* with 'ten green bottles' and they begin 'to accidentally fall' fairly quickly. This provides us with another good example of a contrast between 'the big and the small' in that the drowning of dozens of other survivors who refused to take the journey is used almost as a starting pistol for the survival of our heroes to begin. After a further quarter of an hour we lose Acres, the waiter (Roddy McDowell), down an access shaft into a cauldron of boiling water. Although not unexpected (it is a convention after all) it does give us a little jolt to see such a familiar face go. However, more clinically, he has served his purpose in finding the galley and the other characters have further to go.

Activity 9

AO2 – Explore, respond to and reflect on a range of films and topics

- Are there, or should there be, any rules about who is and who is not killed off in a disaster movie?
- Compare the two posters below.
- How are they similar?
- How are they different?
- Are they trying to do the same thing?
- Which do you prefer and why?

4 *A poster for Alive (1993). Who's next? Gulp! A different take on the 'whittling down' concept…*

Thus it progresses throughout the rest of the film that characters fall away to sustain our interest and make the survival of the final six all the more bitter sweet. On the recent DVD release there is a function where you can actually follow the characters' journey and tally up the deaths throughout the film!

5 *A poster for* Godzilla *(1953)– a big, angry lizard or nuclear payback?*

The remake

It is an interesting exercise to compare an old and new version of a film, if only to see which one we enjoy the best. It is no surprise to find the same codes and conventions at work in *Poseidon* (Warner Brothers, 2006) as in the original. What is interesting is how they are used differently 34 years later.

The disaster is the same except that there is no longer the partial cause of a greedy businessman. As we would expect, the special effects are more impressive and more grisly; the 'in your face' body count is much higher. We still have ten survivors but this time we only get 15 minutes with them before the wave hits. Some of them resemble the original ones but most don't. The waiter is the closest in role and death; the rest seem to have 'moved on'. The survivors are the biggest difference between the original and the remake. We no longer have any old or ugly survivors and the preacher with his ongoing argument with God has gone. Does this make them less representative of the audience? Of a general audience, yes, but in terms of the perceived, much younger, modern cinema audience then the answer may be no.

Which is the best? You will have to watch them both and decide for yourself.

Activity 10

AO1 – Demonstrate knowledge and understanding of how films communicate

AO4 – Use creative and technical skills to construct film products

If you have seen both films, here are some useful comparison questions to ask:

- Where has the corporate 'villain' gone?
- Do the advances in special effects make that much difference?
- Why did the angry doubting preacher disappear?
- Where are the old people (it is a cruise liner after all)?
- Who do we remember most?
- Which do you think was best and why?

Coursework idea

Investigate *Poseidon* (2006) and find out:

- who financed and made it (production)
- by whom and how it was distributed (distribution)
- if it was a box office success (exhibition). (How and where did it earn its money?)

What we have learned

The codes and conventions of the disaster movie are simple. This chapter focuses on the most common conventions, the foundations of the genre if you like. There are others, sometimes specific to sub-genres, e.g. the aeroplane disaster movie. Hopefully you will add to the list yourself as you explore the genre. The basic conventions remain fairly constant – we have a big disaster, we have the survivors and we lose some of them along the way.

Activity 11

- Look at the list of ingredients for a disaster movie you made in the first activity in this chapter (Activity 5). Does it need amending?
- Make any changes you think are needed. Try to explain any additions or subtractions from your list.

Examiner's tip

When dealing with codes and conventions, don't worry about the ones you think you can't remember. Concentrate on the ones you can, or those that feature most heavily in the film you are discussing. Remember to ask questions such as 'Are the codes and conventions being used in a normal way or is there something unusual going on?'

Knowledge check

In this chapter you have continued to deepen your knowledge and understanding of the disaster movie by looking at the variety of ways in which genre is used by producers and audiences. Answer the following questions in order to check you have understood the important areas covered.

1. What are the 'big' and 'small' situations conventionally explored in a disaster movie?
2. Give a brief example of a narrative idea that could be made into a high concept film.
3. Name two stars that you might expect to see in a disaster movie. What sort of role would you expect them to play?
4. Give two examples of stock characters and stereotypes used in disaster movies.

Section B Exploring film

Chapter 3

Themes

In this chapter we will cover:

- what we mean by a theme
- what themes we typically find in disaster movies
- how these themes are handled
- how important they are to the genre.

What themes do disaster movies typically address?

The themes of any film are the issues and subjects that it deals with aside from the disaster itself. Sometimes these may be more important to the film-maker than the disaster. For a mainstream Hollywood genre, the disaster movie is very rich in themes. Most of the themes discussed in this chapter can be found in most of the disaster movies we see. Once again, however, our list is not intended to be definitive.

In common with the disaster movie codes and conventions, the themes split into those centred on the individual and those centred on the general situation or 'bigger picture'.

Examiner's tip

When you look at the themes in a film, try to keep track of which themes are popular at different times, especially in the 1970s and 1990s. You could carry out some research into what was happening during the times the films were made to help with this.

Activity 12

- What themes are suggested by the two posters below?
- Is either theme more serious than the other? Do they have anything in common? Do they take very different approaches?
- What (if anything) do these themes add to these films?

Activity 12 Continued

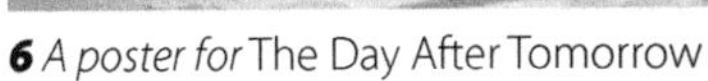
***6** A poster for* The Day After Tomorrow

***7** A poster for* The Core

Activity 13

AO2 – Explore, respond to and reflect on a range of films and topics

- What themes do you think should be/are present in the modern disaster movie?
- Compile a class list and try to rank them in importance.
- Record your ideas so you can look at them again later.

The disaster movie and the individual

Here are some common individual themes used in the disaster movie. They are usually linked to the development of the main characters throughout the film.

- relationships
- self-sacrifice
- redemption
- teamwork

Relationships

These are a vital component in the disaster movie because they extend it beyond the confines of the 'big bang' special effect. As in any film, all kinds of relationships feature – friendship, enmity, love – in fact any kind you can name. The love theme is the most typical – both romantic and family. Love can be straightforward, as in the case of the Rosens (Shelley Winters and Jack Albertson) in *The Poseidon Adventure*. Here we have a couple who lean on their love for one another to get them through the crisis. Even after Mrs Rosen dies, it is her husband's love for her that gets him through. Love can be complicated; Stewart Graff (Charlton Heston) faces the choice between mistress and wife in *Earthquake*. Love can even seem to be the whole point of the story, almost excluding the disaster itself, as in *Titanic*, where Jack (Leonardo DiCaprio) and Rose (Kate Winslet) carry the bulk of the film's interest.

Family is important too and many films see parents and siblings trying to rescue one another:

- Jack Hall (Dennis Quaid) in *The Day After Tomorrow* and his search for his son Sam (Jake Gyllenhaal).
- Jenny Lerner (Tea Leoni) and her relationship with her parents in *Deep Impact* (1998).

The relationship theme in the disaster movie is almost as important as the disaster itself and gives the audience its most common form of emotional 'hook' into the story.

Activity 14

AO4 – Use creative and technical skills to construct film products

- Think of a disaster and imagine your friends or family in it…
- Write a synopsis of the story. How would they react? What would they do? What roles would they have?

Self-sacrifice

Heroes are created in many ways in films. The most common is the character that 'saves the day'. Unfortunately, in a disaster film, the day is almost always beyond saving. This is where acts of self-sacrifice become important for the genre. The human condition is elevated by these deeds throughout almost all disaster movies. Examples are common:

- all manner of people refusing places on lifeboats and giving up life jackets in *A Night to Remember* (1958)
- Reverend Scott's (Gene Hackman) deliberate plunge to save the group and appease his God in *The Poseidon Adventure*
- Sam Royce's (Lorne Greene) heart attack in *Earthquake*, having rescued everybody before himself
- Harry Stamper (Bruce Willis) saving the world in *Armageddon* (1998)
- more powerfully, and ultimately, a film that deals almost entirely with self-sacrifice of a different kind – *United 93* (2006).

The theme of self-sacrifice is unavoidable in disaster movies and provides us with some of the most memorable and emotional individual scenes of any genre. In some ways it is more crucial to the genre's success than the theme of relationships. It is a disaster that allows this theme of self-sacrifice to surface.

Activity 15

AO2 – Explore, respond to and reflect on a range of films and topics

- Try to find real examples of heroism and self-sacrifice, both locally and nationally. Do they differ from the movies? Could you make any of them into a movie?

Redemption

Redemption, or making amends for sins committed, is a theme closely linked to self-sacrifice. Some characters need so much redemption that only an act of self-sacrifice will do. An example of this would be Stanley Tucci's character, Dr Conrad Zimsky, in *The Core*. He is a vain, arrogant and scheming scientist who has jeopardised the planet in the pursuit of career and self. In the end he makes the ultimate sacrifice to try to right the wrongs he has done and manages to laugh at himself as he enjoys his last cigarette. Other examples include:

- Harlee Claiborne (Fred Astaire) the conman who preys on rich, lonely widows in *The Towering Inferno*. He finds a new view on life as if redeemed through his doomed genuine affection for Lisolette Mueller (Jennifer Jones).
- More recently, the part-time selfish father Ray Ferrier (Tom Cruise) in *War Of The Worlds* who only truly shoulders his responsibilities when faced with a disaster of interplanetary size.

There are more subtle and smaller examples of redemption. These can be acts of forgiveness that are brought into focus by the looming disaster. Perhaps it is useful and engaging for the audience to ask 'Should it take the end of the world for someone to do the right thing?'

Activity 16

AO1 – Demonstrate knowledge and understanding of how films communicate

- What do we mean by redemption?
- What different kinds can you think of from other films you have seen?

Teamwork

There are two main kinds of groups or teams that feature in disaster movies: those that are chosen 'by the disaster' and those that are chosen 'for the disaster'. Those that are chosen *by* the disaster are the group of strangers thrown together accidentally in their struggle to survive. Their make-up, as discussed previously, is often an attempt by the film-maker to represent as much of the potential audience on screen as possible. The benchmark for this remains *The Poseidon Adventure*, where young and old and many points in between are in the group.

8 Armageddon – *what a team!*

Those that are chosen *for* the disaster are usually the experts that are sent to deal with the impending disaster. A typical example of this is the range of experts sent to restart the rotation of the earth's core in *The Core*. The roster includes NASA pilots, a weapons expert, a physicist, a university professor and a computer hacker, all highly trained experts in their field.

In both types of team the theme remains the same: humanity as a group is larger than the sum of its parts. The films explore how each person can contribute to, and learn from, the process of working together in the face of a disaster. This raises again the question 'Why does it need the end of the world to promote such cooperation?'

The role of people in a group or team provides us with a bridge between the individual and general themes in the disaster movie. This is because the largest group we all belong to is a society and this is the area where the general themes raise questions.

Activity 17

AO3 – Demonstrate planning, research and presentational skills

- Think of a disaster – who would be in your team?
- As a class, choose your 'perfect' team.
- Who would you choose and why?
- Why are teams so important in the disaster movie?

The disaster movie and society

Common themes that affect society are subject to change. Some ideas are constant, like corporate greed; others have arisen in more recent times, like the potential for environmental disaster.

- corporate greed
- science and technology
- the power of nature or 'nature's revenge'
- human complacency – societal and individual

Corporate greed

Corporate greed is one of the more specific themes that crops up from time to time and in some ways it is the trigger for some of the other general themes. The pursuit of profit by cutting costs and ignoring safety considerations is the 'accident waiting to happen' in many disaster movies.

Unlike the real world, where the source of this blame often remains faceless, disaster movies conveniently focus this on the individual. Such individuals are one of, if not the, most obvious kind of human villain that appear in the disaster movie. We have the historical examples from the *Titanic* films: the negligent and weak Captain Smith and arrogant owner Bruce Ismay. Echoed in similar fictional characters in *The Poseidon Adventure* are Captain Harrison (Leslie Nielsen) and the owner's representative, Linarcos (Fred Sadoff). We also have the purely fictional exemplified perfectly in *The Towering Inferno* by Roger Simmons (Richard Chamberlain), the slimy son-in-law who cuts back on safety standards and tries to jump the queue to safety.

9 The Towering Inferno *with William Holden and Richard Chamberlain – the unacceptable face of capitalism?*

For most of these characters, except some of those who redeem themselves, justice is meted out by death in the disaster they helped to create. However, the divide between fictional justice and reality is highlighted here by the reality-based *Titanic* movies. Bruce

Ismay successfully escapes the ship which he helped to make less safe. The fictional villain 'Cal' Hockley (Billy Zane) may escape the ship but is dealt some measure of justice for his greed by the stock market crash mentioned in the closing narration by Rose.

Activity 18

AO1 – Demonstrate knowledge and understanding of how films communicate

- How do society and business respond to real disasters? For example, how are they depicted in documentaries like Spike Lee's *When the Levees Broke* (2006)?
- Business people – villains or heroes? What do you think?

Science and technology

Our relationship with science and technology has risen in importance in general culture since we potentially authored our own doom by inventing the nuclear weapon. Since then, we have entertained, and been entertained by, many suspect applications of science and technology. Nevertheless, science and technology is often what we turn to in order to avert disaster.

On the negative side, technology may just simply fail – sinking ships, crashing aeroplanes, bursting dams etc. Sometimes it is just not up to the job as society breaks down through its absence, often proving the maxim that we are 'two meals and 24 hours away from complete anarchy'. More recently, our scientific and technological impact on the globe has become a more significant concern. Both *The Core* and in particular *The Day After Tomorrow* find the cause of the disaster in science and technology. It is highly likely that there will be more global warming movies to add to this genre over the next few years.

Activity 19

AO3 – Demonstrate planning, research and presentational skills

Coursework idea

- Play a game as a class or in small groups.
- Take it in turns to suggest one piece of technology to remove from our lives.
- Would it be a disaster? Could any of your ideas be used as the basis for a disaster movie?
- Keep a record of your ideas – they may come in useful later.

On the positive side we can rely on Hollywood (which has itself increasingly relied upon science and technology to maintain its competitive edge) to adopt the more traditional 'science and technology as saviour' position. We need look no further that the two asteroid films of 1998, *Deep Impact* and *Armageddon*, in which the president announces the forthcoming devastation, with the boast that it has happened before but we are the only species in history in a position to stop it. In both films a huge array of devices are used in detecting, planning for and ultimately averting the disaster. Perhaps we need to remember these are 'only movies' and reality has a tendency to 'bring us back down to earth' when looking at science and technology. Whether it is in a positive, or more commonly a negative, way, science and technology as a theme has a key role to play in many disaster movies.

Activity 20

- How is science and technology represented in disaster movies?
- Score a list of disaster movies as positive or negative to decide how science and technology fares. Write up your conclusion.

The power of nature or 'nature's revenge'

In any form designed for the big screen the real sweeping scope and destructive energy of nature is a must. Hollywood enlists them all in the name of spectacle – giant waves, volcanoes, earthquakes, storms, hurricanes, tornadoes, floods, heat, cold, even swarms of killer bees and more. The main reason to put these on film may be to showcase the latest special effects technology and tempt the audience back into the cinemas *en masse,* but this is not the only reason for this theme.

It also allows the film maker to utilise one of the basic responses to any disaster – the fear – and how we are individually reduced in size in the 'face of it all'. Discussing our fragility and who is really in charge of planet Earth leads us into our last theme of complacency.

Activity 21

AO3 – Demonstrate planning, research and presentational skills

- List as many natural disasters as you can.
- Now match films to these.
- Which are the most popular?
- Are there any not featured as films?
- Try to explain what you have found.

Human complacency – societal and individual

The business of doing nothing and ignoring what appears to be the obvious is a very important theme in the disaster movie. On one level it serves to increase and drive the drama of the situation. On the *Titanic* nobody is worried when they are on an unsinkable ship; in *Earthquake* the junior seismologist is just overreacting, nobody expected aliens to come from Mars – but they still did.

10 *The* Titanic *– and they said it wouldn't sink*

In all disaster films this complacency serves to underline normality and what is about to be turned upside down (literally in some movies). As people continue to ignore the signs, the tension builds for we, the audience, knows what is coming – excellent examples can be found of this in most volcano/earthquake movies. The eventual special effects explosion is almost a release of relief for the audience that barely gives us a chance to think 'they told you so'.

This complacency is also part of a wider observation for both the audience as a whole and as individuals. It is the movie as 'warning', like a stern parent wagging their finger and telling us not to leave things until it is too late. Whether it is a visit to the dentist or sorting out global warming now, our main enemy is complacency.

Activity 22

AO1 – Demonstrate knowledge and understanding of how films communicate

- In the films you have seen, who were the most complacent people?
- As a class discuss why you think this might be. Were they just stupid? What would you have done?
- Does this teach us anything? Why?

What we have learned

In looking for themes in the disaster movie we find many different ones with differing levels of meaning for different audiences. They continue to operate on the contrasting levels of 'the big' and 'the small' which we can find in most Hollywood big budget genres. Perhaps the huge size of a disaster compared to the small size of an individual makes the contrast sharper. One thing is almost certain, at least one of these themes will have an impact on even the most unconcerned spectator. Even the thrill seeker who may only have gone to 'watch the fireworks' that a 'big bang' of a disaster offers cannot escape their effect.

Examiner's tip

In dealing with the theme(s) of any film do not forget that what the audience brings to the film is as important as the film-maker's intention. Often the best theme to talk about is the one you feel is most important. Think about how the themes are used by the film-makers – are they serious statements or just easy ways to get a response from the audience?

Knowledge check

In this chapter you have learned what we mean by a theme and you have explored the typical themes that are associated with the disaster genre and looked at how these themes are represented in films. Answer the questions below in order to check your knowledge and understanding of disaster movie themes.

1. Which themes focus upon individuals in the disaster movie?
2. Explain what you understand by the term 'self sacrifice'.
3. Which themes focus upon society in the disaster movie?
4. What is corporate greed?
5. Give an example of a theme in a film you have seen which involved science and technology.

Section B Exploring film

Chapter 4

Iconography

In this chapter we will cover:

- what iconography means
- what the iconography of the disaster movie is
- how iconography is used by the film-maker.

Key terms

Iconography: objects, images, characters, etc. strongly associated with a particular genre, e.g. spaceships and sci-fi, cowboys and the western

What are the key visual features of the disaster movie? **Iconography** in genre films are those items or things that we use on the most basic level to identify where a film 'belongs'. They also have hidden meaning common to the films in which they appear. For example, in a genre like the western we would expect Stetsons (white=good, black=bad), cowboys (the individual) wearing them, six guns (power, law), dusty towns, saloons (the 'west'), Monument Valley style scenery (freedom) etc. In terms of its iconography the disaster movie is less easy to address and its list is less specific. Despite this, even in a general sense, the disaster movie has its own iconography that we can look for.

Examiner's tip

Try to keep a list of iconic things from the films you watch. Which things are used over and over? Which things remain in the memory?

Activity 23

- In some ways, iconography is a visual shorthand. Try to think of as many iconic objects and places as you can. What ideas, thoughts or feelings do certain things evoke?
- Does everybody share the same meanings about all the things you have discussed?

Foreshadowing

Foreshadowing is the film-maker's way of gradually letting us know something is going to happen. It may seem a bit pointless in a disaster movie as we already know this but it is part of the build-up of suspense as we see the clues that most of the participants choose to ignore. The use of foreshadowing can create a particular kind of pleasure. We know more than the characters in the film and want to continue watching to see if we are right about particular events or outcomes.

Key terms

Foreshadowing: warning the audience that something is going to happen or that something will have greater importance as the film progresses; letting the audience see hints about the future that are lost on the characters in the film

As the disaster movie features many different scenarios, these visual clues will take many forms but are iconic because we, the audience, can spot them wherever they are. In ship-based films they are the ignored messages about ice or weather of all kinds. In eruption style films they are the small tremors. In a film like *The Towering Inferno* they are the small malfunctions and fires that we know are about to 'spell disaster'.

This kind of foreshadowing is often found in disaster movies that start with a 'big bang'. In the ones where we are working towards it we have a more formal iconography to look for. Where the disaster movie involves a 'race against time' we will be able to see a countdown. Most iconic are those films that involve a precise 'ETA' (estimated time of arrival); in *Armageddon* the film cuts back to a big clock showing us how much time we have left. Countdowns are also present in more subtle and less precise ways in *Titanic* (and other sinking ship films); the steadily rising water level acts as the countdown any potential survivors must beat.

Activity 24

AO1 – Demonstrate knowledge and understanding of how films communicate

- How is film language used to foreshadow events?
- Compare your ideas in groups or as a class.
- Make a list of the most typical ways foreshadowing is done.

Destruction

The chief icon of any disaster movie must be the destruction itself. To be truly iconic this must be as impressive as the special effects and budget will allow. Even here though there is some room for subtlety. The film-maker can sometimes make choices about what it is they are going to destroy. This allows them to heighten drama and create meaning by using national icons from the real world. New York gets particularly hard hit as there are lots of globally recognisable things to destroy.

Activity 25

- Write down the name of a country on a piece of paper.
- Swap the piece of paper with another classmate. Try to think of an iconic place that *sums up* the country you have got. See if the class can guess your country from your icon.
- Is this just stereotyping? Why?

How many disaster movies pick on the Statue of Liberty or the Empire State Building to emphasise that America has been destroyed? This 'shorthand' is applied across the globe.

In terms of the meaning that comes with destruction it will again depend upon context. There is usually some form of 'judgement' lurking in the shadows that could link to many of the themes discussed in Chapter 3. The warning that 'if that's how you behave then this is what will happen' is the fairly straightforward meaning behind the destruction.

11 *The Chrysler Building being destroyed in* Armageddon

Technology

Humanity's answer to the destruction is technology. Technology is iconic in the disaster movie: it is seen as both a positive and negative force. Often sophisticated technology such as radar systems or computers are shown to fail. This leads to more basic technology becoming more important – pocket knives and ropes (improvised and actual). In fact, it is difficult to think of many disaster movies that do not feature a rope! These failures and successes can signify different things. The failure of sophisticated technology is often about our arrogance and over-confidence – the assumption is that we can do what we like (the 'God complex'). The small things signify how swift our journey 'back to basics' can be. They are a positive symbol of our instinct for survival, our ability to learn from our mistakes and our desire to build a better future.

Aftermath

The day, hour or minutes after the disaster are also iconic to the disaster film. They ask us to reflect and give us time to ask questions. This aftermath has its own iconography: survivors pick their way through the dusty wreckage, usually filled with plenty of abandoned cars. If the aftermath is watery, the quiet survivors observe the floating remains of their immediate past, mixed in with the corpses of those who were not so lucky. If you watch *A Night to Remember*, look out for the rocking horse – it pops up at least three times and each time with a different meaning.

The specialists in aftermath are the nuclear disaster movies (although you can also argue that these are really war films – more fun with genre study). Despite their obvious scale and potential drama, most of these are made for television; examples include the US-made *The Day After* (1983) and *Threads* (1984). These films are all about contemplating the aftermath if anyone was foolish enough to start a nuclear war. Despite their television status, their depiction of that most man-made of disasters is amongst the most horrific – deliberately designed as a powerful warning to all.

The aftermath has perhaps the most subtle meaning of any of the iconography as, taken overall, it asks us to look for our own meanings.

Reality

Just how iconic so many of the disaster movie features have become was brought home savagely to many on 9/11. As the tragic events of that day unfolded, many commentators made the observation linking the real drama to a disaster movie. In terms of iconography, two points should be made. Firstly, *The Towering Inferno* is a very different film when viewed post 9/11; some scenes have more or different meaning now we have seen it for real. Secondly, and most importantly, 9/11 was a day when it was the terrorists who were displaying a keen grasp of iconography, rather than the film-maker, in their choice of target.

12 *New York in* Armageddon *– are we still entertained?*

Examiner's tip

Remember, iconography is not just about remembering a list. We need to think *why* things are iconic. Why do they crop up over and over? Are their meanings always the same? Do film-makers change their meanings? Does our changing world sometimes alter the meanings of the icons associated with the disaster movie?

Knowledge check

In this chapter you have learned what iconography means, especially in relation to the disaster movie. You will also have explored how iconography is used by the film-maker. Answer the questions below in order to check your understanding.

1 What do you understand by the term 'foreshadowing'?

2 Describe two icons you might expect to see in a disaster movie.

3 Which section of *Titanic* would you describe as 'the aftermath'?

Section B Exploring film

Chapter 5

Narrative and plot

In this chapter we will cover:

- narrative and plot
- how disaster movies are typically structured
- whether or not disaster movies have any formulas.

13 *A still from* Twister *with Bill Paxton and Helen Hunt – so I have to go where? When? To do what? Why?*

Key terms

Plot: the more detailed plan of how the story is to be told

As we have seen in Section A, in the most basic terms, a narrative is the story and the **plot** is how this story is constructed. 'Basic' is a good term to use here as one of the criticisms levelled at the disaster movies (and other blockbuster genres) is that the story is too simple and the plot is almost absent. This may be true but we need to consider the narrative and plot that is present.

Activity 26

AO1 – Demonstrate knowledge and understanding of how films communicate

- Think of films from any genre; what elements do there need to be for a story? What are the common story forms? What are people typically doing?
- Are many stories the same? Try to compile a list of the most common stories or story elements.

Narrative

Most disaster movies have a linear narrative that leads up to and away from the central disaster. In *The Poseidon Adventure* and other 'sinking ship' narratives the story leads up to the initial disaster (the freak wave or iceberg) then through the consequences of this as we journey to the now inevitable sinking. When the disaster is towards the end of the film the narrative is even simpler; a 'will they won't they' countdown to doom or escape provides the narrative. This is exemplified in both *Deep Impact* and *Armageddon* as we wait for the asteroid to strike. Given these 'high concept' approaches, there is little need for plot as such because something is going to happen whatever the characters do, otherwise it would not be much of a disaster movie.

Activity 27

AO3 – Demonstrate planning, research and presentational skills

- Does it matter when the disaster happens?
- As a group or a class try to come up with simple story lines that place the disaster at different points in the film.
- Do some work better than others? Try to explain why.

Plot

Key terms

Sub-plot: a story line that runs alongside or interweaves with the main plot

Plot in the disaster movie comes more to the fore in terms of what we call **sub-plot.** The way the disaster movie tells the individual characters' stories is where the plot comes in. The typical plot here is the struggle to survive.

Complications may be thrown in to vary the recipe. In *Earthquake* we have the deranged soldier Jody (Marjoe Gortner) who takes a hostage (another character's sister), Rosa Amici (Victoria Principal); we have Charlton Heston's love triangle and others. In *The Towering Inferno* there is a whole sub-plot involving who is to blame for shoddy workmanship. The ultimate sub-plot can be found in *Titanic*, where the real narrative concerns the doomed romance of Jack and Rose and the actual disaster feels like it has been relegated to the role of sub-plot.

Key terms

Flashback: where a character remembers past events in order to show the audience what happened

Parallel narratives: when two or more characters share different stories that centre on the same event

Framing device: a way of setting up how and where the story happened or is being told (often to place it in a specific context)

Formulaic: where a film contains the same ingredients as others

Although the main narrative idea in many of these films is simple:

- a volcano erupts – what do we do?
- ship hits wave/iceberg – how do we escape?
- asteroid on its way – how can we stop it?

the answers to the questions require plot.

Plot, in terms of the solutions to these problems, is often criticised for its lack of realism and credibility. More important is the plot that engages the audience by dealing with the individuals who are involved in the destruction.

Other narrative techniques can also be found from time to time, such as **flashback** and **parallel narratives**. In *Titanic* the whole story is related as a flashback as the elderly Rose tells the salvage team what happened. It is revealed as a **framing device**, a convenient way to tell the story, as the film shows things she has not seen herself but which are still part of her 'story'. Some disaster movies tell parallel narratives as we watch different people cope in different ways. Most, however, rely on central characters and their interactions. In *Titanic*, Kenneth More's character, Charles Herbert Lightoller, and the unsinkable Molly Brown, are commonly told narratives of characters who do not meet.

Examiner's tip

Try to remember some of the typical very basic story lines. How important is the story to a disaster movie? Does this matter in this genre of film?

The narrative and plot of disaster movies is often referred to as formula or **formulaic**. In other words, many disaster movies are the same film with a new 'big bang' and a different cast. As a typical mainstream genre this observation is quite true. Our job in analysing narrative and plot in the disaster movie is to find and understand the components of this formula.

Knowledge check

In this chapter you have learned how typical disaster movie narratives are constructed. The following questions will help you to check your knowledge and understanding.

1 Write down what you understand by the terms 'plot' and 'sub-plot'.

2 What are parallel narratives?

3 Give an example of a framing device in a disaster movie you know.

4 What do you understand by the term 'formulaic'?

Section B Exploring film

Chapter 6

Style

In this chapter we will cover:

- what style is
- disaster movie style
- how film language is used to create a style
- how different or similar the disaster movie style is compared to other styles of film.

Examiner's tip

When thinking about style it can be useful to think about other genres. The ways in which they look and feel different (or the same) from the disaster movie can help us recognise the style of this genre.

The style of the disaster movie is that of classic Hollywood or mainstream cinema. The word often used to describe this is **verisimilitude**. This refers to credibility – a film's ability to draw an audience in and make them forget they are in fact only watching a series of scenes put together by an editor and director. The 'appearance of reality' is another way to describe it. If we consider most films, it does not take long to think of real things that happen all the time that never seem to happen in the movies. For example, in a film, nobody has a problem finding a parking space, even on the busiest of streets. Does anybody ever need the toilet in 'movieland', especially on all those sinking ships and with all that running water?

Key terms

Verisimilitude: the appearance of reality – the quality of a film that allows the audience to accept it could happen

The use of film language and techniques in the disaster movie rarely strays from the practices perfected way back in the 1930s. Standard uses of the camera, continuity editing, etc. all make sure that, once the audience has 'entered the world' of the film, we are consumed by its narrative.

Activity 28

AO2 – Explore, respond to and reflect on a range of films and topics

- Make a list of things that happen in the real world but don't seem to happen in the movies. Make a second list of things that seem to be true in the movies but aren't in the real world.
- As a class, or in groups, compare your lists. Why are these things true?
- Make a record of the top ten things that only happen/never happen in movies. Does this tell us anything?

Case study: Armageddon

14 *A still from* Armaggedon – *next stop, glory?*

Key terms

Suspension of belief: accepting things that on reflection may be ridiculous or go against the laws of science

How much will an audience accept?

At its most extreme it is referred to as the 'willing **suspension of disbelief**' – where we accept things that on reflection may be ridiculous or even contravene the laws of science. It is only by enlisting Hollywood's familiar style of film-making that the film-maker has a chance of this. Of course, we all have different tolerance thresholds when it comes to credibility. If we look at a movie like *Armageddon*, a modern 'speeded up version' of the mainstream film, we don't need to work for NASA to see how Hollywood is playing fast and loose with possibility.

There are many general criticisms of *Armageddon*, especially in relation to the asteroid and the plan to avert its destruction. If we look at a specific sequence we can pin-point many places where style triumphs over substance. The 20-minute sequence in question involves the astronaut driller's journey to the asteroid itself and raises many questions when considered in terms of 'reality':

- How can the shuttles be launched so closely together without destroying one another?
- Why is there sound in space?

Case study: Armageddon

- If the space station is so old, why does rotating it not break it apart?
- What about weightlessness?
- Would the fuel be oxygen?
- Why do the shuttles manoeuvre like aeroplanes?
- Surely docking two shuttles simultaneously on a moving target is impossible?
- Wouldn't they be destroyed by the explosion?
- Can they really travel so fast?
- 11 Gs will kill a man so how do the heroes survive?
- Why does the body on the windscreen look like it has only fallen out of a tree?
- How can the shuttles survive the crash so intact?

All of these questions probably have answers that conflict with the 'reality' of the movie world in which it is set. The interesting question is where is our threshold? How many of these occur to us as we are caught up in the action? Does the style of the film allow us to enjoy the fantasy without regard to the laws of physics?

Activity 29

AO2 – Explore, respond to and reflect on a range of films and topics

- Do any of the above questions matter when you watch the film? Why?

Key terms

Style: how film language is typically used in a particular genre

The example of *Armageddon* in some ways is extreme in **style**. The director Michael Bay is often criticised for making movies that are too loud, too quick and too stylised. However, their success tells us that even these films do not break with the basic principles of the Hollywood style – 'make them believe the unbelievable'. In the mainstream of Hollywood none of the questions about style seem to matter as long as the most important question 'Does it entertain?' is answered positively.

Even in the disaster movie this is not always true. Very recently, less traditional techniques have begun to make inroads when the reality of true disaster 9/11-style began to make its presence felt in films like *United 93* and *World Trade Center*. In the latter, one scene in particular illustrates a strange crossover between Hollywood and reality when one of the central characters has a vision or hallucination that Jesus is reaching out to him. Jesus is depicted as surrounded by glowing golden light, Anglo-Saxon and stereotypically Hollywood – something that normally would have drawn criticism if not derision. Except in this case the real person depicted has verified this is exactly what he saw, making the on-screen unreality in fact reality.

Examiner's tip

Style can be a very difficult idea to talk about. Keep things simple – realistic and unrealistic are useful terms here. Does the 'feel' of the film help or hinder your enjoyment? Are disaster movies so very different from other films?

15 *A still from* World Trade Center – *Will Jimeno has a vision of Jesus*

Knowledge check

In this chapter you have covered what is meant by the term 'style' and how it is created by the use of film language. You have also explored the differences and similarities in the style of particular disaster movies. Answer the questions below to check your understanding.

1 Give definitions for each of the following terms in order to check your knowledge and understanding:
- verisimilitude
- style.

2 What do you understand by the phrase 'suspension of disbelief'?

3 Give an example of a point in a film you know when you have had to suspend your disbelief.

Section B Exploring film

Chapter 7 Characters and stars

In this chapter we will cover:

- who and what the characters are in a disaster movie
- how important the stars are and how they are used
- representation.

Examiner's tip

Whenever you watch something, try to think if any of the characters are similar to ones you have seen in other films. Who are the stars? Could any other actors take their part? If so, who?

16 *A still from* The Towering Inferno *– Paul Newman and Steve McQueen, two of the biggest stars of the time*

As discussed in Chapter 2, stars are actors who have their own audience beyond the parts they play. Their presence in a film almost guarantees a good-sized audience.

In discussing many Hollywood films there is a tendency to talk about the actor rather than their character. Nowhere is this stronger than in the disaster movie. In perhaps no other genre do stars and characters become most confused and submerged within one another. In a film like *The Poseidon Adventure*, does anyone remember any of the character names at all? When Shelley Winters makes her sacrifice, does anybody refer to it as Mrs Rosen's heart attack?

Activity 30

AO1 – Demonstrate knowledge and understanding of how films communicate

- What do you think is the most common type of character in a disaster movie?
- Discuss the question as a group and try to agree on a top ten of disaster movie character types.

Typical disaster movie characters

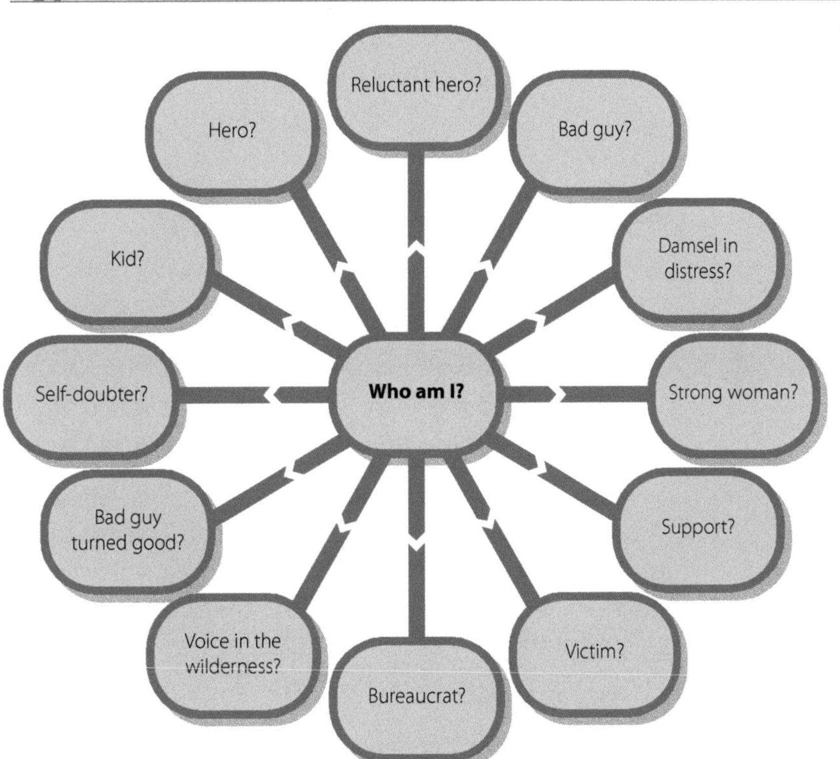

17 *There are several typical disaster movie characters*

We can make a list of some of the typical characters that appear in disaster movies. Although most will fit on this list there will be others.

The hero

This is the straightforward hero, usually male. They are capable from the outset of doing what it takes to survive and/or save the day.

Examples include: Steve McQueen in *The Towering Inferno*, Bruce Willis in *Armageddon* and George Kennedy in a number of films.

The reluctant hero

This is someone who has heroism 'thrust upon them', a character who steps outside their normal job role to save the day. They are good people who 'step up' and do what needs to be done; perhaps how the audience likes to think they would respond.

Examples include: the architect played by Paul Newman in *The Towering Inferno*, Shelley Winters in *The Poseidon Adventure* and Dennis Quaid in *The Day After Tomorrow*.

The bad guy

The bad guy is an out and out 'black hat' (quite often rich) who is out for themselves. This is a character the audience does not mind (in fact relishes) seeing killed off.

Examples include: Richard Chamberlain in *The Towering Inferno*, the deranged soldier in *Earthquake* and Billy Zane in *Titanic*.

The bad guy turned good

The character who starts off as being highly suspect for whatever reason but 'comes good' in the end.

Examples include: the arrogant scientist Dr Conrad Zimsky (Stanley Tucci) in *The Core*, the conman Harlee Claiborne (Fred Astaire) in *The Towering Inferno* and the adulterous Stewart Graff (Charlton Heston) in *Earthquake*.

The self-doubter

Self-doubt is more often a phase that many characters go through rather than making up an actual character type in its own right. It is usually early on in the movie as a team is forming and people are heard to say things like 'I can't go on' or 'This is hopeless'. These are the characters who then often 'morph' into heroes of one type or other.

A good source of these is *The Poseidon Adventure*, where at least half the team is reluctant to follow Gene Hackman and when they do they still don't really believe they can survive. The young singer, Nonnie Parry (Carol Lynley), best exemplifies this as she seems to spend the whole movie exclaiming that she 'can't do it' when faced with the next obstacle.

The kid(s)

Kids are an essential component of the 'women and children first' ethos that dominates many disaster movies. When not being rescued, cute, worried about or underlining sacrifice, they may just be precocious. In other words, like the kid in *The Poseidon Adventure*, quite loud and knowing 'stuff' vital to survival – in this case the layout and technical specifications of the ship.

18 *A still from* The Core *– Hilary Swank, modern woman?*

The strong woman

The strong woman is more common in more modern films.

Examples include: Major Rebecca Childs (Hilary Swank) in *The Core* – an expert pilot and fearless heroine. In older examples of the genre more traditional 'stand by your man', 'roll up your sleeves' and 'get the job done' types include Susan Franklin (Faye Dunaway) in *The Towering Inferno* and Pamela Sue Martin in *The Poseidon Adventure*.

The damsel in distress

An all too common character type in most disaster movies, these are the screaming women who the men rescue.

An example is: Lisolette Mueller (Jennifer Jones) in *The Towering Inferno*. She is a classic example of this when she attempts to perform a rescue which only leads to her having to be rescued.

The bureaucrat

The bureaucrat is usually a businessman or government official, often nameless. These are the characters who ignore the signs through arrogance, greed or both. They were very popular in the seventies!

Examples include: William Holden in *The Towering Inferno*, half a dozen seismologists in *Earthquake* and the pushy ship owner in *The Poseidon Adventure*.

The voice in the wilderness

Often in opposition to the bureaucrat is the character who tries to warn the rest of us; the scientist nobody listens to, the ignored wireless operator or captain. They are ignored usually for one of two reasons: either they lack the power to do anything or their prediction seems just too extreme to be believed (don't these people watch disaster movies?).

Examples can be found in: *Earthquake*, *The Poseidon Adventure* and *The Towering Inferno*. Even the *Titanic* was warned to slow down.

The support

This is a strange category and in some ways it is a 'cop out' as it covers all kinds of characters who don't fit in the other categories. Perhaps 'not quite the hero' would be a better description as these are the characters who help the survival along with encouragement and practical assistance.

Examples include: Red Buttons in *The Poseidon Adventure*, who is one of the best examples of the support character. Whenever things get argumentative he tries to calm everybody down, encourages the doubters and is generally cheerful. Robert Vaughn in *The Towering Inferno* is another example. A remarkably calm and moral politician, he does not seem at all comfortable with William Holden's 'gift' of vintage wine. For most of the movie he hangs around being calm and 'helping out' until he falls out of the window trying to stop Richard Chamberlain jumping the escape queue.

The victim

Finally, the victim is the character type who appears in the greatest numbers in the disaster movie. Many are nameless as they fall, crash, burn and scream and are as much a part of the set as they are actual characters. Yet some of the characters with speaking (as well as screaming) parts are 'victim' types. They are the 'green bottles' that are destined to 'accidentally' fall.

A good example of this is the waiter character in both *Poseidon* films; once the main cast has got to the kitchen their minutes are numbered and, fairly soon after, down the shaft and out of the film they go.

These characters more often than not are thrown together and forced to work out their differences in order to survive. Many of these characters are simple – what is called 'one dimensional'. The audience is expected to recognise them and draw upon all the times they have seen them before to 'fill in the blanks'.

Activity 31

AO2 – Explore, respond to and reflect on a range of films and topics

- Write a list, trying to name at least one character from a disaster film who fits each character type below:
  1. hero
  2. reluctant hero
  3. bad guy
  4. bad guy turned good
  5. self-doubter
  6. strong woman
  7. damsel in distress
  8. bureaucrat
  9. voice in the wilderness
  10. support
  11. victim

One key element in making these characters work involves the casting of stars or the very famous and popular. Actors (and others) who we feel we already know are a great help in engaging the audience's interest in their fate. This is one of the reasons why casting star names is important to the disaster movie – we know these people already, don't we? How much more does the film have to do when we see Tom Cruise in *War of the Worlds* – we know he is a hero, we know he will survive, don't we? Don't forget that the opposite is also true; the convention of 'killing off' means that we will all have expectations as to who we want to see survive or perish. If this involves stars, then the effect and 'enjoyment' is only increased. There are other reasons why the disaster movie needs its stars (we will look at the business reasons in Section C).

Activity 32

AO1 – Demonstrate knowledge and understanding of how films communicate

- As a group, make a list of your favourite modern stars.
- Decide what type of character they would be in a disaster movie.
- Who would you choose and why?
- What about 'playing against type'?

The disaster movie does not just look for one or two familiar faces; in the tradition of the biggest genre films, there is enough room for the 'all star' ensemble cast. Perhaps the best example of this in the disaster movie is *The Towering Inferno*. The main cast list reads as follows:

Actor	Star?	Character type	Killed off?
Steve McQueen	big star	hero fireman	No
Paul Newman	big star	voice in the wilderness/hero	No
William Holden	big star	bureaucrat	No
Faye Dunaway	star	strong woman	No
Fred Astaire	old star	bad guy turned good	No
Susan Blakely	famous face	support	No
Richard Chamberlain	rising star	bad guy	Yes
Jennifer Jones	Oscar winner	damsel in distress	Yes
O. J. Simpson	sports star	hero security chief	No
Robert Vaughn	star	support/victim	Yes
Robert Wagner	rising star	support/victim	Yes

Even if we argue about their star status, this represents a cast of many familiar faces. Unlike some of the other 1970s disaster movies, none of the really big stars fall victim to the destruction in *The Towering Inferno*. Perhaps these stars were too big to throw away in the role of the victim? However, what we see for sure is a group of actors the audience will know in some form or another and this 'knowledge' or expectation is central to drawing us into the story. All Steve McQueen has to do is to arrive dressed as a fireman and we know we can expect a hero who will save the day in any way he can – a character who will never give up. The actor, their star persona and previous work, tell the audience this – the script does not need to establish it, only to use it. It is interesting that perhaps the best film-making judges of this are the stars themselves: Steve McQueen was originally asked to consider the part of the architect (Paul Newman) and it was he who suggested the fireman would better suit his talents.

Activity 33

AO1 – Demonstrate knowledge and understanding of how films communicate

- Go back to your list of favourite modern stars.
- Discuss what qualities you think they bring to a film.
- What other genres of films feature 'all star casts'?
- How important do you think stars are to a movie?

Key terms

Representation: how people, groups, races or religions are shown on screen; the ideas and assumptions about who and what they are that are generally used

Representation

If we take another look at the table it also raises the question of **representation** in the disaster movie. Of the 11 main characters, seven of them are white men. In many ways, disaster movies reflect the general kinds of representation at the time they were made. As more positive representations of non-white male characters became common, so this can be seen in disaster movies. There is an argument that the disaster scenario can act as a 'great leveller', that in the fight for survival all kinds of people 'come into their own'. Examples of this can be found but characters can only come into their own if they are in the film in the first place. If we stay with *The Towering Inferno* we can consider the non-white or non-male remaining four.

Faye Dunaway plays Paul Newman's wife. A career woman, they have a small scene in which they discuss her recent promotion. She does not panic or need rescuing; in fact she helps to keep order on the promenade – at one point refusing to leave. Ultimately, however, she succumbs to the role of 'good woman', promising to be with Paul Newman wherever he goes (despite her own ambitions) and leaving with the other women. Indeed the 'women and children first' ethic is still strong here.

Susan Blakely plays Richard Chamberlain's wife and William Holden's daughter (notice again how we define the character in relation to her male counterparts). Commendably she does not do any panicking – a lot less in fact than her slimy husband. Yet her role is to be not much more than an object for the two men in her life to worry about to greater and lesser degrees.

Jennifer Jones plays a strong woman in terms of a typically Hollywood 'saintly presence'. She is the kindly widow who teaches small children, goes back to save a family (becoming a typical damsel in distress in the process), gives strength to others around her and forgives unreservedly Fred Astaire's conman along the way. Perhaps this is too much for Hollywood as she is the only major female character to die, falling from the glass lift for her trouble.

This leaves the only major black character, played by O. J. Simpson. Although he is heroic and in a position of responsibility (at one point he barks orders at Paul Newman) this entire positive portrayal is undermined somewhat by the fact he is a security guard.

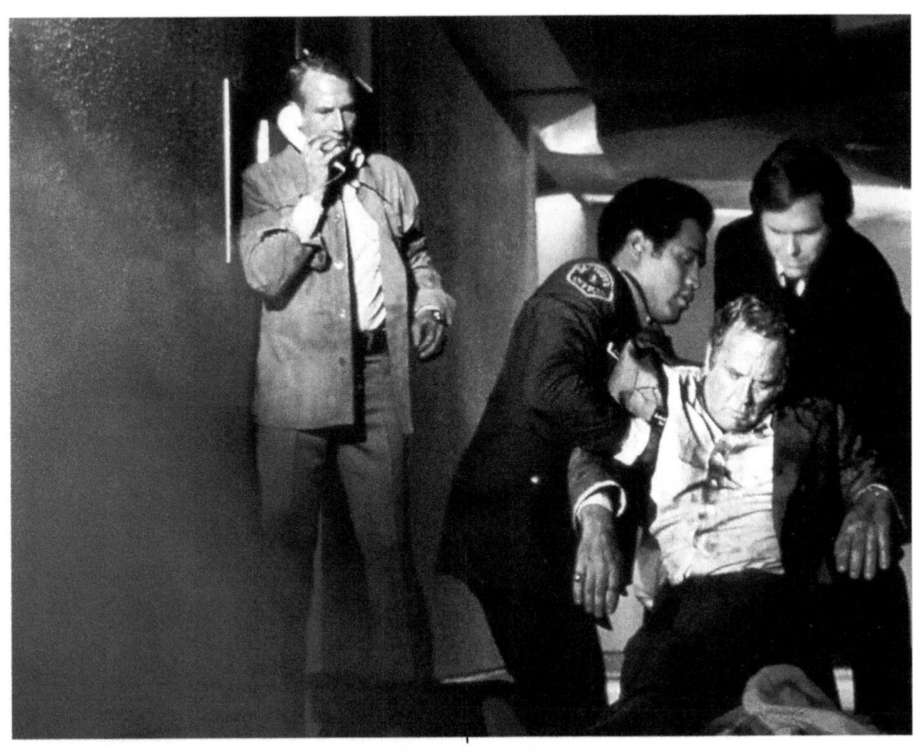

19 The Towering Inferno, *O. J. Simpson – sportsman and hero…*

If we look at representation in disaster movies it would not be very different from much of mainstream Hollywood. In fact, even in more modern films, the traditional formula of the disaster movie tends to mean the hero is white and male and the woman is screaming and rescued.

Activity 34

- women
- the elderly
- white men

- Pick one of the groups above. Write a short answer to each of the following questions :
  1. How is this group represented in disaster movies?
  2. Is this representation fair and accurate?
  3. Why is the group represented in this way?

Examiner's tip

When thinking about characters, try to find the kind that crop up over and over again. Why is this? Does the actual character change very much in disaster movies of different ages? How are you, and other people you know, represented? Is this fair?

***20** Morgan Freeman breaks new ground in* Deep Impact

Knowledge check

In this chapter you have studied representation with a particular focus on the typical characters that can be identified in a disaster movie. You will also have explored the importance of stars and the ways in which they carry meaning in a film. Answer the following questions in order to check your understanding.

1 List the typical characters you may expect to find in a disaster movie.

2 Describe in detail two typical characters from a film you know.

3 Give a definition of the term 'star'.

Section B Exploring film

Chapter 8 Ideology

In this chapter we will cover:

- what ideology is
- which ideologies we can find in disaster movies
- how ideology can lead to different films
- how a changing world has altered the ideology of the disaster movie.

Key terms

Ideology: a system of values, beliefs or ideas that is common to specific groups of people

Ideology is a system of values, beliefs or ideas that is common to a specific group of people. All movies will have these, often whether they like it or not. As most of the big disaster movies are American, US ideology is ever present. In most disaster movies American leadership and supremacy come to the fore. It is usually up to them to 'save the world'. A number of films exemplify this – the space missions in *Deep Impact* and *Armageddon*, the 'terranauts' of *The Core* etc. In all these films, 'can do' heroism and a return to almost pioneer-style values of the old frontier rule the day. This kind of 'flying the flag' for 'the good old US of A' is often criticised for being over the top. Nevertheless, it remains an easily spotted form of ideology that is a very important driving force for many of these movies.

Activity 35

- Try to think of as many different ideologies as you can. How many of these do you think regularly feature in films?

Examiner's tip

Ideology is about belief and ideas; try to think how a change in any of these might affect a film. Look at films from different countries to see how ideology is more obvious than we might think.

Case study: The 'Titanics'

21 Titanic – *an American dream?*

What do the 'Titanics' say about us?

An interesting example of both ideological and cultural identity is the difference in attitude between the British *Titanic* film, *A Night To Remember*, and the American version, *Titanic*.

In the 1958 film *A Night To Remember* the characters focused upon are almost exclusively British. The token American characters serve only to remind us of where the ship is going and provide some light relief in terms of manners and behaviour. The movie is all about the right way to do things, the stiff upper lip, and how, if we all pull together, adversity can be overcome. Indeed, much of the behaviour in the film elicits phrases such as 'the Dunkirk spirit' or the 'spirit of the Blitz'. Any bad behaviour is seen as unsporting and not very British. A frequently discussed plot point of the drama is why a ship, the SS *Californian*, ignores the sinking *Titanic*, even though she is only 10 miles away.

The main hero of the piece is Kenneth More's second mate, Charles Herbert Lightoller, a typically middle-class officer who seems to almost single-handedly salvage the situation. He is rewarded with survival and an understated summary of the situation.

I've been at sea since I was a boy. I've been in sail. I've even been shipwrecked before. I know what the sea can do. But, this is different. Because we were so sure. Because even though it's happened, it's still unbelievable. I don't think I'll ever feel sure again, about anything.

All of this conveys the tragedy and doom of the situation with a typical British reserve.

22 A Night To Remember – *the British stiff upper lip?*

Case study: The 'Titanics'

Activity 36

AO2 – Explore, respond to and reflect on a range of films and topics

- What ideas or attitudes are suggested by the two posters on page 105?
- Which poster do you think is more effective? Discuss which film you would go and see. Who might be more likely to go and see the other one (if anybody)?
- What (if anything) do these posters say about these films and the people who made them?

The American film of 1997, *Titanic*, is very different. To begin with, all mention of a ship called the SS *Californian* is gone and we are left to wonder why. The whole tone of the film is radically different; American characters come to the fore and a more fictitious story comes to dominate. The *Titanic* becomes a 'ship of dreams' rather than that of tragedy and disaster. This dreaming and optimism is very American, culminating in the appearance of that most powerful of symbols – the Statue of Liberty. In *Titanic*, the British are a source of blame and behave as badly as everyone else. The officer, played originally by Kenneth More, only makes a cameo appearance in the form of Jonathan Phillips. The main British officer, First Officer William Murdoch (Ewan Stewart), is depicted as panicky and corrupt; he loses his head, shoots a passenger and then kills himself – no 'stiff upper lip' there then.

Basically, the sinking of a British-owned liner becomes an American story – a reflection of the 'American dream' ideology replacing any stiff upper lip 'Britishness' that may or may not have been present on the actual night in question. If such contrasting ideologies can be at work in two films about the same real event, this shows us how powerful and all pervading ideology can be.

Religion

Religious ideologies are also quite common to the disaster movie – after all, there is nothing quite like the end of the world (even just the end of our world) to focus a character's attention on God. The movie where this is strongest is *The Poseidon Adventure* where we watch Gene Hackman's character engaging in an active debate with his God throughout the film. Discussing his faith, and what form faith should take, shapes his leadership of the survivors throughout the film. His final sacrifice seems to be his ultimate answer to the God who 'helps those who help themselves'. Even when religious ideology is not as obvious as this, people still pray, church bells ring, services are attended and God is thanked and cursed throughout most disaster movies.

Environment

Our relationship with the environment and planet is another important ideology in a genre of film that often involves Mother Nature 'taking her revenge'. We mess up, pollute and bring about environmental disaster on all scales in many films.

Sometimes it is a plot device, as in *The Core*, when our meddling begins to destroy the earth's magnetic field. In other recent films, like *The Day After Tomorrow*, we are presented with a global warming scenario. As the debate continues about the values surrounding climate change, the ideology involved will continue to feature in movies.

Activity 37

AO2 – Explore, respond to and reflect on a range of films and topics

- How different are the ideas in the disaster films you have seen?
- Why are they different? Is there anything else they should talk about?
- How important do you think ideology is to the enjoyment or success of disaster movies? Does it matter to you?

Key terms

Ethics: accepted codes or values of right and wrong

Ethics

Ideology is often linked to **ethics**: accepted codes or values of right and wrong. One event questioned the ideology and ethics of the whole disaster movie genre itself. On 9/11 where two ideologies, or cultures, came into real conflict, we all watched a real disaster unfold live on television. For some time after, the events of that day raised many ethical questions for the film business. Some were answered by delaying film releases and editing others – most famously the removal of the World Trade Center from *Spider-Man*. Many people asked whether Hollywood would ever be able to make another disaster movie. The scenes, watched in horror, had been served up many times before as entertainment, but suddenly 'trashing' New York did not seem fun any more.

For a while, the ideology of exploiting such events seemed to have changed; at the very least the question was 'How soon is too soon to make movies like this again?' This showed how important ideology can be in making movies. Inevitably, as feelings calmed down and curiosity asserted itself, movies were made. Five years on we have *United 93* and *World Trade Center* 'disaster movies' that deal directly with the 9/11 events. Ideologically, however, they are much more sensitive to all sides and are not as celebratory or 'gung ho' as their fictional predecessors.

Activity 38

AO2 – Explore, respond to and reflect on a range of films and topics

- Do you think people's attitudes to disaster movies have changed since 9/11?

Examiner's tip

Ideology can be a controversial area open to much debate. Consider whether it is a good or a bad thing for a movie to deal with. What about your ideas? Do you agree or disagree? Have you changed or picked up any ideas from films?

Knowledge check

In this chapter you have learned what is meant by the term 'ideology'. You will have explored the different ideologies contained within disaster movies and traced the ways in which a changing world has altered the messages and values evidenced in these films. Answer the following questions in order to check your understanding of this difficult area.

1 What does the key term 'ideology' mean?

2 Can you identify any beliefs, values or ideas that are evidenced in James Cameron's *Titanic*?

Section B Exploring film

Chapter 9 Industry, genre and audience

In this chapter we will cover:

- what we mean by the film industry
- production, distribution and exhibition
- how finance interacts with genre
- the importance of audience and its size
- different kinds of audience
- where movies are consumed and the changing ways we can buy films.

Examiner's tip

This is a big topic. Always try to relate it back to your own experience and behaviour. What have I seen? Where did I see it? What have I bought? Why? Remember you are a member of the film industry's most important audience group – why?

Activity 39

- Why is it called the film 'industry'? What does it have in common with other industries (if anything)?

Key terms

Production: activities involved in the actual making of the film

Distribution: deciding where a film will be shown and publicising this

Exhibition: where the film is shown – cinemas of varying types

Industry and genre

The film industry – with its **production**, **distribution** and **exhibition** – is no different from any other business in its need to make money. Profit is needed to keep shareholders happy and ultimately to make more movies.

One of the main reasons we have genres in the first place is that Hollywood saw these as formulae for success, recipes that they could reuse to achieve the financial returns they needed.

It is a common criticism that these movies are 'formulaic' yet financially it is a deliberate strategy to 'recycle'. This recycling of ideas is an attempt to reduce risk and sell a product with a good financial track record. Hollywood feels little pain when accused of a lack of originality if the box office receipts are high enough. Often the critics forget that this is how this branch of the arts/entertainment industry has always functioned. The remake or reused narrative is as old as the American film industry. Even before the emergence of Hollywood, some films were remade three, four or even five times or more if they proved popular enough.

Activity 40

AO2 – Explore, respond to and reflect on a range of films and topics

- Look at the disaster movie timeline. Can you see any patterns?
- Try to find out reasons why this might be so.

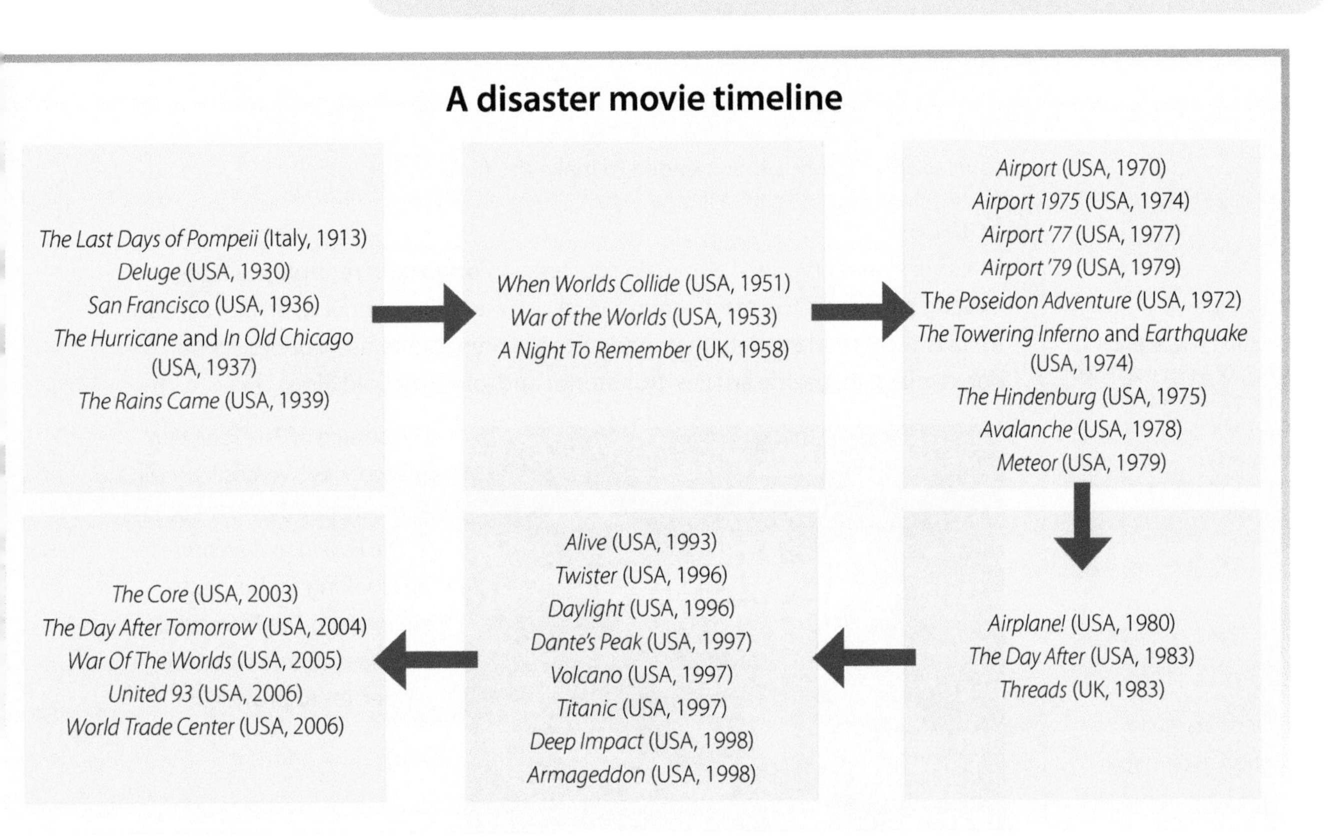

Key terms

Cycle: a period of popularity for a certain kind of film – when the audience is big enough then the industry will keep giving people what they think they want

Disaster movies are a good example of films that are remade; the 1970s and 1990s provide us with two cycles where the genre was popular. In the 1970s, *Airport* and *The Poseidon Adventure*, started a **cycle** that ran throughout the whole decade. These films remained popular with studios and producers right up until *Airplane!*, a parody that brought the cycle to a close as ideas ran out and audience interest fell. In the mid to late 1990s we had many disaster-themed movies – *Twister*, *Daylight*, *Volcano*, *Dante's Peak*, *Armageddon*, *Deep Impact* and others.

Key terms

Producer: the person or people in overall charge of how the film is put together

Genre and stars

Certain personalities or people are often the key to the success of the genre formula throughout a particular cycle. Stars are the most important of all to this success. Disaster movies are expensive to make and this makes them risky. One way a studio or **producer** can try to reduce this risk is to make sure 'big names' are part of their package. If an expensive film is to make money it will need every advantage it can get, particularly the 'built-in' audience a popular actor or star can bring with them.

Sometimes other names come to prominence – producers and directors may make an impact. In the 1970s the name 'Irwin Allen' was synonymous with the disaster movie; he became known as the 'master of disaster'. Audiences came to expect a certain level of spectacle from the producer of both *The Poseidon Adventure* and *The Towering Inferno*.

Case study: The Towering Inferno

Production

Every film begins with an idea. This idea can come from a number of different sources and money is then needed to make the film.

Sources

Films are based on one of two main sources – an **original screenplay** or a pre-existing **property**. The most common is the pre-existing property, mainly because there is such a wide variety that producers are prepared to use – books, comic books, plays, magazine articles, true stories and, of course, old films.

Key terms

Original screenplay: a script for a film not based on any other source (an original idea)

Property: any source of ideas that has been used to create a film

Examiner's tip

Your coursework section allows you to find out about the ways in which films are made. The information and activities below will help you when you come to research your own film and create your own pre-productions and productions.

23 The Towering Inferno – *the mother of all disaster movies?*

The source of *The Towering Inferno* was two books. Irwin Allen, inspired by the success of *The Poseidon Adventure*, was looking for his next big project; *The Tower* and *The Glass Inferno* were the properties to provide it.

Case study: The Towering Inferno

Activity 41

AO3 – Demonstrate knowledge and understanding of how films communicate

- Try to come up with as many different kinds of property that could be turned into a film.
- Is there anything that cannot be turned into a film?

Finance

The **rights** to the books cost $790 000 dollars. As this would be a massive project and a big risk, two studios, Warner Brothers and 20th Century Fox, joined together in a unique **co-production** deal to provide the $14 million **budget** (around $58 million at today's prices). The growth and industrial size of modern Hollywood means that a $58 million dollar budget these days would not be considered large. In return for their investment, Fox took the US profits and Warner Brothers took the rest of the world profits.

Key terms

Rights: the legal permission that allows one person to use another's ideas

Co-production: when two or more organisations jointly finance and make a film

Budget: the amount of money producers plan to spend on making a film

Distribution and exhibition

Activity 42

- Look at any of the film posters used in this section of the book. What do they 'say'? How do they 'say' it?
- Discuss which you feel are the most effective.
- How important is the poster to marketing the film?

As we already know, distribution is the business of actually getting the film from its producers and into the cinemas. Many of the activities most important to a film's commercial success take place at this stage of a film's life.

The distributor is largely responsible for the marketing of the film to both audiences and the exhibitors. The marketing of a film involves many activities, gimmicks and schemes and, just when we think we have seen them all, distributors come up with new ones.

Whatever activities they decide on they all serve the same ends, to get people into the cinema – increasingly for that all important **opening weekend**. Over the last decade or so the performance of a film has been judged on the **box office** returns from its first weekend on release, particularly in the case of the mainstream, like disaster movies. In the case of *The Towering Inferno*, the distribution rights were split between the co-financiers of Warner Brothers and 20th Century Fox.

Key terms

Opening weekend: the money a film takes during its first weekend of release

Box office: the money a film generates in ticket sales; a reference to where people traditionally buy their tickets

Case study: The Towering Inferno

The distributor makes their profit by charging the exhibitor a rental fee for the print of the film. The fee for a print can be a flat fee, i.e. a one-off payment. It could also be, more commonly, a percentage of the ticket sales which are usually at their highest over the first week of release. To make a good profit from a film, a cinema will try to show it for as long as possible. If you have ever wondered why the popcorn and 'extras' are so expensive, and why the cinema is so keen on you not bringing your own, this is part of the reason. In the case of many films, the cinema is forced to treat it as a **loss leader** – an opportunity to sell its refreshments where it can keep all the profits.

A **print** is a copy of the film shown by the cinema. These are quite expensive to produce and this is why UK cinemas show most films later than American ones – so they can reuse the US prints. It is only the biggest budget films that may be afraid of piracy that can afford a simultaneous global release.

Key terms

Loss leader: a product sold at a loss by a business to promote the sale of its other products

Print: the copy of a film shown in cinemas

Activity 43

AO3 – Demonstrate knowledge and understanding of how films communicate

- Research some recent box office figures. Which films raised the most in the UK and abroad?
- Do you think too much importance is put on the 'box-office'?

Whatever **release pattern** the distributor adopts, they will have a marketing strategy for most films. This can be increasingly complicated and very expensive. The marketing budget for a blockbuster which is expensive to produce will be several tens of millions of dollars – much more than the production budgets for many other films.

Key terms

Release pattern: how often and where a film will be shown – general release is as wide as possible, limited release may only be in London or specialist cinemas

Where does this money go? We need to take a deep breath if we are to try and list all the things it pays for. The main ones can be divided into two categories:

- Print media – posters appearing in newspapers, magazines and on billboards.
- Broadcast media – trailers appearing in cinemas and on television and radio.

(To see some of the publicity activities devised for exhibitors of *The Towering Inferno*, look on the website: http://www.thetoweringinferno.info under the promotions section.)

Although interesting relics from another marketing age, these do show us how the role of marketing has grown in importance over the decades since the release of *The Towering Inferno*. Despite lacking glamour, they demonstrate that the exhibitor had more of a role in generating the 'buzz' a film needs for success. Increasingly the exhibitor relies on the inventiveness and financial power of the distributor to deliver its audience. These days, the all important poster/lobby display and trailer are the main weapons in the exhibitor's armoury.

Key terms

Franchise: where a film (and its sequels) are part of a larger business entity composed of multiple tie-ins and merchandise licenses; these have become more deliberately planned in recent Hollywood history, e.g. *Star Wars*

Tie-ins: an individual piece of a franchise, designed to 'cash-in' on the interest generated by a film; these take many forms – for example, the book of the film, or, more recently, the computer game of the film

Product placement: when a film features products and brands prominently

Activity 44

AO2 – Explore, respond to and reflect on a range of films and topics

- How many different marketing activities can you think of?
- Compile a class list.
- Which would you use to promote a film? Would you invent any new ones?

Other sources of income and publicity

Generating interest in a blockbuster film does not end with the marketing involved with distribution and exhibition. When we hear the term '**franchise**', it does not just refer to films that will have sequels. Within the concept of the franchise is the massive world of merchandise and **tie-ins**. All kinds of other businesses become involved at this stage, from toy and fast food companies, to those that are involved at the production stage with **product placement**. Product placement involves the film featuring products and brands prominently and has become increasingly obvious as production budgets grow and money is required in greater amounts and from wider sources. As an example, an actor may look at his Rolex watch several times during a film and we are 'treated' to a close-up of the watch face, complete with manufacturer's name.

24 The Core ... *Pepsi – well placed...*

Activity 45

AO2 – Explore, respond to and reflect on a range of films and topics

- Can you think of any product placement in a movie?
- Discuss whether this spoils the movie.
- Do you think there should be any rules or guidelines to control product placement?

Not only do these activities earn extra publicity, they also generate direct revenue from the fees that must be paid for the licences that allow the other businesses to become involved in the film.

Songs

One tie-in activity that is almost a disaster movie tradition is the hit record or Oscar-winning movie song. From 'The Morning After' (*The Poseidon Adventure*, best song Oscar) and 'We May Never Love This Way Again' (*The Towering Inferno*, best song Oscar) to 'My Heart Will Go On' (*Titanic*, best song Oscar) they have been very important. Getting a song played on the radio and featured in the charts might not raise a lot of revenue for the film studios but it does generate massive amounts of free publicity for their movie.

Unique selling points

We cannot leave this section on 'other' sources without mentioning the occasional gimmick that Hollywood comes up with to increase the interest and give their film a new USP (unique selling point). The 1970s were no exception; in some of the later disaster movies 3D was planned for or used. The most notable was the development of 'sensurround' for the movie *Earthquake*. This involved using the sound system and low frequency sound to create a rumbling sensation that felt like an actual earthquake in the cinema. Despite its effectiveness, it remains a gimmick that never caught on.

What we consider to be a gimmick can change – early moving pictures were themselves considered to be a mere novelty item. Many other technical advances such as sound, colour and widescreen were considered as gimmicks initially as they were responses to a competitive threat from other studios or television. This may be about to recur as 3D technology is under development once again. That modern 'master of disaster' James Cameron (*Titanic*) will release his next film in 3D and other powerful film-makers such as Steven Spielberg and George Lucas are also championing the new technology. Who knows, with the level of cinematic spectacle about to rise again, perhaps the disaster movie might be due another cycle?

Activity 46

AO4 – Use creative and technical skills to construct film products

- What new 'gimmicks' would you invent or like to see?

Afterlife

Increasingly, the money a film can make is not limited to the cinema. The disaster movie producers of the 70s could have only dreamed about the money that the home market generates for the film industry. Once a film leaves the cinemas, it can earn its producers and distributors more revenue from cable television fees, terrestrial television fees and the all important DVD release.

DVD and people watching the film at home is probably now as important (if not more so) for most films as the money from exhibition. These days the film comes out on DVD almost immediately after cinema release (in a few cases simultaneously) and is a vital source of income for the industry. This is particularly true for non-mainstream films that do not find a distribution deal or a cinema audience. Many people now prefer to watch films in the comfort and privacy of their home with a picture and sound quality that is often better than the cinema. This gap in quality will continue to widen as cinemas stick with film prints and home systems move increasingly towards high-definition television (HDTV) and Blu-ray levels of quality.

Activity 47

AO3 – Demonstrate knowledge and understanding of how films communicate

- Research the latest technological changes that have or will affect how we watch films. Try to think about whether they will make a big or a small difference.

25 *Movie audiences – how do we know what they want?*

Audience

Key terms

Audience: a group of people with similar tastes and/or characteristics

Like genre, **audience** is about groups with similar characteristics and in the case of audience we are talking about groups of people. All this business of putting things into groups is an attempt to make film success easier to understand and predict. Indeed, Hollywood considers the studying and 'second-guessing' of these groups to be even more important to the financial success of their movies.

So just who are these groups?

The most common way to define an audience is by age. 'Children', 'teenage', 'young adult', 'adult' are some of the labels that are used. Often they will have ages attached such as 14 to19 etc. and usually they will fall in line with the film industry certification boundaries. Which group is the most important? Hollywood refers to the 'key demographic' as the 15- to 18-year-old group as this is the one that visits the cinema most often. This goes some way to explain why there are so many 15 and so few 18 certificate films.

An audience's status is also important. Are they single, couples, male, female, families? This will influence the certificate, and ultimately the content, of a film. Many films will be aimed at an audience different to that gained by the original material in order to secure the largest potential number of viewers. A film like the first *Spider-Man* was based on a comic book aimed at older teenagers. The film itself 'needed' family attendance and was aimed at the new 12A certificate, which allows parents to decide if it is too violent or scary for their children. I wonder how many parents refused to take their children to see the original *Spider-Man* movie?

Activity 48

AO3 – Demonstrate knowledge and understanding of how films communicate

- Try to find out the different categories people in the film industry, and business in general, use to define their audiences.

Whatever categorisation is used, and there are many more in the world of marketing, the idea that a film needs an audience is fundamental to film production. Films will often be denied distribution because the distributor cannot work out just how to sell them and who they should sell them to. The only thing we can really count on is that most films given some sort of distribution (even straight to DVD) will find an audience; only the size is in question.

Fans

Fans are those people with a specific passion for a film, films or genre. Whether they are fans of art house, foreign, sci-fi or horror, they all belong to a loyal, small(er) but significant audience. Their attitudes, practices and spending habits could be the subject of another book. Studying them can be valuable as they demonstrate the kinds of behaviours that are both manipulated and that manipulate Hollywood. Individual movie fans can rise in importance (think of Harry Knowles and his 'Ain't It Cool News' website that can make or break a film); groups of fans can be highly influential (think of *Star Trek* enthusiasts) – the studio will rely on them to at least cover the costs of a new movie in the franchise. At the time of writing, the next Star Trek film is in pre-production; Paramount, the studio responsible, will be very aware of not upsetting the fans too much as, without their attendance, the film could sink without a trace.

Disaster movies, like other genres, have their fans too. Many of the websites you will find, and at least one of the books you can buy, are authored by fans of the genre who want to share their passion and, in the case of the older movies, 'keep the flame alive'.

Activity 49

AO2 – Explore, respond to and reflect on a range of films and topics

- Research some 'fans' – they could be fans of something you like.
- What do you think of their behaviour? How much influence do you think they really have?

Overall, the film industry needs to be confident that people will want to see their movie. They try to have as clear a picture of this audience as they can from the very outset of pre-production. If an audience is small then it will need to be loyal so a smaller budget can be recovered from the project, even if this is not until after the DVD revenue comes in.

Examiner's tip

The film industry is constantly changing. Keep looking for news stories about films – discuss them in class and try to keep track of them, always thinking 'How does it affect me? How does it fit in with what I have learned?'

Occasionally studios find the 'holy grail' of film production – a small film that captures the imagination and finds a massive mainstream audience. Films like *The Full Monty* (1997) or *The Blair Witch Project* (1999) have managed this. If one 'industrial phenomenon' sums up the magic of movies it is films like this, as try as the industry might it cannot turn their successes into a reusable formula. This is good for the audience for as long as the film-makers are kept guessing about who the audience is and what they want, they will keep trying an ever-growing range of ideas.

Knowledge check

In this chapter you have learned about the relationship between the film industry, film audiences and the disaster genre. You will have looked at the ways in which the film industry is organised, focusing on production, distribution and exhibition. You will also have had the chance to explore creatively the ways in which films are 'sold' to producers and to audiences. To test your understanding, answer the following questions.

1. Provide a definition for the following key terms:
   - production
   - distribution
   - exhibition.
2. What is an original screenplay?
3. Give two examples of 'property'. How does a property differ from a screenplay?
4. Why is the opening weekend of a new film's release so important?
5. What is a 'loss leader'?
6. What is being referred to when we talk about a film's box office return?
7. Explain what is meant by the term 'release pattern'.

Section B Exploring film

Chapter 10 Disaster movies – a conclusion

In this chapter we will cover:

- what we have learned
- how focusing on a specific genre can be useful
- how our knowledge can be applied to other genres
- how different or similar the disaster movie is to other styles of film
- knowing what a disaster movie is.

26 Dante's Peak – *our conclusion might not be so dramatic!*

In many ways the disaster movie is an ideal genre to explore the world of Hollywood, both artistically and industrially. Its somewhat big-budget formulaic approach makes it a genre that is typical of Hollywood. It encompasses all that is good and bad at this level of industrial film-making.

It can be observed on closer inspection that the disaster movie is a very 'flexible' genre to tackle at this level. The fact that its boundaries, as with a lot of other genres, are not definitely fixed is one of the main aims of genre study. It is not the elasticity of these boundaries that is important. What is important is that we are aware they can be stretched and how this stretching can be used by both audience and film-maker alike. When a genre is subverted or parodied, as in the *Airplane!* movies, this often gives us the clearest idea of what it means to be an example of such a genre.

Examiner's tip

When looking back over a whole topic, try to use your own interests and experience to help with your understanding.

Examiner's tip

Do not worry about trying to remember all the facts and examples. Try to use the terms and theories with films you like and watch to increase your understanding of them. It is not always how much you know that matters – it is what you do with what you have learned that counts.

Activity 50

AO1 – Demonstrate knowledge and understanding of how films communicate

- As a group, come up with as many reasons as you can in favour of studying the disaster movie or any film genre. Try to agree an order of importance.
- What have you got out of the study? What are your top three reasons for studying a film genre? Discuss the question and try to agree on a top ten of disaster movie characters.

Genre is best seen as making meaning through the use of familiar tools rather than as an inflexible checklist of items that will always break down because of its exceptions. The simplest question to ask paraphrases an old piece of movie dialogue:

Does it look like a disaster movie? Does it smell like a disaster movie? Does it taste like a disaster movie? Does it feel like a disaster movie?

If the answer to any of these is 'Yes' then our job is to set about proving why and how it is a disaster movie.

Knowledge check

In this section you have learned how a mainstream Hollywood genre uses both micro and macro elements to create meaning and achieve its aims. You have explored the modern Hollywood system and how it manages production, distribution and exhibition. You have also examined the nature of audiences and how and why we consume the films we do. The final part of this chapter has also given you an example of the kind of exam questions you may expect when you take your Exploring Film paper. The best way to check your knowledge now is to work through Assessment practice 4 on page 122, using the tips given to answer parts a) to e).

Assessment practice 1

What will I have to do in the exam?

The box below includes a sample examination question from the Exploring Film paper where most of the work you have done on the disaster film will be tested. The boxes around it contain ideas about the kinds of things you will have to do to earn the marks available.

This might be close-up, zoom, pan, tracking and so on, dependent upon the extract. For 1 mark you will have to use the right term and describe the use of the shot. For example, *A close-up to highlight a character's emotion or reaction.*

Always read and follow these instructions very carefully.

This is a longer question worth 8 marks so will demand more from your response. The choice of film language and the use of the whole extract means you will be repeating parts (a) and (b) in much more depth. The choices you make and how much discussion and analysis you include will be vital. How this is marked is listed in the box below.

Paper 1: Exploring Film

Read the paper prior to viewing extract.

Answer **all** *the questions.*
The film extract will last approximately 20 minutes.
You should spend one hour ten minutes completing the questions.

1. (a) Identify one camera shot. [1]

(b) Why is it used? [1]

(c) How are **two** of the following used to create panic and tension in this extract? [8]

- sound
- editing
- mis-en-scène
- colour and lighting

Here you will need to talk about the reason the film-maker chose this shot. What meaning or effect were they trying to create? For example, *They zoomed in to highlight just how angry X was; the close-up makes the emotion more 'in your face'.*

(c) A02 Explore, respond to and reflect on a range of films and topics using key film concepts and appropriate terminology.

For each explanation of a micro feature:
Basic explanation: written communication sufficiently accurate to make meaning clear = 1 mark
Adequate: written communication reasonably accurate = 2 marks
Detailed: written communication controlled, clear and generally accurate = 3 marks
Excellent: written communication is in appropriate style and clearly and coherently uses specialist terminology. High degree of accuracy = 4 marks.

Assessment practice 2

What will I have to do in the exam?

The box below includes a sample examination question from the Exploring Film paper where most of the work you have done on the disaster film will be tested. The boxes around it contain ideas about the kinds of things you will have to do to earn the marks available.

Here you will have to give one of the codes and conventions, icons, etc, that define the genre you have learned about. For example, a particular character type or special effect.

Always read and think **very** carefully about what the question wants you to do.

This is a longer question worth 6 marks so will demand more from your response. You will be expected to discuss the features of the extract that tell us it is a disaster movie. It will be useful if you can analyse whether it is being used in a typical way or is being subverted or used differently in some way. How this is marked is listed in the box below.

2. (a) Identify **one** typical feature of disaster films in this extract. [2]

(b) Why is it typical? [2]

(c) Show how **one** of the following genre characteristics is used in the extract and in a disaster film you have studied. [6]

- setting
- costume
- characters and relationships
- themes
- representation

For this question you will have to explain why it is typical. State examples of other films it is used in and why it is common and associated with disaster movies.

(c) AO1 Demonstrate knowledge and understanding of how films communicate meanings, evoke personal responses and engage audiences.

How each genre characteristic is used:

Basic explanation: Written communication sufficiently accurate to make meaning clear = 1 mark

Limited explanation = 2 marks

Sound explanation: Written communication reasonably accurate = 3 marks

Clear and confident explanation = 4 marks

Very good, detailed explanation: Written communication controlled, clear and generally accurate = 5 marks

Excellent explanation: Written communication is in appropriate style, clearly and coherently uses specialist terminology. High degree of accuracy = 6 marks

Assessment practice 3

What will I have to do in the exam?

The box below includes a sample examination question from the Exploring Film paper where most of the work you have done on the disaster film will be tested. The boxes around it contain ideas about the kinds of things you will have to do to earn the marks available.

Make sure you give at least two reasons here. Do not limit yourself to discussing the poster as a whole. Focus on different parts of the image. Is there more than one image? Do not forget the job all posters are designed to do.

Always read and follow these instructions **very** carefully. Spend time thinking about the poster. The exam tests your thinking, not your ability to write fast for an hour and a half!

For longer answers your arguments will have to have a bit more in-depth.

Remember persuasion is about the distributor trying to get a positive response. How do you think they think this will get people to go and see the film? Try to discuss each of the suggestions you are given. Better answers will try to judge how effectively each of these elements has been used. How this is marked is listed in the box below.

3. Look carefully at the film poster for *The Day After Tomorrow*, then answer the following questions.

(a) Why do you think these images have been selected? [4]

(b) How does the other information on the film poster persuade audiences to see the film? [6]

In your answer, you may refer to:

- quotations
- stars
- tag lines
- awards
- director

(b) AO2 Explore, respond to and reflect on a range of films and topics using key film concepts and appropriate terminology.

Only one item of information given = 1 mark
Only one item given with basic explanation. Written communication sufficiently accurate to make meaning clear = 2 marks
More than one item with basic explanations = 3 marks
More than one item with clear explanations. Written communication reasonably accurate = 4 marks
More than one item with detailed, accurate explanations = 5 marks
More than one item with excellent explanations. Written communication is in appropriate style, clearly and coherently uses specialist terminology. High degree of accuracy = 6 marks

Assessment practice 4

What will I have to do in the exam?

The box below includes a sample examination question from the Exploring Film paper where most of the work you have done on the disaster film will be tested. The boxes around it contain ideas about the kinds of things you will have to do to earn the marks available.

Try to be as imaginative as you can here. Use your knowledge of other disaster movie titles. Explain the reasons behind your choice.

Take your time. Write a few notes. Hopefully this is something you have thought about before. If you want to use ideas used before, mention what has inspired you and how and why you will use them.

Don't forget what effect a film climax should have and how you would use film language to achieve it. How the marks will be awarded is listed in Box 2.

Here again, try to use your imagination and avoid just copying exactly another film you have seen. How the marks will be awarded is listed in Box 1.

4. Create a new idea for a blockbuster disaster film.

(a) Give the film a title. [2]

(b) Briefly outline the story of your film. [4]

(c) Briefly describe the climax of the film and show how either special effects or camerawork are used to attract audiences. [6]

(d) Choose two stars for the film, giving reasons for your choice. [4]

(e) When do you think will be the best time of the year to release your film? Briefly explain why. [4]

Make sure you talk about two stars – why they will be right for your film and what kinds of things they will bring with them. For example, 'I would choose Brad Pitt as I want my film to be successful and he has lots of fans, and I can't think of a disaster movie with him in it so this would make mine a little bit different.'

Try to think about the times of the year different kinds of films are released. When would people expect this kind of film? When would there be competition? What about awards? Plus do not forget the commercial needs of your film.

Box 1 Question (b) mark scheme

A basic outline. Written communication sufficiently accurate to make meaning clear = 1 mark

An adequate outline. Written communication reasonably accurate = 2 marks

A well-structured, plausible outline. Written communication controlled, clear and generally accurate = 3 marks

A creative and well-structured, plausible outline. Written communication is in appropriate style, clearly and coherently uses specialist terminology. High degree of accuracy = 4 marks

Box 2 Question (c) mark scheme

A basic description. Written communication although basic sufficiently accurate to make meaning clear = 1 mark
An adequate and effective description. Written communication reasonably accurate = 2 marks
A detailed, resourceful and highly effective description. Written communication is in appropriate style, clearly and coherently uses specialist terminology. High degree of accuracy = 3 marks

Overall:
A basic sense of how feature attracts audiences. Written communication although basic sufficiently accurate to make meaning clear = +1 mark
An adequate sense of how feature attracts audiences. Written communication reasonably accurate = +2 marks

A clear sense of how feature attracts audiences. Written communication is in appropriate style, clearly and coherently uses specialist terminology. High degree of accuracy = 6 marks

Section C New horizons

Chapter 1 Exploring film outside Hollywood

In this chapter we will cover:

- the differences and similarities between films made in mainstream Hollywood and those made in other parts of the world
- the social and historical context of a selection of the close study films
- the characters, narratives, themes and issues raised within the non-Hollywood close study films
- the ways in which people, places, events and issues are represented
- the organisations which produce the films and the audiences who respond to them
- your own response to the film and the forms in which this critical response may be expressed.

Key terms

A list: the list of stars who are currently attracting the highest salaries and most prestigious film deals

Dialogue: conversations between characters

Work through Activity 1. How many of you chose the Hollywood film? Sometimes it's the prospect of having to read subtitles that puts us off watching films made in non-English speaking countries. Perhaps the desire to see one of our favourite **A list** Hollywood stars appeals to us much more than watching actors who we have never seen before. Often we base our viewing choices on what we already know and like. We don't want to be disappointed so we pick familiar films of a specific genre, containing our favourite stars. We may even have a director that we really admire, for example, Tim Burton (*Beetle juice* (1988), *Edward Scissorhands* (1990), *Charlie and the Chocolate Factory* (2005)). We like the **dialogue** to be in our own language and a badly dubbed film somehow spoils our overall enjoyment of the cinema experience.

In short we all have a set of expectations when we watch films. Many of the films you have studied for this course will have been made in Hollywood. Often when we think of cinema, we automatically think of Hollywood and then we compare other kinds of cinema to it.

When we talk about 'British cinema' or 'French cinema' or 'Australian cinema' we perhaps assume that the films made in these countries are somehow quite different to Hollywood cinema. This is not necessarily true and although you may notice several differences in terms of style, or settings, between your chosen focus film and a typical Hollywood film, there will also be striking similarities.

Activity 1

A01 – Demonstrate knowledge and understanding of how films communicate

A02 – Explore, respond to and reflect on a range of films and topics

- Look carefully at the three posters.
- Which is the Hollywood film, which is the French film and which is the British film?
- What kinds of clues do the posters contain to help you identify their country of origin?
- What kinds of expectations are set up through the choice of images, the titles, genre or stars?
- Which film would you prefer to see? Why?

1 *Posters for* Clueless *(1995),* Amélie *(2001) and* The Full Monty *(1997)*

Activity 2

A01 – Demonstrate knowledge and understanding of how films communicate

A02 – Explore, respond to and reflect on a range of films and topics

- Research a typical week's programme at your nearest multiplex cinema.
- How many films are American?
- How many are from other countries?
- How do we identify, for example, a French film?
  - Is it because all or most of the money to make the film came from France?
  - Is it because the principal actors were French?
  - Is it because it was set in France?
  - Is it because it tells us more about French history or culture?

The non-Hollywood films for this part of your course have come from all over the world:

Amélie	France
Bend It like Beckham	Great Britain
The Devil's Backbone	Mexico
Ghosts	Great Britain
Goodbye Lenin! (2003)	Germany
Ratcatcher	Great Britain
Spirited Away (2001)	Japan
Tsotsi	South Africa
Whale Rider	New Zealand
Yasmin	Great Britain

They have been chosen because we think they are really enjoyable. They contain some brilliant performances by actors that you may have never seen before. The story lines may be funny, sad, exciting or thought-provoking. Some of the settings may be unfamiliar but the problems or situations which face the characters are not.

Tsotsi and *Ratcatcher*, for example, deal with the problem of poverty and the importance of family. *Amélie* deals with love and loss. *Bend It like Beckham*, *Yasmin*, *Whale Rider*, *Ghosts* and *Goodbye Lenin!* feature the difficulties of prejudice and living within a fast-changing world. *Spirited Away* and *The Devil's Backbone* create worlds where ghosts and spirits guide the central characters through difficult situations. All the films have the experience of young people within the world at the heart of their narratives. All explore what we call 'universal themes' – situations and problems that affect us all at certain points in our lives.

Activity 3

A02 – Explore, respond to and reflect on a range of films and topics

- What characteristics do you expect when we talk about being French… being Australian… being Italian?
- Imagine you are going to make a film set in either Great Britain or France. What kind of setting would you choose for the opening sequence? Give reasons for your choice.

We all have certain ideas about what other people and places are like. Often these ideas are based on the ways we have seen them represented in film, television or other forms of media. Although these representations are chosen in order to make the people and places as believable as possible, they can often be quite stereotypical.

If you look at, for example, the settings you chose in Activity 3 for your British or French films, how many of you chose London, or Paris, for your establishing shots? Did you use a specific iconic landmark to let the audience know where the film is set, for example, London Bridge, Big Ben, the Eiffel Tower or the Champs-Elysées?

Examiner's tip

When you are asked about themes and issues you should think carefully about the ways in which they are represented. Representation also requires a consideration of style and genre. Although you may have learned about these areas separately, they all work together in order to communicate the film's key messages and values. When you have completed your case study practice, answer the questions on the specimen exam paper at the end of this section. Pay close attention to the examiners' tips attached to each part of the paper and always spend more time on questions that carry higher marks.

Often the opening sequence of a film can be really important, not just in terms of establishing where the film is set, but in introducing key ideas and themes. Whichever film you have chosen to study in this section of the course you will need to closely analyse key sequences, beginning with the opening sequence. The work you have already completed on the macro and micro elements of film language will help you to explore how the central characters and some of the 'universal' themes, or issues, mentioned above are represented in your close study film.

In the case studies which follow you will be given the chance to learn more about some of the films. Case studies for those set films not covered in this section are available on the Heinemann website: www.heinemann.co.uk. The work you will be asked to do will prepare you for your exam. It will also give you ideas for your coursework. Everything that you learned in the film language section (Section A) will help you to understand and analyse these films.

Each case study will begin with a synopsis (a brief outline of the story) and an introduction. This will be followed by:

- themes and issues
- genre and style
- representation
- creative tasks
- additional resources.

Section C New horizons

Chapter 2 Case study: *Ghosts*

In this chapter we will cover:

- the ways in which the true story of the Morecambe Bay tragedy informed the making of *Ghosts*
- the themes and issues raised within the film
- the ways in which people, places and events are represented
- the style and genre of the film
- possible creative responses to the film.

2 *A still from* Ghosts

Country: UK

Production year: 2006

Director: Nick Broomfield

Certificate: PG

Main awards: Official Selection Sundance 2007, Official Selection London Film Festival 2006

Case study: Ghosts

Activity 4

AO3 – Demonstrate planning, research and presentational skills

In pairs, work on a definition for each of the following terms:

- asylum seeker
- immigrant
- illegal immigrant.

Synopsis

Ghosts is the first feature film made by the well-known documentary director Nick Broomfield. It tells the story of a young single mother, Ai Qin, on her journey from Fujian province in China to Great Britain.

Ai Qin despairs of ever providing a better life for herself and her young son in China, so she borrows a vast sum of money to be smuggled to England. The journey proves to be truly terrible and the destination (Thetford, Norfolk) little better. At first, Ai Qin works in a food packing factory only to find that she is earning less than the English girl who works beside her and that the 'agency' is deducting large sums of money each week from her wages for 'taxes'. She then works back-breakingly hard, picking spring onions for Sainsbury, Asda and Tesco only to find she is unable to afford even to buy a bunch when she visits her local supermarket. Finally, she is forced to leave the house she has shared with 12 other illegal immigrants and travel to Morecambe in order to join the gangs of workers picking cockles in the bay.

Introduction

Ghosts is based upon a real-life tragedy. On 5 February 2004, a group of Chinese workers were collecting cockles in Morecambe Bay, Lancashire, when they were cut off by the incoming tide in the bay at around 9.30 p.m. Previously the group had been attacked during the daytime by a group of local cockle pickers who had tried to force them off the beach. So the workers had decided it was 'safer' to work at night after the locals had left. However, they did not realise that this was very dangerous as the bay was well known for quicksand and fast tides.

Many of the Chinese workers could not swim. The weather was bad that night and they quickly became trapped by the rising waters. They didn't know how to contact the emergency services and instead several called their families back in China in order to say their last goodbyes. Although the emergency services were eventually alerted they were only able to rescue one of the workers trapped by the rising waters.

A total of 21 bodies, men and women between the ages of 18 to 45, were finally recovered from the bay. Fourteen people managed to scramble to shore unaided; two more bodies were never found. All the workers were illegal immigrants, mainly from the Fujian province, and have been described as untrained and inexperienced. They had been earning less than the national minimum wage; the 'agencies', or gangmasters, that found them work also deducted money from their pay. They had been living in shared houses with perhaps ten or 12 others, for which they were forced to pay huge rents. Many also had families in China who were entirely dependent on the money they sent back from their earnings each month.

Nick Broomfield was so moved by the story of these workers that he decided to make a film about the tragedy. By focusing on the story of one woman, Ai Qin, he wanted to highlight universal themes such as poverty, racism and exploitation.

Activity 5

AO3 – Demonstrate planning, research and presentational skills

- Now see if you can find newspaper reports on the Internet about the 2004 Morecambe Bay cockling disaster and the 58 Chinese migrants found dead in a lorry in Dover in 2000. The Wikipedia website will help you and provide other external links for your research.
- Discuss these reports with the rest of the class.
  - Where did the majority of the immigrants involved in these tragedies come from?
  - Why do you think so many had come from this particular Chinese province?
  - Which of your definitions for asylum seekers, immigrants or illegal immigrants (see Activity 4) seem to best 'fit' the people who died in both of the tragedies you have researched?

Themes and issues

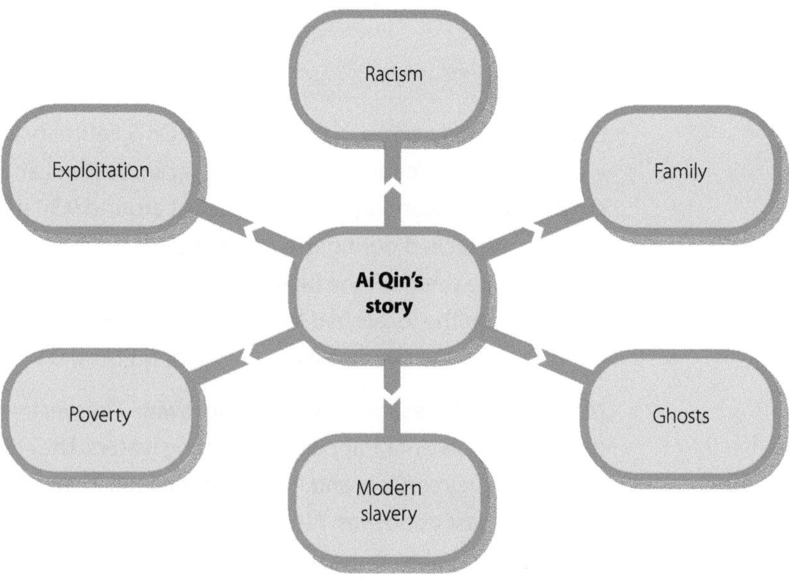

3 *Themes and issues in* Ghosts

Case study: Ghosts

The diagram on page 130 highlights some of the themes and issues contained within *Ghosts*. These are explored through Ai Qin's story as we follow her journey from the Fujian province of China where she lives with her family and her little boy to England. All of these themes and issues are connected. It is poverty that allows others to exploit people like Ai Qin and traps them into working long hours for little or no pay. It is poverty and the desire to make a better life for their family that forces them to pay huge sums of money and to break the law in order to come to England. In the sections below we shall consider the importance of poverty and ghosts and the ways in which they are represented within the film.

Poverty

Activity 6

AO1 – Demonstrate knowledge and understanding of how films communicate
AO2 – Explore, respond to and reflect on a range of films and topics

- Watch the opening sequences of the film once more (11 minutes). As you watch, make brief notes on the following questions.
  - There are two captions which come between the opening credits and when we see Ai Qin working in the fields. What do they tell us?
  - What reasons does Ai Qin give for wanting to go to England? Is the decision to leave easy? Why not? Do her family want her to go?
  - How much do the snakeheads want from Ai Qin in order to get her to England? Why is it so expensive?

The captions in the opening sequences underline important facts that seem to underpin the whole film. Firstly, we are told that the film is based on real events which took place in 2004. Then that:

> *Three million migrant workers in the UK form the 'backbone' of the food supply system and the construction, hospitality and health industries.*

Nick Broomfield obviously thinks that we need to know just how useful people like Ai Qin are in Great Britain, because they work in our hospitals, factories, shops and hotels.

The final caption is shown as Ai Qin works in the fields in Fujian; it tells us that workers like her only earn £30 a month. This shot showing Ai Qin bent double, up to her knees in water, reminds us of an earlier shot, before the flashback as she bends to rake up the cockles on Morecambe Bay. In both places she is forced to work long hours in terrible conditions in order to support her family. She is very poor; this means she has few choices in life and it is easy for others to take advantage of her desperate need to build a better life for herself and her little boy. The conversations between Ai and her mother and father underline the importance of this theme and the difficulty Ai has in making the decision to go to England. As she says her final goodbyes at the coach station she tells her mother, 'I don't know if this is the right thing to do.'

Case study: Ghosts

You may have already noticed certain recurring **motifs**: the importance of family and of keeping contact by mobile phone. As Ai Qin leaves Fujian we see her crying with her face pressed up against the window of the coach; this motif is to be repeated throughout the film. It seems to emphasise just how trapped she is by her poverty; her desperation to break free is shown though her body language and facial expressions.

Key terms

Motif: an image or idea that is repeated in a film

Ghosts

'Ghost' is a Chinese slang word used to describe white people. In Nick Broomfield's film the word takes on a whole new meaning. The 'ghosts' are people like Ai Qin who come to Great Britain secretly, who are forced to take low-paid jobs, and stay hidden from the rest of us in case they are found and sent back home. They are the illegal Chinese immigrants; the people that our own society chooses to ignore or exploit.

4 *A still take from the final sequence of* Ghosts

Look carefully at the image above taken from the final sequence of the film.

- It seems as if Ai Qin and her fellow workers have been washed up on a vast, alien shore, in a world of cruelty, prejudice and indifference. The close up of Mr Lin at the front of the frame underlines the hopelessness of their situation.
- The workers in the background look tiny and vulnerable against the huge expanse of sand, sky and sea. Some are on their knees.
- Everything seems grey and bleak and hopeless.
- The ghosts are the illegal immigrants themselves, dead in spirit, drifting unacknowledged in and out of rundown, overcrowded accommodation and poorly paid employment.

Case study: Ghosts

Activity 7

AO2 – Explore, respond to and reflect on a range of films and topics

Read through the following extract from a critical review:

> *Like Ghosts, the Chinese immigrants remain invisible to most of us and yet they are everywhere, touching the fabric of our lives without us ever knowing. We do not see them, we do not acknowledge their presence, but they are there. Whenever we shop at a supermarket, or eat in an expensive seafood restaurant, they are there. We rarely stop to think about our link in the chain of cheap labour and the exploitation of these workers. Perhaps after we have seen this film we will...*

- Why does the critic believe the Chinese immigrants are 'invisible'?
- How can they be in a supermarket or an expensive seafood restaurant?
- Do you think that films really can change our attitudes and opinions about social problems or other people?

Genre and style

Ai Qin's story is told in a stark, documentary-like way. Every character in *Ghosts* is cast using non-actors. The English cocklers are real cocklers; the Norfolk natives are from Norfolk. Aiquin Lin who plays the central character Ai Qin left China herself at the age of 22 and was smuggled into England. She thought her journey would take only a few weeks – it took four and a half months. She found she could only get low-paid work and her hopes of sending money back to her family were quickly dashed.

The experiences of the central character of *Ghosts* closely mirrors Aiquin's real-life experiences. Indeed, throughout the film the line between fact and fiction is constantly being blurred.

Activity 8

AO2 – Explore, respond to and reflect on a range of films and topics

- In pairs spend a few minutes trying to arrive at a definition of 'fact' and 'fiction' and then, as a class, write up on the board the definitions that seem to define these terms best.
- List some examples of fictional films and factual films underneath your definitions.
- Do you think that by casting 'real' people, the film becomes more believable or credible than many other fiction films?
- *Ghosts* is a British film and yet most of the actors speak in their native Fujianese or Mandarin. Do you think this makes the film more difficult to watch? If so, why do you think Nick Broomfield, the director, made this decision?

Case study: Ghosts

At first, Ai Qin works in a food packing factory, where the drudgery, monotony and exhaustion of 12-hour days are represented starkly by Broomfield. He 'forces' the audience to experience the monotony by shooting long sequences which focus on the repetition of tasks and which highlight the cold 'prison-like' factory environment.

Ghosts is shot in a way that makes us feel that the camera is observing and following the people and places encountered during Ai Qin's journey. The colour has a 'bleached out' quality, shots are naturally lit and often characters are silhouetted by the natural grey light that floods in behind them. The camera is used subtly and faces and expressions are important. However, these are usually brief shots before the camera moves on, constantly shifting, seldom settling, always anxious, looking over shoulders, just like the immigrants themselves.

Ghosts is a really interesting film because the documentary conventions used give us the shock of the 'real' – this is a story about 'real people' and 'real problems' – we have the newspaper reports to prove it. It's not a fiction film and yet it's not a **documentary film**. Perhaps it's best described as a **docudrama**: a dramatic recreation of 'real events' by 'real people'.

Key terms

Documentary film: a film that presents a version of events which viewers are intended to see as 'fact' rather than 'fiction'

Docudrama: a dramatised film based on real events

Activity 9

AO2 – Explore, respond to and reflect on a range of films and topics

Nick Broomfield always saw *Ghosts* as a drama and not a documentary. He wanted to blur the line between drama and documentary by using real people and improvised dialogue whilst keeping a narrative structure throughout. He wanted to create a drama that felt 'real'.

- Do you think *Ghosts* is better because it uses real people and improvised dialogue or do you think it would have been better with well-known actors who had to stick strictly to the script?
- What reasons can you give to back up your opinion?

Representation

Characters

Because *Ghosts* is based on a real story, Nick Broomfield tried to make the characters as 'real' as possible too. Ai Qin and the other principal characters are played by former illegal immigrants who draw on their own experiences of life in order to give passionate, authentic performances.

Ai Qin is both the name of the character in the film and the person who plays her. She speaks in her own language and we have to rely on the subtitles to tell us what she says. Ai Qin is able to portray the suffering she endures without overacting; much of her dialogue was improvised, and often we know what she is thinking and feeling because her face is so expressive. She is tiny, quietly spoken and does not complain and yet we know that she is strong. She has left her child in order to make money for a better life and has survived the terrible journey to England nailed into a wooden crate.

Case study: Ghosts

Activity 10

AO1 – Demonstrate knowledge and understanding of how films communicate

- Look carefully at the still of Ai Qin as she travels in the minibus on her final journey out into Morecambe Bay. What does her expression tell you about her mood, her hopes and her fears?
- We constantly see Ai Qin trapped within her environment. Look at the still below. What does the bathroom remind you of? How often do you see Ai Qin gazing through a window with a similar expression on her face?

Ai Qin gazes through the window of the bus

6 *Ai Qin gazes through her bathroom window*

Setting

Nick Broomfield begins and ends his film on the Morecambe beach: not the haven for holidaymakers that we might have expected in the past, but a huge, empty, cruel space which looks like something from the end of the universe.

- If you review the opening and closing sequences you will notice that the bay seems almost to take on a life of its own.
- The wind makes strange and frightening noises.
- The incoming tide seems to have tentacles which grab and pull under anything that is left on the sand.
- The sound of the water becomes louder and more threatening.

Case study: Ghosts

Activity 11

AO1 – Demonstrate knowledge and understanding of how films communicate
AO2 – Explore, respond to and reflect on a range of films and topics

- Now study the still on page 132 which shows the Chinese workers on the beach and then listen to the opening moments of the film with your eyes closed.
- How do the sound and images combine to create a feeling of the supernatural or spirit world?

Although the camera has a restless quality throughout the film there are times when the motion stops and the camera and characters take in the fullness of the scene. There are also moments when parts of England are seen as beautiful rather than threatening.

- Review the scene in the orchard and the one when Ai Qin first sees the rainbow over Morecambe. These scenes have a sad, eerie beauty. What do you think they might be saying about Britain in the past or Ai Qin's expectations before she came to this country?
- Note down what Ai Qin says when she sees the rainbow over Morecambe Bay. Think about the ways in which the dialogue combines with our knowledge of what is about to happen to create a powerful, affecting sadness to the scene.

Examination practice

Key terms

Chronological: a number of events arranged in order of their occurrence

The opening and closing sequences of any film are often really important in terms of exploring key themes and issues. *Ghosts* begins and ends on Morecambe beach but, although we finish almost at the point we joined the film after the initial flashback, most of Ai Qin's story is told **chronologically**. If we revisit the opening and closing scenes we are able to see how key themes and ideas are represented.

Examiner's tip

This work will give you some valuable tips for writing the answers in your examination. It will also give you ideas for the sorts of things you will need to put in your first piece of coursework – the close analysis of a film sequence.

Activity 12

AO1 – Demonstrate knowledge and understanding of how films communicate
AO2 – Explore, respond to and reflect on a range of films and topics

- Watch the opening once more and make notes on the film's language. You may wish to think about: mise-en-scène (setting, costume, props, lighting and colour), camera movement and framing, editing and sound.
- Remember to say what you see! Compare your observations with the analysis written on the following page.

Case study: Ghosts

Key terms

Diegetic: sound that is a part of the film's world, e.g. dialogue, wind, traffic

Close analysis of opening sequence

The sequence begins in darkness with the **diegetic** sound of the sea and the wind. A series of captions inform us, in a factual way, that this film is based on the true story of a terrible tragedy involving Chinese immigrant workers. The opening wide-angled long shots allow us to take in the huge sky and seascape.

A white van travels along the shore sandwiched between the shore and the sea and angry sky. An interior shot of the van allows us our first glimpse of Ai Qin. She has her cheek pressed against the window of the vehicle as she looks out. Her nose is bleeding slightly and her expression is sad and anxious. This motif is repeated throughout the film as Ai Qin views an alien Britain through windows, trying to make sense of this strange and terrifying place that she has risked everything to come to. The motif also underlines the fact that she is trapped and unable to break free from the poverty that imprisons her.

The next long shot shows the workers bent double, silhouetted against the silver-grey sky looking like small crabs scuttling around on the surface of the sand searching for food. I think this shot shows how hard it is for the Chinese workers to make a living in such a threatening environment. A circling shot, followed by a close-up, shows Ai Qin's growing anxiety, confusion and exhaustion.

A beautifully shot sequence follows in which the sea almost seems to take on a life of its own. Frames are speeded up showing the tide coming in; the waves grab at the shore like long tentacles and the sound of water and wind drowns out everything else as the light fades to almost complete blackness. We then see the white van again surrounded by water; the Chinese workers are on top of the van. We know what is about to happen to them but since we know little about them we are not too emotionally involved, just curious about how the drama will be played out.

A flashback then moves us through time and space to Fujian province in China where Ai Qin is cycling through the town with her little boy. A caption tells us that we have gone back in time to a different place. We then learn about Ai Qin and her family. The conversations between Ai and her mother show just how hard the decision to leave China is for both of them.

In this short sequence we realise that Ai Qin is the central character. We know that she will be one of the workers involved in the tragedy but we don't know if she will survive. In the flashback we learn how poor she is, how important her family are, and how she is exploited by the snakeheads who arrange for her to get to England. We also see how hard the cockle pickers have to work and how threatening the environment is that surrounds them.

(508 words)

Case study: Ghosts

Key terms

Juxtaposition: to place side by side; in film, placing particular shots alongside each other in a sequence to create a specific effect

Irony: the use of language which may have one meaning for the speaker and those they are talking to and another for a privileged audience, e.g. we know the Chinese workers may be about to die and yet they spend their last moments discussing sending money to their families

Activity 13

AO1 – Demonstrate knowledge and understanding of how films communicate

AO2 – Explore, respond to and reflect on a range of films and topics

- Now watch the closing sequence of *Ghosts* and write an analysis of film language and audience response. The following questions and observations should help you to do this.
- The final sequence begins in exactly the same way as the opening sequence. Sound and silence communicate a feeling of growing dread. Focus carefully on sound and try to describe what you hear and the effect it has upon the audience.
- Although what has happened is repeated, do we respond differently to this scene now that we know the characters and their stories?
- Focus carefully upon camera movement and framing. How are the growing feelings of panic conveyed and where are we placed? Consider the **juxtaposition** of interior and exterior shots, the low level shots in which the sea appears to lap up against the camera, the use of zooms and the hand-held camera.
- What is the sad **irony** of the final calls made on mobile phones to families and loved ones back home?
- The film ends just after the final repeated motif of Ai Qin looking out of a window – this time she is on a plane going home. We see her reunion with her family and the final credits are preceded by captions which tell us the British government has done nothing to help the families of those who died. We are asked to contribute to a fund set up by Nick Broomfield. Do you think if this were a mainstream Hollywood film the ending would have been different?

Creative responses to Ghosts

Activity 14

AO3 – Demonstrate planning, research and presentational skills

AO4 – Use creative and technical skills to construct film products

- Imagine you are a Hollywood director and you want to make a film based on the Morecambe tragedy. Think carefully about the ways in which it would be different from the British *Ghosts*.
- Look in the final coursework section of this book and read the section on 'pitching' on pages 167–183. Now write a pitch for the Hollywood version of *Ghosts*. You may want to give the film a new title – perhaps a fictionalised Nick Broomfield character would be at the centre of the narrative. Would the ending be different? Include a consideration of the stars you would target to play key roles like Mr Lin or Ai Qin.

Case study: Ghosts

Activity 14 Continued

- Read the following review of *Ghosts* written using only 55 words:

  In Ghosts, *Broomfield, our leading documentary maker, uses the docu-drama form to create a powerful picture of modern-day slavery in Britain. This moving, unsettling film follows Ai Qin as she endures the terrible journey from China only to be exploited by greedy British bosses and ultimately risk her life picking cockles in Morecambe Bay.*

  A must see 10 out of 10.

- Now try to write your own review using no more than 50 words! This is great practice for your exams because you really have to think hard about the important things you want to include. Don't forget to give the film a mark out of 10.

Additional resources

- DVD extras: *The Making of Ghosts:* an excellent one-hour documentary which highlights the importance of casting and the detailed research that Nick Broomfield carried out before making *Ghosts*
- Hsiao-Hung Pai's articles on the Morecambe Bay tragedy in *The Guardian*
- 'The Stowaway's Story' by Decca Aitkenhead, *The Guardian*, 6 January 2007
- 'Modern slaves without a ghost of a chance' by Nick Broomfield: Guardian Unlimited: Arts blog-film

Section C New horizons

Chapter 3 Case study: Tsotsi

In this chapter we will:

- explore the differences and similarities between specific films made in South Africa and Hollywood films
- find out about life in South Africa – its culture and history
- focus upon key themes and issues within *Tsotsi*
- explore the ways in which film language is used to communicate ideas.

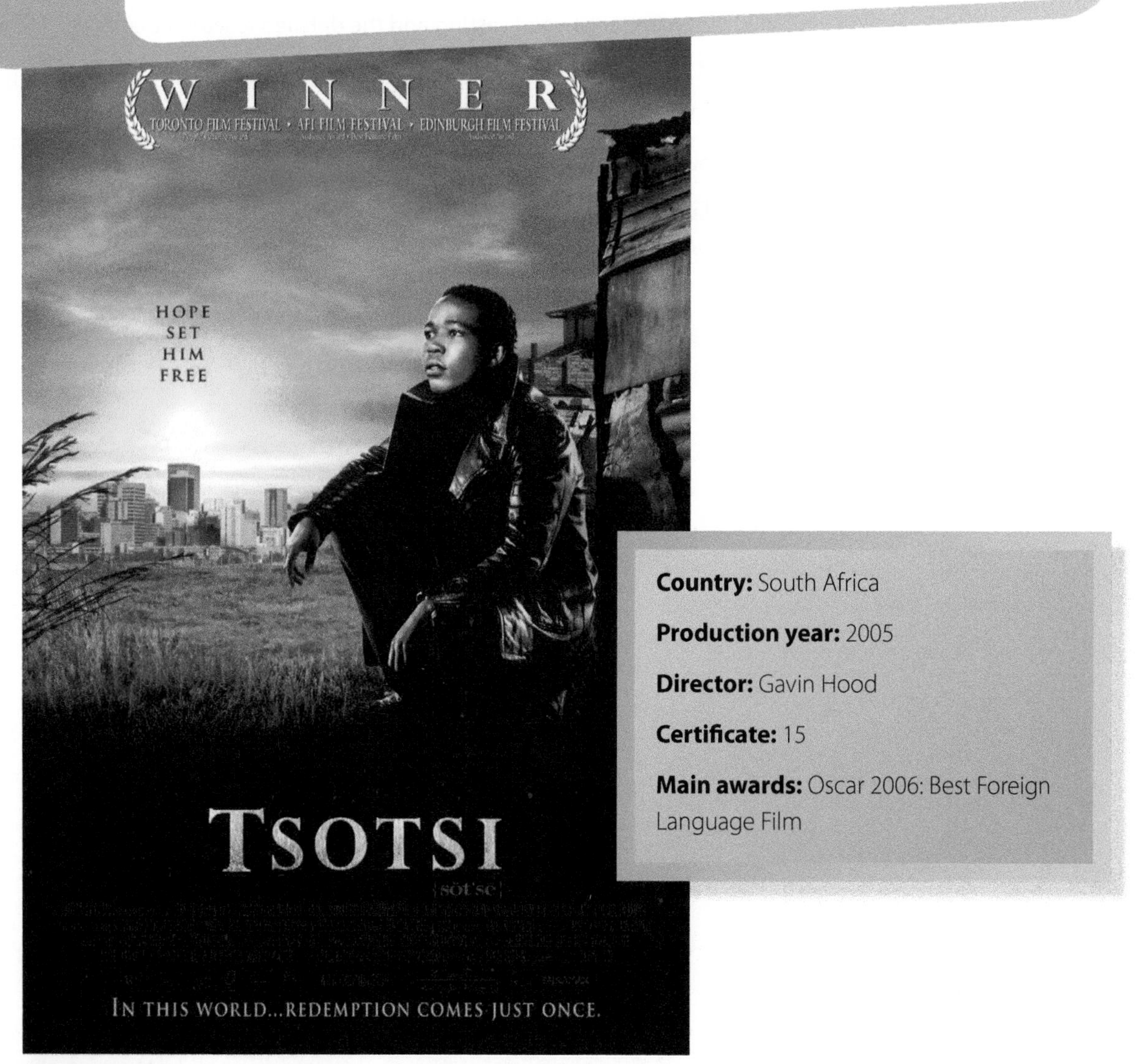

Country: South Africa

Production year: 2005

Director: Gavin Hood

Certificate: 15

Main awards: Oscar 2006: Best Foreign Language Film

7 *A poster for* Tsotsi

Case study: Tsotsi

Synopsis

Tsotsi is a film about a young South African tearaway. He is the leader of three other criminals: Boston, Butcher and Aap. After killing a man on a train Tsotsi argues with Boston, the most intelligent gang member, and runs off into the night. Later, as he crouches under a tree for shelter he seizes the opportunity to steal a car. He bungles the robbery and shoots the female driver, then drives off into the night not realising her baby is in the back of the car. The baby changes Tsotsi's life and the film traces his journey from a nameless thug to someone who finally finds the strength to do the 'right thing'.

Key terms

Tsotsi: slang word for thug/young black criminal

Activity 15

AO3 – Demonstrate planning, research and presentational skills

- In small groups brainstorm a list of things that you already associate with South Africa.
- Pool your ideas with the rest of the class and divide them into two columns: *positive* associations, e.g. sunshine, wildlife; and *negative* associations, e.g. hunger and poverty.

Introduction

Key terms

Oppositions: an opposite thing, or person, or term; a focus on oppositions is often a useful way of analysing film narratives

When we watch or read news about South Africa, it is often the negative associations that are highlighted, such as the rapid spread of HIV/Aids over the past 20 years or so. When we watch travel programmes, or read holiday brochures, we get a much more positive view of breathtaking mountains, luxury hotels and up-market game reserves. South Africa is also famous for the production of diamonds from its diamond mines. Unfortunately, the black workers in these mines have benefited relatively little from the wealth they have produced. These **oppositions** are apparent even when we know a comparatively small amount about South Africa.

South Africa is a vibrant, stunningly beautiful country, full of lively, colourful people who are still coming to terms with relatively new-found freedoms following the collapse of the oppressive apartheid system.

South Africa has had a violent, troubled history. Apartheid, an unjust, dehumanising and demeaning system, was introduced by the white government in the late 1940s. Many countries all over the world opposed apartheid. However, it wasn't until some 50 years later, in the early 1990s, that economic and political pressure from Great Britain and the rest of the world finally brought about the collapse of the racist apartheid system. Today, South Africa is governed by those who represent the majority of its people. It has abundant natural wealth, together with a rich, vibrant

Case study: Tsotsi

culture, and yet a huge majority of its people live in poverty. The film *Tsotsi* reflects these contrasts in contemporary South African society:

- economic wealth with terrible poverty
- political freedom and optimism with crime, disease and drug addiction.

Activity 16

AO3 – Demonstrate planning, research and presentational skills

- Research the term 'apartheid'. Find out as much as you can about what apartheid meant in South Africa.
- Why was Nelson Mandela an important figure in South Africa's history?
- Find out at least two 'facts' about the following linked issues in South Africa today:
  - unemployment
  - poverty
  - housing
  - crime
  - HIV/Aids.
- How many different languages are spoken in South Africa?

South African film industry

The South African film industry is relatively undeveloped when compared to, for example, the British or other European film industries. During the apartheid years the government only funded Afrikaans language films so, effectively, black people had no 'voice' in their own cinema. The only 'black' films produced were badly made Zulu language films which falsely showed South Africa's black population as supporting apartheid.

8 *Richard Harris and James Earl Jones in* Cry My Beloved Country *(1995)*

In the 1990s, after apartheid, Hollywood began to make films set in South Africa. These films usually featured Hollywood stars such as James Earl Jones and Denzel Washington playing well-known South Africans who had fought against the apartheid system. Hollywood chose to ignore the fact that 11 different language groups interact in South Africa by adopting a particular kind of accent/dialect based on the assumption that all black people in South Africa spoke in the same way and could be easily understood by English-speaking audiences!

Until recently it was at least 20 per cent cheaper to make a film in Cape Town than in Australia, and roughly 40 per cent cheaper than filming in the USA. Because film-makers could save significant sums of money by making films in South Africa, the industry tended to concentrate on making commercials, or films, for other countries such as America. However, the country's economy has become stronger in the past few years so consequently making films for other countries in South Africa has become more expensive. The South African government has started to fund the film industry and there has also been much more interest in producing films that contain an authentic South African 'voice' which reflects South African culture.

When *Tsotsi* won the Oscar for the Best Foreign Film in May 2006 it was seen to mark a really important turning point for the South African film industry. In the past ten years the number of people employed within the industry has risen from an estimated 4000 to well over 20,000. There is certainly a sense that a new generation of South African directors is emerging who want to tell their own stories; but this is still not without its problems.

Audiences

Today, on television at least, there is a healthy representation of black South Africans and soap operas attract a large, growing audience. It is hoped that these audiences will provide a market for locally produced feature films. However, poverty is a huge problem and again the gap between the 'haves' and the 'have nots' becomes apparent. Most cinemas are in white shopping malls and have very high ticket prices. State funding through the national Film and Video Foundation is helping a little but, while the huge problems of poverty and unemployment remain, it is difficult to envisage an industry which truly reflects the lives of black South Africans. It has been said that as long as most audiences are white and middle class, only certain types of films will be successful in South Africa. *Tsotsi* is an example of a film that seems to have attracted both black and white audiences. For example, it has had good box office returns in both the black and white areas of Johannesburg. Nationally, it took 40 per cent more than the co-funded *The Constant Gardener* (2005).

Themes and issues

Tsotsi is a film about a young gangster who lives in one of the many shanty townships situated just outside Johannesburg, one of the largest cities in South Africa. It is based upon a short novel written in the early 1960s by South Africa's most famous playwright, Athol Fugard. In his early notes when writing the book Athol noted down important elements of Tsotsi's character:

- his fear of being moved emotionally
- his journey from a place 'shrouded in darkness' where 'Nothing is precious. Nothing is worth keeping' to a final realisation of the value of life and love.

Originally, the story was set in the 1950s, ten years after South Africa had introduced apartheid. Gavin Hood, a young, white South African director who had trained in a Californian film school, thought the book could be turned into a really good film, so he decided to update Athol's story and set it in modern post-apartheid South Africa.

Case study: Tsotsi

***9** Gavin Hood accepting his Academy Award for* Tsotsi *(Best Foreign Film 2006)*

> **Key terms**
> **Indictment:** something that serves to condemn or censure

It is perhaps a sad measure of just how little things have changed today that Athol Fugard's powerful **indictment** of racism, poverty and inequality in apartheid South Africa could so easily be transplanted into the twenty-first century. Hood did this by making at least one policeman black and placing the black parents of the stolen baby within a smart gated community in a wealthy area of Johannesburg.

The film is a brilliant, powerful exploration of the huge differences between the 'haves' and the 'have nots' in South African society. However, Tsotsi's story is not just about a young black South African. Gavin Hood, the director, consistently points out that there are countless young people like Tsotsi all over the world who struggle to exist and are brutalised by a violent, uncaring society.

Viewing the trailer

The purpose of any film trailer is to persuade the audience to go and see the film that is being advertised. The trailer for *Tsotsi* is no different. When we watch it, a series of fast edits forces us to concentrate on the images chosen to attract us to the film. The sound creates atmosphere; we are given short snatches of dialogue between characters from within the film's world, and a voice-over continues to 'sell' the film to us, giving us information about the characters and the narrative. The trailer is designed to arouse our curiosity. If we want to find out what happens we must watch the film.

Case study: Tsotsi

Activity 17

AO1 – Demonstrate knowledge and understanding of how films communicate

AO2 – Explore, respond to and reflect on a range of films and topics

- You can find the trailer in the extras section of the DVD. Watch it three times and note down at least one of the voice-over comments about Tsotsi, the central character.
- Also pay close attention to the word wall which creates the backdrop for images and sound several times during the trailer. Try to note down as many of the words as you can which make up the wall while you watch.
- Note down any images that you find particularly interesting. Are any images repeated? If so, why do you think this has happened?
- What sorts of music or sound are used within the trailer? Do these set up any expectations or create a specific kind of atmosphere?
- Share the things that the narrator has said about Tsotsi, and the words you have noted down from the word collage, with the rest of the class.
- Now watch the whole film. Keep your list of words and phrases from the trailer in front of you as you watch. Note down the points in the film where they seem to be important or relevant.

Genre and style

In your study of genre so far you will have learned that some films are really difficult to categorise. Think about *Tsotsi*, where the central character is a small-time gangster with his own gang. They steal money and cars and in the opening we see them as violent individuals.

Activity 18

AO1 – Demonstrate knowledge and understanding of how films communicate

AO2 – Explore, respond to and reflect on a range of films and topics

- In small groups, make a list of the five characteristics that we analyse when considering genre:
  - setting
  - characters
  - props or significant objects
  - narrative style
  - themes.
- Briefly note down under those headings what we might expect from a 'typical' gangster film.
- Now use the headings to note down what you have learned about *Tsotsi*. The following questions will help you:
  - Is the setting typical?
  - Is *Tsotsi* a conventional gangster film? If not, why not?
  - Do gangster films usually feature babies? Mobiles? Dogs?
  - Are the themes typical? How different is the story and how is it told?

Case study: *Tsotsi*

Clearly *Tsotsi* is a complex film that doesn't easily fit into a genre category. *The Guardian* called it 'a modestly budgeted social thriller'. Certainly, it keeps the viewer 'on the edge of their seat', especially when watching the ending for the first time, so it does 'thrill'. Whenever you come across the word 'social' you can expect references to the way we live, interact, organise and group within a culture. *Tsotsi* explores important aspects of society. Because the problems that affect the characters are difficult ones which don't necessarily have easy solutions we don't get answers, or the neat resolution we may expect from many Hollywood films.

Representation

From your initial look at the trailer for *Tsotsi* and from your first viewing of the film, you will have noticed a number of themes and issues are raised. We are going to focus on those themes and issues and begin to explore the ways in which they are represented through the film's language.

You will remember in Chapter 2 we said that the opening sequence of a film can often give us lots of clues about what may happen in the film.

10 *Aap, Tsotsi, Butcher and Boston in the opening sequence of* Tsotsi

So let us go back and review the opening sequence. Before you do, read through the questions in Activity 19.

Examiner's tip

The questions you will be asked in your Exploring Film examination are similar to those in Activity 19. Answering these questions will help to prepare you for that exam as well as the 'Exploring Film Outside Hollywood' paper.

Case study: Tsotsi

Activity 19

AO1– Demonstrate knowledge and understanding of how films communicate

AO2 – Explore, respond to and reflect on a range of films and topics

- In groups of between three and five, read through the questions below. Decide which of the questions each of the group members will concentrate on.
- Now watch the opening sequence of *Tsotsi* up to the point when we see two boys sheltering in a stack of huge concrete pipes (approximately 10 minutes 20 seconds).
  - On first viewing just watch the film.
  - On second viewing make notes.
- Answer your questions. When you have finished, share your answers with your group and see if they have noticed anything that you may have missed. When you are sure you have finished you can compare your answers to those of the other groups in the class.

1 What images accompany the title credits? What kinds of shots are used? Why do you think the director, Gavin Hood, has chosen these shots to begin his film?

2 What do you learn about Tsotsi's personality during the opening sequence?

3 Concentrate on the way sound and silence are used when Tsotsi and his gang 'stake out' their victim and follow him onto the train. How is it different from the sound in most of the rest of the sequence? Are there any other points where diegetic sound tells us what is happening within the emotional world of the characters?

4 Each of the gang members reacts differently to the murder on the train. How are these differences shown? Think about body language, facial expressions and gestures. Notice the kinds of camera shots that are used.

5 Are there any images that are repeated in the sequence? Why do you think they are used more than once?

6 At the very end of the sequence who do you think the little boys are that are sheltering in the pipe? What clues are we given to their identity and their relationship?

Examiner's tip

Make sure you have learned the names of the important characters and the actors who play them in your close study film and that you can spell their names correctly. You wouldn't dream of answering a question on a book or play that you have studied for English if you didn't know the names of the central characters in those texts, and studying a film is very similar to studying a book!

A close analysis of the representation of characters, relationships and themes in the opening sequence

Gavin Hood wastes no time in introducing us to many of the central characters and establishing the ways in which they relate to one another. The film opens with a series of close-up and extreme close-up shots of Boston, Aap and Butcher's hands. Aap and Butcher are playing dice – we see the die turning in the air and then falling – we also see a long sharp bradawl which is being turned in one of the player's hands. Ideas about chance and destiny, fate and fortune are immediately signalled. The dice land with a five and four upwards.

A mid-shot shows the dice players and Boston sitting around a table in a small room. The mise-en-scène here already shows Tsotsi as alone, apart from the rest of the gang. He has his back to the action as he gazes out of the open door at the red setting sun. Butcher claims he has won with 11 (neither he nor Aap can add up). Boston's intelligence is immediately established – he is the only one of the group who can count. He informs them with a wry smile that four and five make nine. However, it is obviously Tsotsi who is the leader; they all leave the hut on his signal, the older gang members acknowledge him as he passes them and he decides on the victim who is to be robbed.

Throughout this sequence Tsotsi only speaks two words. Gavin Hood has said he wanted the film to have minimal dialogue and for the story to be told through images and interactions which show what is happening in the inner world of the characters.

Boston's reactions to the killing are clearly expressed in the series of close-ups showing the shock, pain and horror he feels. He is physically sick. Because he has education he is also able to express what he feels in words and actions. In the following scene in the bar, he cuts himself and tells the others this is how he felt inside after the murder. He taunts Tsotsi, asking him if he knows the meaning of the word decency (another recurring theme).The others do not have the words to express their feelings.

Aap is obviously panic stricken after the murder; we see this through the close-ups showing his eyes rolling with fear, but he seems to put it out of his mind fairly quickly. Perhaps he is used to surviving in a hostile, violent world? His physical build, facial expressions and costume (a battered hat that seems too small for his large head, trainers and tracksuit bottoms) mark him out as the slower, more comic member of the gang.

Butcher's name seems to tell us all we need to know about him. He looks straight into the eyes of his victim and shows no remorse for the killing.

Tsotsi's character is harder to read. We know his name means 'thug' or 'criminal' but Boston tells us this isn't his real name. Perhaps then, we are meant to think that there is far more to him than we at first see? His expression gives us mixed messages – sometimes it is fearful, sometimes stony, and often his face seems fixed, almost expressionless. When he finally shows some emotion and attacks Boston (as the storm in the background builds) it comes as a shock to the audience. It is interesting to note the 'trigger' for his violent outburst. He has kept his temper while Boston attacks him with questions about his name, his father and his mother, but when Boston finishes with 'Not even a dog you have cared for?' he completely loses control. Again, a puzzle or enigma is introduced. Why? In this opening sequence, several important themes are suggested by the repetition of certain motifs.

As the gang walk into the station, a high angle shot shows them dwarfed by a huge poster which states 'We are all affected by HIV or Aids'. In the foreground of the frame, which shows the gang on the football stand where Boston is being sick, top lighting picks out a similar poster spelling out the same message and advertising the Lottery. Why might these elements of mise-en-scène be important?

Did you notice the number of close-ups which focus upon hands? If you spotted these or any other recurring motif when you watched the opening sequence, think about the ideas or themes within *Tsotsi* that they may introduce.

Names and voices

In the opening sequence Boston tries to goad Tsotsi into telling him his name, saying 'Every man must have a name'. As the film progresses we find out more and more about Tsotsi's past through a series of flashbacks. As we learn about the hardships he has had to endure, and witness the way in which he refuses to abandon the baby, we begin to see that he is far more than the thug his adopted name suggests. The sequence in which he goes to see Miriam for the second time is a really important one. Let's review it once more and think about the ways in which it seems to mark huge changes within Tsotsi.

11 *Tsotsi talks to Miriam*

Narrative, style, themes, ideas: the final sequence

We have already noted just how important the opening sequence of *Tsotsi* is in terms of establishing characters, themes and ideas which may be explored later in the film. In your work on narrative and genre earlier on in the course you will also have looked at the ways in which certain enigmas (puzzles/questions) are set up which excite our interest and make us want to continue to watch. You will also have looked at the different ways in which a story can be organised.

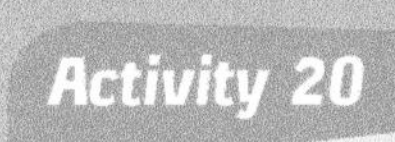

Activity 20

AO1 – Demonstrate knowledge and understanding of how films communicate
AO2 – Explore, respond to and reflect on a range of films and topics

- Watch the sequence which begins with Tsotsi taking the baby to Miriam's house for the second time (Scene 5 run for 8 minutes 33 seconds) up to the point when he insists that Boston is taken back to his house.
- What name does Tsotsi give the baby and why is both the name and the naming process important?
- What do we learn about Tsotsi's past in this scene? What is it that 'triggers' these memories?
- This scene proves to be the turning point in the film's narrative. What changes happen to Tsotsi? Why do you think they happen at this particular moment? You should consider Tsotsi's relationship with Miriam and Boston together with the importance of ideas about a possible future for the first time in the film.

Case study: Tsotsi

In your work on the second sequence you will have examined the ways in which flashbacks gradually reveal more and more about Tsotsi's past.

Tsotsi's story is a simple one but it is told in such a way that it keeps us watching. At the start of the film Gavin Hood sets up a series of enigmas:

- Where does Tsotsi come from?
- Where are his mother and father?
- What is the importance of the beggar?
- What will he do with the baby?

When we reach the final sequence it is really hard for the audience not to feel some kind of sympathy for Tsotsi, in spite of the terrible things that he has done. We know that most mainstream Hollywood films end with some kind of resolution when many of the questions that have kept us interested throughout are answered. Often the ending is happy and we leave the cinema with a warm glow, knowing that the central characters, both good and bad, have got what they deserve. Let's look at the final sequence of *Tsotsi* and explore our feelings as the film ends. Let's see if all our questions are answered and decide whether there is a final resolution to Tsotsi's story.

Activity 21

AO1 – Demonstrate knowledge and understanding of how films communicate
AO2 – Explore, respond to and reflect on a range of films and topics

- Watch the final sequence once more. Note down what happens in the end. Is this the way you wanted the film to finish? What do you think will happen to Tsotsi after his arrest?
- Now watch 'The Alternate Endings' on the DVD extras menu. How many endings were considered by Gavin Hood? Note down what these endings were.
- Why did Gavin Hood decide that these endings were not the best ones for his film?
- What response from the audience did Gavin Hood want to achieve? How successful do you think he was?
- Which of the endings do you like best? Give reasons for your choice.

Gavin Hood leaves the final question 'What happens to Tsotsi?' for us to answer. However, although *Tsotsi* is a story about one boy, the film also raises more universal questions or problems. Remember, Tsotsi is not really a boy's name, it is a term meaning 'young, black gangster or thug'. Tsotsi could be any one of the hundreds of thousands of young people all over the world who have no family and are forced to live in poverty.

The universal questions in this film are often raised by the repetition of certain motifs. We have already looked at the importance of hands, dice and gambling, and AIDS posters in the opening sequence. When you watch the film for the second time think about the importance of these motifs and others such as:

- mobiles
- decency
- hope
- family
- a 'proper' name.

What kinds of universal concerns do you think these may communicate? See if you can spot any other recurring ideas or motifs. Note them down and share them with the rest of your class.

Creative responses to Tsotsi

12 *The concrete pipes that shelter homeless children in* Tsotsi

Case study: Tsotsi

In your examination, the question will allow you to show your knowledge and understanding of the ways in which *Tsotsi* communicates all the issues and ideas that you have explored and discussed in class, in a creative way. You may, for example, be asked to:

- write a review for a specific target audience
- create a poster
- design a page for a website or
- produce a 'blog'.

Whatever task you are given, it is important that you include a consideration of performance, issues and themes, people and places and combine these with your personal response to the film. As with any examination, practice is important so here are some activities which will help you to prepare for this question.

Activity 22

AO3– Demonstrate planning, research and presentational skills

AO4 – Use creative and technical skills to construct film products

- Buy a copy of *Empire* or *Total Film* from your local supermarket or newsagent. Firstly, read and enjoy it! When you've finished reading it, carry out some research on the target audience for these publications. Obviously they are aimed at people who watch and enjoy films but can you find out anything else about the target audience?
- Now imagine you are about to write a review of *Tsotsi* for one of these magazines. Think carefully about the kinds of things that an audience expects to find out when reading a review and note these down.
- Visit www.imdb.com and go to the *Tsotsi* page. Along the left hand side of the page you will find a column which contains 'external reviews'. These reviews have been written by film critics or journalists with specific audiences in mind. Read through some of these reviews and note which publication or platform they were written for. Print off two that you find interesting.
- Go back to the *Tsotsi* page. Just under the main credits you should find a heading called 'User comments'. Click on this and read through some of the comments that 'ordinary' viewers have posted onto the website. Print off two interesting or challenging examples. Are these reviews different to the external reviews you have looked at? If so, why?
- Look through your four reviews carefully and make notes on what the writers have included. You should end up with a list like this:
  - language
  - themes and issues raised
  - performance
  - music
  - narrative
  - cinematography
  - awards won
  - critics' personal responses.
- Decide where you want your review to go. If you choose *Empire* or *Total Film*, look carefully at the style and language used in these publications. If you decide on a user review, why not post it directly onto the IMDb website (www.imdb.com)?

Additional resources

- DVD extras: your teacher will ensure you have several opportunities to explore *Tsotsi* in a creative way. Watching the DVD extras can give you lots of information about the way in which the film was made, the difficulties encountered and the differences in attitude to the film-making process within the white and the black populations in South Africa. They also allow Gavin Hood to outline the 'director's vision' – what he wanted to communicate through the film's language and the importance of music. Actors such as Presley Chweneyagae (Tsotsi) and Terry Pheto (Miriam) talk about their own experiences of growing up in the townships and give us an insight into the ways in which their performances seem to contain such power and truth.
- Film Education Study Guide: *Tsotsi*: Film Education have also produced an excellent free study guide on *Tsotsi* which can be downloaded from their website www.filmeducation.org. This guide will give you invaluable information about South Africa, characters and relationships, motifs and themes and story and narrative. It also provides help on writing a review, posters and artwork, promotional campaigns and marketing.
- Internet resources include:
    - www.imdb.com: a superb site for all research and an excellent 'portal' into other useful sites
    - http://film.guardian.co.uk: reviews of *Tsotsi* and connected articles published in *The Guardian*
    - http://www.southafrica.net: research on the current and historical situation in South Africa.

Assessment practice 5

What will I have to do in the exam?

The pages which follow include sample examination questions from Paper 2: Exploring Film Outside Hollywood. The boxes around them contain ideas about the kinds of things you will have to do to earn the marks available.

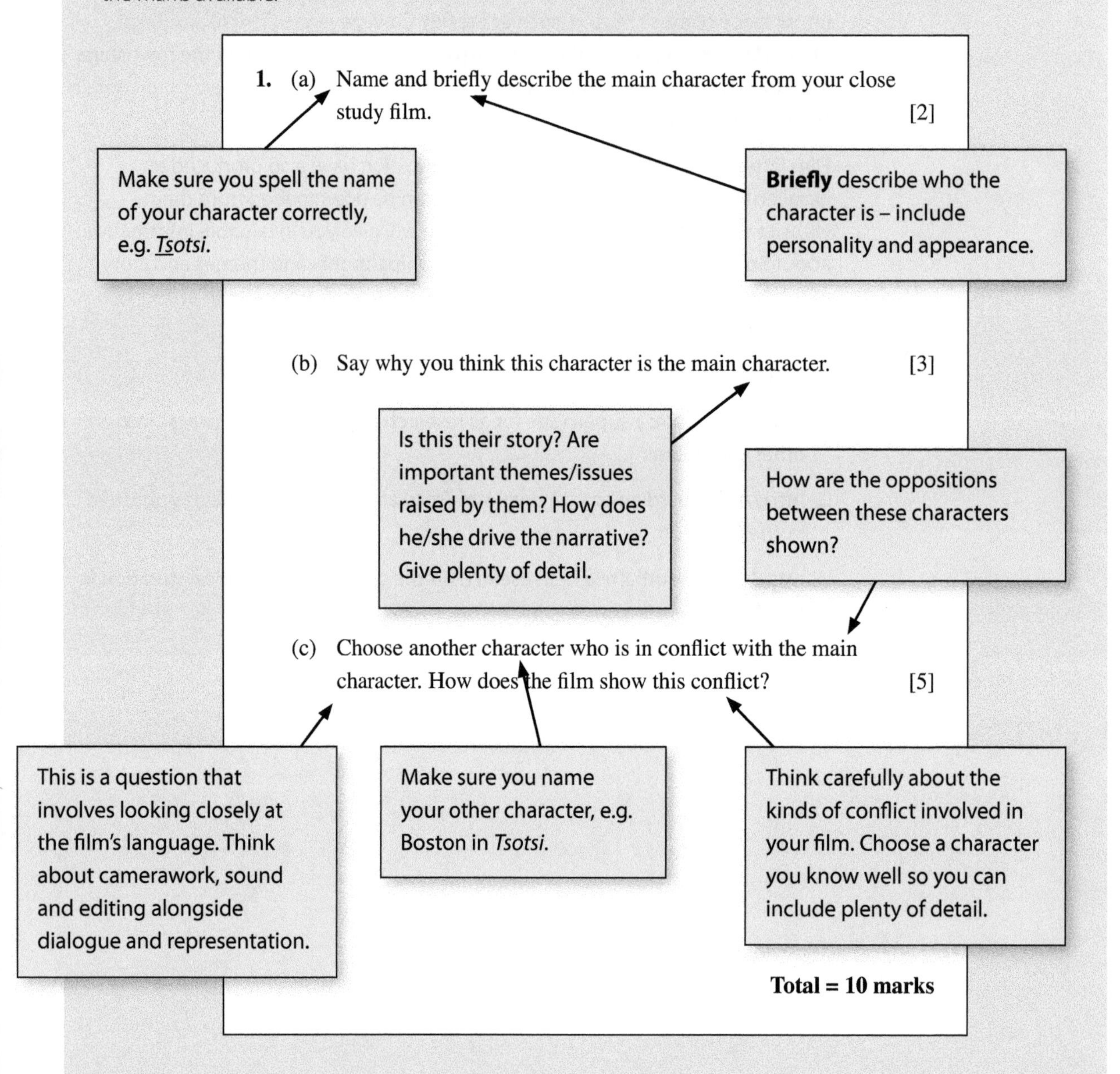

1. (a) Name and briefly describe the main character from your close study film. [2]

(b) Say why you think this character is the main character. [3]

(c) Choose another character who is in conflict with the main character. How does the film show this conflict? [5]

Total = 10 marks

2. (a) Identify one key theme or issue your chosen film raises. [2]

Think carefully before you choose your theme or issue; make sure it is one that you can write about in detail.

(b) Briefly summarise what the film suggests about the theme or issue. [6]

Remember that your film may have explored a particular theme or issue in different ways *and* that different audiences may respond differently to these.

(c) Choose one important sequence from your close study film. Explore how the film represents its key theme or issue. [12]

In your answer you may wish to refer to the role of one or two of the following:

- mise-en-scène (setting, costume, props, lighting and colour)
- camera shot and movement
- editing
- sound.

This question carries high marks; make sure you give clear, detailed explanations of the ways in which film language is used to represent your chosen themes and issues.

Don't ignore these 'memory jogs' – they provide a clear structure for your answer.

Total = 20 marks

3. Write a user review of your close study film for a website. You can discuss what you have liked or disliked about the film. Here are some important questions you should include in your review:

- Why was the film entertaining/not entertaining?
- Were there any funny/powerful/moving performances?
- What questions are raised by the film's issues?
- What have you learned about people and places from this film?

Total = 20 marks

Think carefully about the platform, format and audience for your review. You may have done something very similar for your coursework. Think about those ideas.

You can put in ideas of your own – your personal response is very important.

Don't ignore these questions! They will help you to demonstrate your knowledge and understanding.

Section D Coursework

Chapter 1 Approaches to coursework

In this chapter we will:

- carry out a short research project on one of your favourite films
- find out how the film was made and who made it (production)
- discover who sold it and how (distribution)
- explore why and where audiences have chosen to watch the film (exhibition)
- learn how to produce a close analysis of the ways in which film language creates meaning and response in a short film sequence.

Activity 1

AO4 – Use creative and technical skills to construct film products

- In groups make a list of your favourite films.
- Discuss the reasons why you found these films particularly enjoyable.
- Share your group's list of films and the pleasures you got from them with the rest of the class.

You have probably been asked in the past what your favourite film is. Perhaps you always think of a film that you enjoyed fairly recently. There are lots of factors that may influence your enjoyment of a film. Think about your mood at the time. Were you watching with a friend who loved the film too? Did a star that you particularly like give a superb performance? Were the special effects really amazing, as in *Transformers* (2007)? Was there a 'new take' on a familiar genre (*Scream*, 1996) or did the ending have an unexpected twist (*The Sixth Sense*)?

In this section you are going to find out a lot more about a film that you really enjoyed. The great thing about Film Studies is that you can amaze your family and friends with your in-depth knowledge of particular films. At the same time you often find that the more you know about a film the more pleasure it gives!

1 *A still from* The Sixth Sense *(1999)*

Activity 2

AO1 – Demonstrate knowledge and understanding of how films communicate

AO2 – Explore, respond to and reflect on a range of films and topics

AO3 – Demonstrate planning, research and presentational skills

- Decide which of your favourite films you would like to learn more about. There may be lots of things you like about the film. Try to find a short sequence (about 5 minutes) which could show the rest of the class just how good it is.
- Prepare a short talk which explains the reasons for your choice and highlights what you really rate about it. This could be the camerawork, the sound, performance, genre, or any other element of the film's language that you enjoyed.

Production

Now it's time to find out more about your chosen film by doing some industry research. First of all, you are going to explore the ways in which the film came to be produced.

All films begin with an idea which then gets turned into a screenplay by a screenwriter. You are going to begin your research by finding out who wrote the screenplay of your chosen film. Usually www.imdb.com provides a good starting point. One frequent source for stories is a newspaper. If you study *Ghosts* for Paper 2: Exploring Film Outside Hollywood, you will find that Nick Broomfield, its director, based the film on newspaper reports of a real tragedy involving 21 Chinese workers. Often old films are remade and sometimes plays or novels are adapted for the 'big screen'.

Activity 3

AO2 – Explore, respond to and reflect on a range of films and topics

AO3 – Demonstrate planning, research and presentational skills

Research task

- Find out where the idea for your film came from and who wrote the screenplay.
- Who directed the film? Has he or she directed any other well-known films?
- Who starred in the film?
- What was the budget for the film?
- Where was it made? Did funding come from more than one country?
- Did you find out any other interesting facts about the production of your film?

Keep all your research in a working notebook and don't lose it! Your teacher will give you a Film Exploration Proforma (FL2) to fill in when you have completed all your research. The Proforma shows what you have learnt about your film and is sent away with your coursework.

If a film has major stars in it the production budget could easily be more than $80 million. Generally the screenwriter is paid between 2.5 per cent and 5 per cent of this budget. So a screenwriter with a really good screenplay could expect to earn $1 million. An excellent incentive for you to begin your screenwriting career *now* and choose this option for your pre-production coursework!

Distribution

Once any film is made it has to travel in order to reach its audience. Distribution involves acquiring a film from its producers and trying to make it reach the widest possible audience by selling it to the places where films are going to be shown – to exhibitors. Distributors need to make sure that when a film reaches its destination there are lots of people waiting to see it. So, we need to know about the film before it arrives at its exhibition destination. A film usually needs to make about two and a half times what it cost to produce just to ensure it doesn't lose money.

Activity 4

AO3 – Demonstrate planning, research and presentational skills

Think it through

- In small groups, note down the various ways in which we might find out about a film before it arrives at our local cinema.
- Share your list with the rest of the class.

Key terms

Test screening: a private screening of a film to an invited audience before its release

Test audience: an invited audience who watch and give feedback on a film before its release

Test screenings

Distributors have a number of roles to fulfil. Firstly, they try to find out what kinds of audiences might like the film enough to go and see it. Often this involves arranging **test screenings** for **test audiences** about three months before its release. The test audience will be asked a number of questions about the film.

Activity 5

AO2 – Explore, respond to and reflect on a range of films and topics

AO4 – Use creative and technical skills to construct film products

Think it through

- Make a list of the kinds of questions a distributor might want to ask a test audience after they have watched a film.
- Share your list with the rest of the class.

Test screenings are really important. Often the audience can spot problems that the film-makers haven't noticed. They may think the film is too long and that some scenes are not really necessary. There may be parts of the narrative they find difficult to understand. They may not like the star of the film. The distributor is really anxious to know whether people in the test audience would recommend it to their friends. Often the films we choose to go and see are the ones our friends have 'raved' about so recommendations are an important way of ensuring a film's success.

Marketing and publicity

Often our choice of film is also based on the kinds of expectations that have been set up by the various marketing and publicity campaigns organised by exhibitors. Large sums of money are spent on these campaigns. For example, a summer blockbuster may cost as much as $100 million to promote!

Posters

Most campaigns start with a poster – this is usually the first time we become aware of the film.

Activity 6

AO2 – Explore, respond to and reflect on a range of films and topics

AO3 – Demonstrate planning, research and presentational skills

AO4 – Use creative and technical skills to construct film products

Think it through

- Try to find a poster advertising your film on the Internet or in a film magazine. If you can't find one for your film, choose a poster you really like.

Write it up

- How does your chosen poster appeal to its audience? Make brief notes on some or all of the following areas:
  - genre elements including props, costume and setting
  - the use of stars (how important are they?)
  - special selling points, e.g. awards
  - target audience
  - references to other films, books, music or television programmes
  - the images that are used (which colours and why?).

Key terms

Merchandising: the process whereby manufacturers incorporate elements of a forthcoming film into their products

Posters make us aware of a forthcoming film but there are also other important ways of making sure we know about it and will pay to see it.

Merchandising

Merchandising is the name given to the process whereby the manufacturers of other products, or the suppliers of other services, incorporate elements of a forthcoming film into their products. This may be anything from pyjamas with Spider-Man on the front to birthday cakes topped with *Lion King* images. Probably the most famous example of merchandising is McDonald's, the fast-food chain, who regularly tie in their products with films designed for a family audience, most notably new Walt Disney releases.

Activity 7

AO3 – Demonstrate planning, research and presentational skills

AO4 – Use creative and technical skills to construct film products

Talk it through

- In groups of three or four, discuss any examples of merchandising that you have noticed in the past few months. Make a list of the kinds of products and films involved.

Coursework idea

- Plan a merchandising campaign for a new film.
    - Decide on the target audience for the film then think about the kinds of products that would appeal to them.
    - Pick at least three items and draw a design (or create one on a computer) for each item.

This kind of promotion has become extremely important. If we consider that about 21 million people all over the world go to a McDonald's outlet every day, where they are surrounded by film posters, served meals in boxes emblazoned with film images, and served drinks in giant paper cups covered with pictures, we begin to see just how powerful merchandising can be.

2 *Promoting* Pirates of the Caribbean

Festivals and premieres

Often films are entered in important film festivals before their release. If they win an award, or are well received by critics and audiences, the resulting 'buzz' of publicity will help to attract wider audiences. However, there is a risk involved for producers and exhibitors as there are no guarantees of success and a negative response could affect ticket sales.

The French Cannes Film Festival is the most prestigious of all the festivals. It is held annually, attracting international attention and huge media coverage. Usually, producers, directors, stars and actors attend in order to intensify the publicity. If a film gains an award it is invariably used on posters, trailers and other publicity in order to 'sell' the film.

Timing

When the film has been marketed and publicised we come to the point when it is finally 'released' and can be shown in cinemas. The timing of the release is vital. Look carefully at the programmes in your nearest cinema around Christmas or during the summer holidays. What kinds of films are being shown? Can you spot any differences to the programmes for times when there are no school holidays? The first weekend of release can be crucial in terms of a film's success. Often it can account for between 50 and 75 per cent of its overall takings.

Activity 8

AO3 – Demonstrate planning, research and presentational skills

Talk it through

- Discuss with your partner the last time you went to see a film as soon as it was released at a cinema near you.
- How important was it for you to see it as soon as possible? Why?
- Why do you think film critics are allowed to see films before they are released? Do you ever read reviews before you go to see a film?

Exhibition

This is the last of these three interconnected areas (production, distribution and exhibition). It's the point where we finally get to see the film (providing it is classified as suitable for our age group).

The ways in which we view a film are changing rapidly. Before most homes in Britain owned a television (up to the late 1950s) most towns had at least one cinema and many had more. In Great Yarmouth, for example, there were four cinemas, with two more only a short bus ride away. Today, Great Yarmouth has only one cinema left and there are no others nearby. However, many more people now travel some distance to the nearest multiplex and still have a choice of a range of films. Alternatively, they can rent a DVD or video from their local video shop and watch in the comfort of their own home. The ways in which we view films are constantly changing. What other ways can you think of in which we get to see films?

Reviews

Earlier, you will have touched upon the importance of reviews for both the audience and the exhibitor. Distributors often provide press packs for journalists that include cast interviews and photographs. Premieres, galas and festivals are arranged in order to generate publicity.

However, if critics across the world really dislike a film, they can bring about its failure at the box office. Of course this isn't always the case and sometimes critics misjudge the appeal of a film. For example, when James Cameron's *Titanic* was released in 1997 it was the most expensive film ever made. It was backed by a massive publicity campaign. Yet on its release it was almost universally 'panned' by the critics. But still:

- audiences loved it
- Celine Dion had a number one hit with a song from the sound-track
- it consolidated Leonardo DiCaprio's star status
- it elevated the British actress, Kate Winslet, to stardom.

In spite of its huge production and distribution costs, it became one of the most successful films ever made.

Activity 9

AO3 – Demonstrate planning, research and presentational skills
AO4 – Use creative and technical skills to construct film products
Exam preparation

- Find three reviews of your film which have been written for different publications, e.g. *The Guardian*, *Empire* and *Total Film*.
- What elements of the film are focused on (genre, narrative, director, star etc.)?
- Can you identify the target audience from the way the review is written and its content?

Film language: the close analysis (20 marks)

By now you will have learned a lot about the ways in which your favourite film was made, distributed and exhibited. You will also have learned a lot about the micro and macro elements of film language at the beginning of this course. So let's go back to the sequence you brought into class to talk about (Activity 2 on page 159). It should be about 5 minutes long. You may know it quite well already but have you closely analysed the film's language in order to consider why you think it's good?

Activity 10

AO1 – Demonstrate knowledge and understanding of how films communicate

- Look at Sarah's analysis below of the ways in which camera framing and camera movement combine to create meaning in the opening sequence of *Tsotsi* (one of the non-Hollywood close study films).
  - The **red text** indicates the parts where she shows her understanding of key concepts and when she uses the appropriate terminology accurately.
  - The **green text** indicates the points where she identifies camera shots or movement and then goes on to examine the meanings/effects that are created by their use.
  - Finally, and this is very important, the **blue text** shows the places where Sarah has given her own response to the sequence – how it made her feel and why.
- Now decide on a short sequence that you want to analyse. Choose just two of the micro elements of film language (e.g. editing, sound, mise-en-scène, camera framing and movement) to focus on.
- For homework, watch your sequence through at least three times, making notes as you do so. You may want to pause the film at certain points, or rewind if you think you've missed something. Remember your main focus areas but, like Sarah, you may want to mention other elements of film language when they combine to create meaning. Take your notes into class and work on the first draft of your analysis.

An analysis of how camerawork is used in the opening sequence of Tsotsi

The opening scene is introduced with a game which involves dice. There is a close-up of the dice to symbolise that life is a game of chance as nobody can choose who their parents are and how they end up in life sometimes. There is also a repeated motif of close-ups of hands which could show their working class background and the fact that they are used to doing manual labour. It could also show that we all have the power to change in our hands.

Because of the camera framing we are able to identify the main character who is Tsotsi. He isn't really introduced straight away until a powerful close-up that is emphasised by the music kicking in at the same time. The non-diegetic sound-track is parallel to the image of the four boys walking down the street as it highlights their authority. After we've seen them walking down the street there is an establishing shot that lets us know the circumstances they have to live in. It is a high angled shot indicating that the people in the township are small and powerless over their surroundings.

After this Tsotsi and his gang go to do a job which seems to be a regular occurrence. As they arrive at the train platform there's a panning shot so that we can pick them out of the crowd. At first it is hard to see them as they are blending in so as not to appear suspicious. Another high angled shot, this time looking down on the crowd and the gang, shows a massive orange banner centre frame. It is highly noticeable and attracts our attention straight away as it reads 'HIV affects all of us'. This is a terrible virus that has unfortunately taken its toll on Africa where, if you are lucky enough not to contract the disease, you will more than likely know someone who has.

The scene which follows shows the gang scouting for their next victim. A series of medium shots are used to pick out a range of possible victims. However, the shot of a chirpy old man is longer which, instantly tells us that something is going to happen to him. Also he is portrayed as a jolly old man who smiles as he buys a gift from a stall. We have already formed an opinion of him and have warmed to him. An extreme close-up then shows us Tsotsi's eyes which show no expression; this connotes that he has no conscience. He stares intently at the man. It then quickly edits back to the victim and zooms in on an envelope of money; here the audience click on to the fact that Tsotsi is going to steal the money.

I think this opening sequence really sets up the story well. We learn a lot about Tsotsi and his gang, their environment and what they are about to do through the camerawork. Very little dialogue is used but a feeling of real tension is built up very quickly and we want to watch on to find out what will happen next.

Sarah Boyd
535 words

Examiner's tip

The first thing to notice is how few words Sarah wastes. Almost everything she writes refers to the sequence and she closely analyses specific shots rather than re-telling the story. It is safe to assume that your moderator will know your film and you certainly don't want to waste words, or more importantly marks, by writing down the story.

Examiner's tip

As with any new area of study, getting used to understanding the ways in which, for example, lighting and sound (two of the micro elements of film language) can combine to create a particular kind of atmosphere in your chosen sequence takes time and practice. Remember professional writers always draft and redraft their work. Your teacher will make sure that you have plenty of help and lots of opportunities to explore the ways in which film language communicates. You will need to re-watch your sequence several times. It can be guaranteed that with each viewing you will notice something new and each time you do so you're probably going to gain marks!

Knowledge check

In this chapter you have learned about the processes involved in the making of your favourite film, how other films are funded and some of the stages involved in the production of a film. You have further explored what is involved in the distribution of films and how they are exhibited and reviewed. You will also have investigated the connections between the production, distribution and exhibition processes and learned what makes a good analysis of a film sequence.

In order to check your knowledge and understanding of this chapter answer the following questions.

1 Where can ideas for film stories come from?
2 Who generally turns these ideas into screenplays?
3 What is a test audience?
4 Give an example of a recent merchandising promotion.
5 Which 'micro' elements of film language combine to make meaning in a film sequence?

Chapter 2

Coursework: pitching and pre-production

In this chapter we will:

- find out how ideas for films are sold to possible producers
- learn about the typical format and codes and conventions used in pre-production work
- experiment with ways of selling your own ideas to prospective producers.

The pitch

Key terms

Pitch: the overview of a film idea presented in a way that would attract interest from investors (think of a sales pitch)

Screenwriter: a person who writes film scripts (screenplays)

Pitching has been around since the early days of Hollywood film production. It refers to the **screenwriter** 'pitching' an idea to a producer in the hope that he or she will receive funding to develop the idea into a full screenplay. A screenwriter may have less than a minute to convince a producer that the idea is bankable and worth pursuing. As many writers in Hollywood are freelance (self-employed) they may be pitching an idea that they have already written or trying to assess whether an idea is worth pursuing.

***3** Producers can be very busy people!*

A good pitch should explain the premise or basic idea for the film. Screenwriters may make reference to other (successful) films and specific stars as a way of quickly getting the producer to imagine the film. In some cases the screenwriter may pitch the film as a middle ground between two already successful films or well-known stories, for example, *Romeo and Juliet* meets *Gone in Sixty Seconds* (2000). This isn't to suggest that the original characters from the films mentioned would be included, but it gives ideas about the types of characters and events that would be.

Even outside Hollywood, films are pitched to potential investors who want a brief summary of the film without having to read the script.

Producers will usually assess a pitch based upon **concept** and **castability**. Referred to as the two Cs, these are the major factors that could ultimately sell a film.

Key terms

Concept: is the idea good?

Castability: would it be suitable for certain stars?

Logline

A logline is a one sentence summary of the film's narrative. Sometimes these can be very direct.

Activity 11

AO3 – Demonstrate planning, research and presentational skills

AO4 – Use creative and technical skills to construct film products

Talk it out

- See if you can recognise the films below from their single sentence logline.

1. *A little boy is schooled in the art of wizardry.*
2. *A young man and woman from different social classes fall in love aboard an ill-fated voyage.*
3. *When a Roman general is betrayed, and his family murdered by a corrupt prince, he comes to Rome as a gladiator to seek his revenge.*
4. *A clueless Kazakh journalist visits America to make a documentary and to marry Pamela Anderson.*
5. *A young magazine assistant gets a rude awakening in the fashion world when she meets her difficult new boss.*

Think it through

- In small groups, pick three films which you have all seen (these could be films watched as part of the course).
- Each person should write a logline for the films.
- Discuss these and decide which is the best logline for each of the films.
- Write a short summary of what you think makes a good logline.

Turning the idea behind a whole film into one sentence can be tricky, but this could be the deciding factor if a potential producer/investor wants to hear more or would rather pass on the idea.

Creating a logline

Once you have an idea for your imaginary film, creating a logline is a good way to focus your ideas. If we imagine a logline is the answer to a question (what is your film about?)

then we can approach it in this way. If a producer were to ask you this question you should try to cover:

- **character** – at least the main character
- **genre** – what genre is the film?
- **narrative** – what makes it unique?

Remember, a potential investor is looking for the two Cs; your job is to show them that there is a clear concept and that the film is castable.

Activity 12

AO2 – Explore, respond to and reflect on a range of films and topics

Think it through

- Look at the following three loglines. Rank them in order of which you think is the most likely to get investment.
- In groups, discuss why you think this is.

1 *A man seeks revenge when his wife is killed by gangsters.*

2 *A naive country boy travels to the city for the first time to take part in a national shooting competition.*

3 *Missing presumed dead, Captain James Tucker returns home to find his family have vanished and his identity has been erased... He wants answers.*

Creating your pitch

Having aroused the interest of your audience with your logline, the pitch must now give an overview of the narrative in less than 150 words. One way of doing this could be to list the major events that happen in your film as bullet points from beginning to end. Your study of narrative should have given you ideas for different frameworks for approaching this. You may wish to simply state the film's genre in your pitch (*'it's a musical'*) or this could be more implicit, referring to generic conventions.

Key questions you should ask yourself include:

- Is there a clear sense of narrative structure (beginning, middle and end)?
- Does my pitch develop ideas about the main character(s)?
- Are there suggestions as to who could play the main character(s)?
- Is the film's genre clear?
- Are there references to other films?
- Is the overall concept clear?
- Is the film easily castable?

This may require a couple of drafts to get it under 150 words. Remember, the actual pitch is verbal, so use language that you and your audience will be comfortable with.

Activity 13

AO3 – Demonstrate planning, research and presentational skills

AO4 – Use creative and technical skills to construct film products

- Pitch your idea to one of your classmates. They should use the table below to measure the success of your pitch. Afterwards, you should identify areas where your ideas were unclear and try to rectify these before submitting your finished pitch.

	Very clear	Clear	Unclear
Overview of narrative			
Outline of main characters			
Ideas for actors to play main characters			
Genre			
Are there references to other films?			
Is the overall concept clear?			

Assessment practice

Create a 150-word pitch which begins with a logline. It should contain basic ideas about narrative and genre and make reference to at least one other film. It could include ideas about suitable stars.

Key terms

Shooting: this refers to the actual filming of a script

Pre-production

Pre-production refers to all of the work done before a film starts **shooting**.

Following a successful pitch, a film will be developed. This may simply refer to drafting and redrafting the script, but with larger films it will include initial work on marketing.

Coursework options

As part of the coursework you must do one of the following pre-production activities:

- Produce a screenplay extract for the opening of your film.
- Generate possible merchandising ideas.
- Create a storyboard for a key sequence from the film.
- Produce a mock-up of two teaser posters.

Script/screenplay

A film script is generally referred to as a screenplay in the industry as the term 'script' is usually used for stage plays; a professional screenplay contains much more visual information.

There are several important elements to the script/screenplay:

- **Scene** – screenplays are divided into scenes. A scene is a piece of dramatic action that takes place in a specific place during a particular time.
- **Slug line** – another term for the scene heading. It tells us whether the scene is inside or outside, where it is and what part of the day it takes place in. It is usually written in capital letters, e.g. EXT. THE PARK. AFTERNOON.
- **Scene direction** – this refers to the things that you would see if you were watching the film. It should be detailed enough to allow a reader to 'picture' the film in their heads. Details of sounds (although not visual) should also be included here. It is always written in the present tense.
- **Character heading** – the name of the character who is about to speak. Usually written in capital letters and centred above the dialogue.
- **Dialogue** – this is what the characters say.

Remember that film is largely a visual medium. So what we see can be more important than what is said. You may choose to produce a 500-word screenplay for the opening of your film and this may legitimately contain no, or very little, dialogue. In the example below there is much more detail about what the audience would see.

Scene 1
EXT. THE PARK. AFTERNOON

A group of boys are playing football. The smallest boy on the team is Chris. He strikes but misses and the ball goes rolling down a hill.

OTHER BOYS
Oh Chris!

Chris runs after the ball. The ball picks up speed as it rolls down the hill. Chris is getting out of breath. The ball rolls through some big scary gates. Chris slows down and stops as he gets to the gates. The gates are old and huge. There are plants growing up them. Behind the gates is a big house which looks as though it is falling apart. Chris leans in to look through the gates. He does not notice an old man behind him.

OLD MAN
I wouldn't go in there if I were you.

Chris jumps around with his back up against the railings.

CHRIS
But my ball is in there.

The old man leans forward. Chris is afraid and presses himself against the railings.

OLD MAN
The old lady who lives there doesn't like to be disturbed. She doesn't like children and she doesn't like football.

In the background there is a pop. It is the sound of the ball being burst. Chris quickly turns around to look through the gates but he cannot see anything. When he turns around again the old man has gone.

Your study of film language will hopefully have highlighted the importance of a film's opening sequence in conveying ideas about narrative, genre and character through film language. Remember, it is your ability to communicate visual ideas that will be assessed rather than your ability to write good dialogue.

Professionally, the format and appearance of a screenplay will follow strict guidelines, making every page equivalent to 1 minute of screen time. You don't have to do this but you should try to make your screenplay as professional as possible by using scenes, slug lines, screen directions and following the conventions for the layout of your script. Film Education have an excellent free study guide which gives you lots of examples of screenplays for popular films. You can download the guide from www.filmeducation.org/secondary/studyguides/screenplays.pdf.

Assessment practice

Write a screenplay of no more than 500 words for the opening of your film.

Merchandising

Merchandising has become one of the major ways the film industry generates revenue. It refers to **ancillary products** which are directly linked to a film through the use of characters and images. In some cases the film could be viewed as an advertisement for the merchandise. Just think of Disney and the way it has used the characters from its films to become a major player in leisure and retail through its theme parks and stores all over the world.

Unlike most other forms of marketing which cost money, merchandising generates income, as well as promoting the film. For this reason it has been a major area of development over the past 20 years.

Key terms

Ancillary products: products that are made which use film characters or images

Does it spin-off or tie-in?

Most merchandise fits into either the **spin-off** or tie-in category, and films that are successful in making money from merchandising make use of both approaches.

Key terms

Spin-off: when a new media product (for example, a website, computer game, television programme or sound-track) is created using the ideas established by a film

***4** Computer game versions of popular films may be developed before the film is released*

The key to successful merchandise is the way it makes use of imagery from the film. Both tie-ins and spin-offs will make use of the artwork (such as logos and specific images) relating to the film.

Even though the name of the film *300* (2006) doesn't really stand out or say anything about the film, the creation of effective artwork meant that the film's title could be used across a range of products, including hats, bags and key chains, to promote the film.

The logo for 300

Activity 14

AO3 – Demonstrate planning, research and presentational skills

Think it through

- Using a recent popular film (Hollywood films are probably best for this) search the Internet for merchandise relating to the film.
- List the different types of merchandise that you see (you do not need to list every individual product) continuing the list below:
  - stationery, action figures, mouse mat…
- Identify the different groups being targeted by the products (age, gender etc.).

Examiner's tip

Some films are more suited to merchandising than others. You should carefully consider whether your film lends itself to tie-ins and spin-offs before opting for this pre-production activity.

Some films are more suited to merchandising than others and films aimed at younger audiences can be very successfully merchandised. But it is not restricted to younger people: films like those from the James Bond franchise have generated many successful ancillary products over a long period.

Merchandising your imaginary film

You are required to produce a portfolio of possible merchandising ideas for this activity.

You need a clear idea of your target audience and the types of products they need or would want. The most successfully merchandised films will have a range of products that target different genders and age groups. There is no requirement to physically produce items of merchandise but the portfolio must show that you have developed your ideas.

The student examples below are T-shirt designs for an imaginary film called *Vengeance*.

***6** These T-shirt designs were made by a student for an imaginary film called* Vengeance (Source: Aqil Kamran)

Assessment practice

You must design three to five items of merchandise for your imaginary film.

Activity 15

AO2 – Explore, respond to and reflect on a range of films and topics

AO3 – Demonstrate planning, research and presentational skills

Think it through

- When you have completed each merchandise design, you should show them to a friend and then ask them to answer the following questions:
  - Is there a clear link between the film and the item of merchandise?
  - Is there a clear audience for this type of product?
  - Does the product make use of the film's artwork? Are there visual links between the products?

Storyboarding

A storyboard is an artistic impression of what a film will look like.

If you would like to see a good example of storyboarding go to the Film Education website at www.filmeducation.org/secondary/studyguides/storyboard.pdf and look at 'P is for Psycho' on pages 2–3 of their excellent study guide.

Storyboarding is an essential part of the planning process and most mainstream films will be storyboarded before any filming begins. The storyboards allow all of the people involved in the production to visualise what the film will look like. As well as planning the types of shot used and key aspects of the mise-en-scène, they include information on camera movement and give an indication of how the film will flow (through editing and, on a broader scale, narrative).

Storyboards may be produced by a professional storyboard artist. It is the artist's job to turn the ideas of the director and cinematographers for every single shot in the film into a small drawing.

Storyboards are broken down into frames and each frame represents a shot from the film. If we consider that films may contain a huge number of different shots, it is a time-consuming process. But it can help to identify potential problems and save time when filming begins. This may include identifying:

- locations that are required
- sets which need to be constructed
- special/visual effects that must be planned for.

In their most simple form, storyboards could be a page of boxes representing frames and space for other information at the side. This can be seen below.

7 The basic frame of a storyboard

Storyboards should contain:

- written information
- visual information.

Written information

The amount of information contained on professional storyboards can vary and you may find examples with very little or very detailed information. For your own production, you should try to include as many of the following as possible as this will help to demonstrate your understanding of film storytelling and show the knowledge that you have picked up elsewhere on the course:

- **Shot number** – on a real film this would relate to the shooting script so that it is clear which part of the film the storyboard represents.
- **Shot description** – camera angle, distance and any camera movement. It is acceptable to use abbreviations here (for example, high angle XLS).
- **Action** – a written description of the action to take place in the shot.
- **Cut type** – this will indicate the type of transition to the next frame (cut, dissolve, wipe).
- **Shot duration** – how long the shot lasts.
- **Sound** – this could be broken down into dialogue, music and noise, as films often have several different elements making up the audio track.

You may want to use a template to remind you of the information needed, like the slightly more complicated storyboard shown below.

1.

Shot description:

Action:

Duration:

Dialogue

Music

Noise

Cut type:

8 *A more detailed storyboard template*

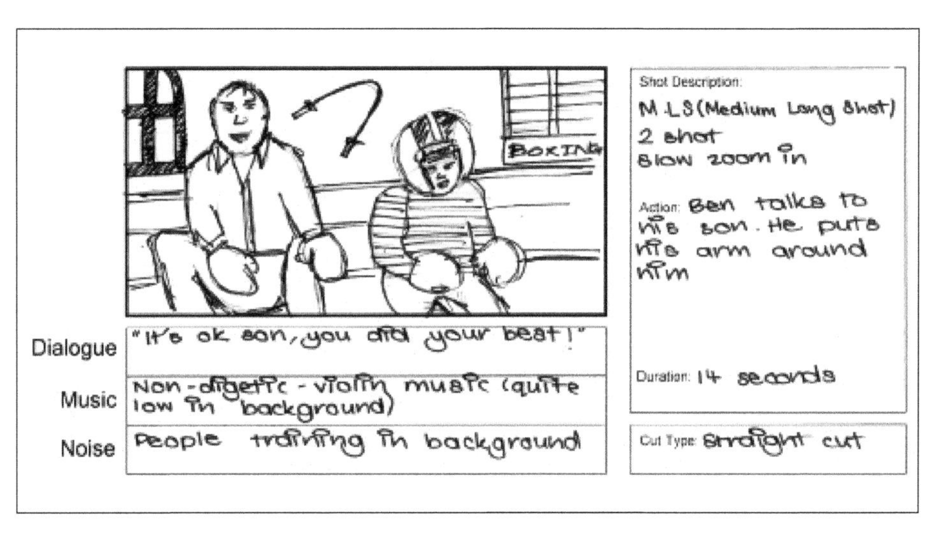

9 *An example of a student's detailed storyboard (Source: Zalika Mardenborough)*

Visual information

Along with the written information and the drawings, the following techniques could be used to give a sense of movement to the sequence.

10 *Adding a sense of movement to a frame*

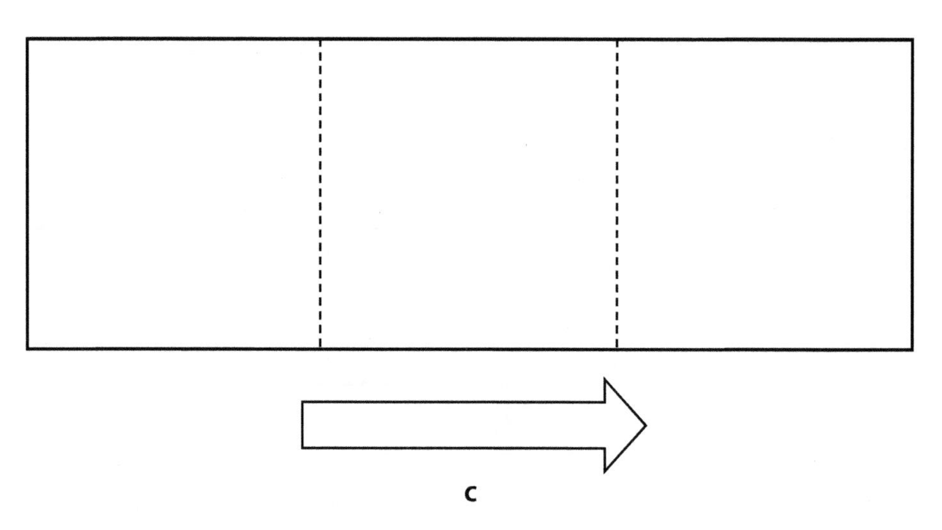

11 *Pan movement as shown in a storyboard*

- A = Arrows *in* the frame indicate movement within the frame (for example '**tilt** up' or '**pan** left'). This could relate to the movement of characters or objects.
- B = Arrows *outside* the frame are used to show camera movement.
- C = Overlapping/linked shots (floating frames) come in many different shapes and sizes and are good for demonstrating more complicated camera movement. The example above should be used in a storyboard where a pan movement is required. The wide frame is made up of three frames (the dotted lines represent the original frame size).

Key terms

Tilt: camera is fixed and tilts upwards or downwards

Pan: the horizontal axis of camera movement when turning from left to right

If you are using a storyboard template, arrows relating to camera movement may be more difficult to include. Professional storyboard artists would not use a template and you may find that drawing the storyboard from scratch gives you more creative freedom, like the examples drawn by a student below.

12 *This student has added movement to their frames by using arrows (Source: Tahirah Khatun)*

Activity 16

AO3 – Demonstrate planning, research and presentational skills

AO4 –Use creative and technical skills to construct film products

Think it through

- Select a chapter from a DVD of a film from a similar genre to yours.
- Using slow motion or pause, list the first 15 shots in the sequence. You should make reference to the following for *each* shot:
  - shot duration
  - camera angle

Activity 16 Continued

- camera distance
- camera movement
- sound (dialogue, music, noise)
- cut/transition to next shot.

Write it up

- Write down the overall duration for the 15-shot sequence.
- You may wish to repeat this for a second or third example.

The information that you have listed for the sequences looked at in Activity 16 would be the information needed in a storyboard sequence. Looking at how each sequence is constructed should give you some ideas about the range of things you must consider when producing your own storyboards.

Producing storyboards

The best way to prepare for making your own storyboard is to decide on the sequence you would like to produce from your imaginary film. Try to pick a sequence where something interesting is happening. For example, you may choose the opening sequence.

Storyboarding the opening sequence should provide you with plenty to do as you must try to establish character and location. You will need to think carefully about what you are trying to tell the audience about this character through the mise-en-scène, costume, hair and physical movement, which should all combine to create a sense of personality.

Once you have decided on the sequence you wish to storyboard, you should list the shots frame by frame and write all of the information you wish to convey in the shot. At this stage you should also include all of the features of film language you are going to use. An example is given in the table below.

Shot 1: Wendy waking up

Action	Wendy is at home in bed and is starting to wake. She stares around the room looking very confused.
Mise-en-scène	The bedroom is a mess, Wendy's hair is all over the place and she still has make-up on which is smudged. The bed linen is white, in contrast to the rest of the room.
Cinematography	XCU of Wendy's eye. This should be out of focus to begin with and then slowly come into focus as her eye opens. Then there is a slow zoom out where we start to get a sense of the chaos in the room.
Sound	Alarm clock. This should be muffled at the start then become more crisp (as the image comes into focus).
Editing	Cut to next shot.

Activity 17

AO3 – Demonstrate planning, research and presentational skills

Think it through

- Make a copy of the grid above and fill it in for your own opening shot.

Planning each of your shots in this way will make the storyboarding process much easier. It is also a good way of identifying if shots are actually needed. For each shot you should ask yourself, 'What does this shot add to the audience's understanding of what is going on?'

You may decide to add duration once you have started to produce the storyboard as you can then go through each shot with a stopwatch to see if the timing is realistic.

Once you have all of your shots planned, you can start to draw up your storyboards.

You are being assessed on your ability to tell a story using cinematic devices, not your ability to draw. However, to make your storyboards as successful as possible you really need to move beyond 'stick people' and try to give a sense of the mise-en-scène.

Tips on storyboarding

- Make your storyboards small (there is less space to fill and your drawing skills – or lack of them – may not be as noticeable).
- Try to cover as many shot types as you can.
- Identify some movement in every frame (camera movement or action).
- Avoid large blank spaces.
- Make sure the frames are labelled correctly.
- Use a stopwatch to check shot duration isn't too long or too short.

Teaser posters

Teaser posters are usually produced for big budget Hollywood films as a way of alerting potential audiences to the fact that a film is going to be released in the future. They may be produced before filming has even begun.

The type of information given on a teaser poster is different from a poster used to publicise a film when it is on release.

Teaser posters usually rely heavily on the film's artwork; this could be a logo or an image that will be used throughout the publicity campaign. In some cases the image may be one with which the audience are already familiar, for example, the Super-Man emblem. Hollywood's current trend for producing pre-sold and franchise films provides opportunities for this. Other teaser posters may introduce us to new images which they hope will become iconic and instantly recognisable – like the Jurassic Park logo.

13 *A teaser poster for* Misery *(1990)*

Teaser posters may only highlight one particular aspect of a film and most teaser posters will highlight one of the following features:

- the star
- the genre
- the basic premise.

There may be little other information as the film is unlikely to have a certificate at this stage and a release date will probably not have been scheduled. Occasionally teaser posters will give a broad idea of when the film is likely to be released (for example, Summer 2009).

Teaser posters will be placed where potential audiences are most likely to see them (usually at cinemas or on the Internet).

Producing teaser posters

Before deciding to produce teaser posters, you should consider the suitability of your imaginary film. Certain film genres are much more suited to this form of publicity than others.

Looking at teaser posters for other films should give you ideas about the layout and different approaches.

Activity 18

AO2 – Explore, respond to and reflect on a range of films and topics

AO3 – Demonstrate planning, research and presentational skills

Think it through

- Look at the teaser poster for *Batman*.
- List the information being conveyed by the poster.
- What information that you would normally expect to see on a film poster has been left out?
- How does this poster try to get audiences interested in the film?

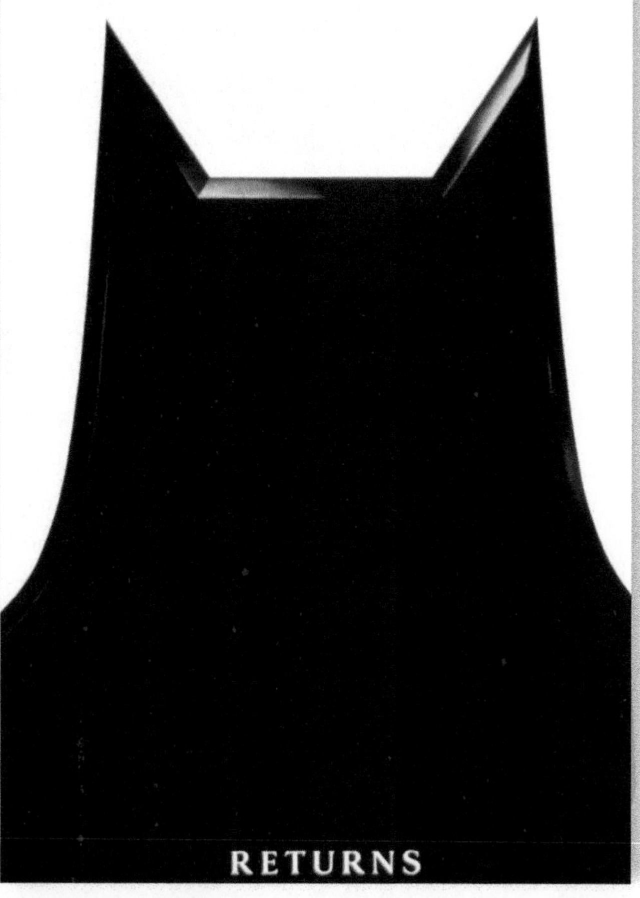

14 *A teaser poster for* Batman

Activity 19

AO3 – Demonstrate planning, research and presentational skills

Think it through

- Using the Internet, find three examples of teaser posters. (A good starting point would be to look for films which you know are coming out later this year.)
- Make notes on each in terms of:

Star	
Genre	
Basic premise	

Write it up

- Write a summary of which you think is the most successful based upon these three areas.

Assessment practice

You must produce a minimum of two designs for your poster. You should decide on the central image of your posters and what information you want to include. You could choose to produce two alternative posters or two which complement each other, highlighting different elements of the film.

Knowledge check

In this chapter you have learned what a logline and a pitch are and how to create and deliver a logline and sales pitch for your imaginary film. You have also explored how to produce a storyboard and a script and found out what a teaser poster is and how it is created. You will also have investigated the importance of all of the above in terms of the production and distribution of films. The questions below will help to test your knowledge and understanding.

1 Give a brief definition of the following terms:
- pitching
- concept
- logline
- castability.

2 Which three important elements should you include in a logline?

3 What are slug lines and scene directions in screenplays?

4 Write down the six pieces of essential information that should be included in a storyboard.

5 What is a teaser poster?

Section D Coursework

Chapter 3 Coursework: production

In this chapter we will:

- investigate the ways in which films are produced and marketed
- plan, research and create a film-based product
- experiment with a range of ways in which we can use/improve our technical and creative skills
- explore the ways in which we can demonstrate knowledge and understanding through creative production work.

The production is a substantial piece of work and is designed to give you the opportunity to pull together all of your learning from the course. Whichever brief you choose, your product should show that you can demonstrate:

- knowledge and understanding of how films communicate meaning and engage audiences
- planning, research and presentation skills
- the use of creative and technical skills.

The production is a more substantial piece of creative work than your pre-production piece but you can make use of work you have already done by basing the production on your original pitch and pre-production idea. For example:

Idea	Pre-production	Production
Horror film	Storyboard	Filmed sequence
War film	Script	Web page
Sci-fi film	Merchandising	Portfolio of stills

Alternatively, you may come up with a completely new idea which could give you more opportunities to show the extent of your knowledge and understanding.

To get the best marks you should try to work in a different medium to your pre-production task as this will give you more chance to get the best marks. For this reason it may not be a good idea to produce teaser posters for pre-production and select the poster campaign option for production.

Filmed sequence

The filmed sequence is the best way to demonstrate your understanding and ability to apply what you have learned about film language. The sequence must create atmosphere. It could be from any point in an imaginary film and might be the first 2 minutes of what could clearly be a much longer sequence. You must have access to basic camera and video editing equipment if you are to undertake this task successfully.

The sequence should show that you understand how all of the following features contribute to the creation of meaning:

- mise-en-scène
- camera/cinematography
- editing
- sound.

Groups

The filmed sequence is available as a solo production or as a group (with a maximum of four people). You may want to discuss these options with your teacher and members of your class. Below are some ideas of how the practical work may be split. You will notice that there is no specific 'director' as this is not really required on a project of this scale; the role that really covers this would be the person in charge of mise-en-scène and camera/cinematography. The group of four has two people sharing responsibility for editing as this is such a challenging and time-consuming role. You should note, however, that they must each produce their own account of their role.

Solo project

You should give careful consideration to working alone as it can be a very time-consuming and demanding task.

Group of 2

Student A	Mise-en-scène, camera/cinematography
Student B	Editing, sound

Group of 3

Student A	Mise-en-scène, camera/cinematography
Student B	Editing
Student C	Sound

Group of 4

Student A	Mise-en-scène, camera/cinematography
Students B and C	Editing
Student D	Sound

Research and planning

Initially 2 minutes may seem restrictive but you should look at short films for examples of how much can be achieved in a short space of time. Short films can be viewed in many places on the Internet and there are even online competitions dedicated to films that are 90 seconds or less.

AO3 – Demonstrate planning, research and presentational skills

AO4 – Use creative and technical skills to construct film products

Think it through

- Select a film and watch a 90-second clip.
- Make a note on every shot and edit (if you have slow motion facilities on a DVD player this is easy).
- Repeat the exercise for two more films and compare the range of shots used, the type of transitions and shot duration and the sound.
- Look for similarities between the three.

Activity 20 should give you some ideas about what things you need to include in your sequence.

Choosing the sequence may be the hardest thing you do. The purpose of the task is to show that you can apply your knowledge of film language so you should try to select a sequence that will provide opportunities to show what you know about mise-en-scène, cinematography, editing and sound.

Roles

There are many different roles on a film set. In this section, we will explore some of the roles you will need to assign when producing your film sequence.

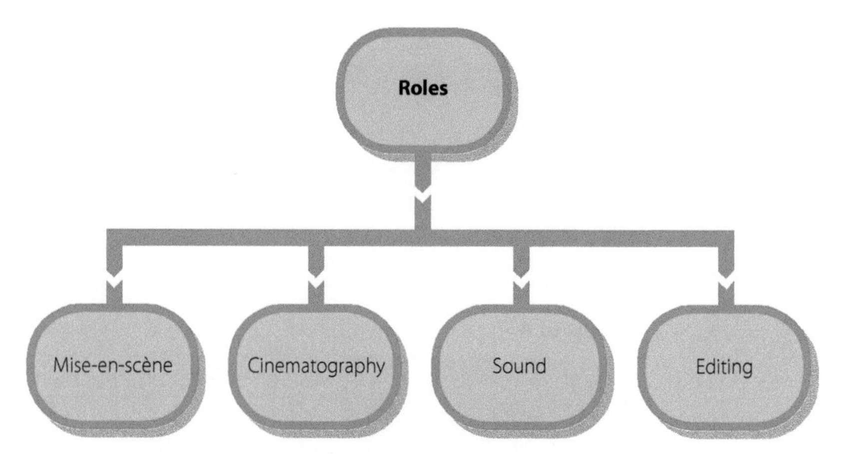

15 *You will need to assign a number of roles when you are producing your filmed sequence*

Mise-en-scène

The person in charge of mise-en-scène on this production is really covering the roles of several people on a real film set. They will be in control of the following aspects:

16 Mise-en-scène must be carefully organised

- **Location** – where are you going to film? Why has this location been chosen?
- **Set dressing** – does anything need to be added to the location to help the audience understand what is going on?
- **Props** – what props are required? Are these available? Will they have to be made?
- **Lighting** – natural light or artificial light? How can this be used to create atmosphere?
- **Costume** – what does this tell us about the characters? Could this be used to show understanding of genre?

Camera/cinematography

Key terms

Shot-reverse-shot: usually used when two characters are talking to each other – alternating shots are used and as each character speaks we see them in shot

The person in charge of the camera must try to make sure that a range of different shots are used in an appropriate manner. On a production of this size, the cinematographer will also be the camera operator. Try to use shots which help you convey meaning to your audience. For this reason, 90 seconds of **shot-reverse-shot** may not be the best way of demonstrating your camera skills. You should aim to have ten or more different shots in the sequence and try not to repeat the same type of shot more than twice.

17 A range of specialist equipment is used to achieve particular effects

Think about the following aspects:

- **Camera distance** – try to include at least one close-up, one mid-shot and one long shot. An establishing shot is a good starting point for any sequence.
- **Camera angle** – look for opportunities to use angles other than eye level in the sequence. You should aim to include at least one other angle (high or low) if you feel it is justified.
- **Camera movement** – movement can be hard if you do not have specialised equipment. If you have a tripod you should be able to include a pan or a tilt, and a tripod with wheels may provide more scope for movement. Avoid hand-held cinematography unless you are trying to show a character's point of view. You should also avoid using the zoom as this can look very poor; if you must use it then do so very slowly.
- **Focus** – the cinematographer must make sure that shots are in focus. If the camera you are using has automatic focus, avoid sudden movement and set the camera recording a few seconds before the action takes place, which will allow the auto focus to adjust.
- **Framing and composition** – think about what is included within the frame and what is left out. Good framing comes in many guises and so you will need to use your common sense. If you are not sure about the framing, move the camera to a new set-up to film the same shot; this will give you more opportunities later.
- **Filming for the editor** – you should try to make the editor's job as easy as possible by making sure you film enough for the sequence to make sense. You should consider filming **cutaways** and **insert shots** that the editor can use if there is a gap in the footage. You should also try to observe rules such as the **180° line** and the **30° rule.**

Key terms

Cutaways: shots which cut away from the action, usually to add interest or information

Insert shot: usually a close-up inserted to offer an essential detail of a scene, e.g. a close-up of a gunfighter followed by insert extreme close-up of quivering hand

180° line: two characters in a scene should always have the same left/right relationship

30° rule: states that the camera should always move at least 30° between shots in order to soften the effect of changing shot distance

Editing

The editor is responsible for shaping the sequence from the footage supplied by the cinematographer. It may be worth looking back at your notes on different types of editing from your study of film language.

18 *Inside an editing suite: today most editing is done on a computer*

As well as getting to know the software that you are using, the editor must also show that the following features have been considered:

Key terms

Rushes: footage that is developed, printed and has sound added, usually overnight, so that it can be viewed by the director/crew

Match on action cuts: cutting just before a character moves out of frame

- **Choosing cuts** – your raw unedited footage can be referred to as your **rushes** and it is your job as the editor to go through these and select the best take of each different shot (providing that there is more than one take of each shot). It is best to keep all cuts that do not have an obvious flaw and label them, as sometimes one may look better than another alongside the shots that come before and after.
- **Shot duration** – you want to make sure that your shots are long enough for the audience to see what is going on, but not so long that the audience are waiting for the cut. One way of overcoming this is to include as many **match on action cuts** as possible. This means cutting as someone moves out of the frame rather than waiting for the frame to be empty before the cut to the next shot. As a rule of thumb the longest shots are usually at the beginning of a sequence and the shortest at the end. As the sequence is designed to build atmosphere, the rhythm of editing that you create will be one of the main ways this is achieved.
- **Transitions** – most films use straight cuts unless there is a specific reason not to. Look back over your notes on transitions and what they signify. The task is not to dazzle viewers with as many different transitions as you can – you should only use those that contribute to the atmosphere of your sequence.
- **Editing effects** – most software packages contain a variety of editing effects such as split screen or picture-in-picture. Just because they are available doesn't mean you have to use them and you should only use effects that you identified as relevant when you were planning.

***19** A sound recordist at work on the set of* Superman Returns

Sound

The creation of a sound-track can provide opportunities for some very creative work and it is vital that sound is considered for every shot at the planning stage. The audio track will be assembled during or after the sequence has been edited, but the planning of this will determine how successful this is in the finished piece.

The following points must be considered:

- **Dialogue** – there is no requirement to have dialogue in the sequence as this can be very hard to do well without the right sort of equipment. If you are including dialogue you should make sure that the camera (or the microphone, if you are fortunate enough to have access to one) is close enough to pick this up clearly. You should also consider using dialogue in other ways, perhaps adding a voice-over.
- **Music** – in atmospheric sequences the most common form of music used will be written specifically for the sequence (**score**). This is not to suggest that you need to write the music, but the score will often be simplistic and not have any lyrics. You may want to use music from an existing film. You should try to avoid playing 90 seconds of your favourite song unless this really adds something to the meaning. The volume of the music is another good way of showing your understanding of how music can enhance the communication of your ideas by having it louder in some places and softer when there are other things happening on the audio track.
- **Sound effects** – this doesn't need to be the sound of explosions and laser beams; even someone's footsteps is a sound effect and in a real film it is likely that this will have been recorded separately. Not relying on the sound recorded by the camera is a good starting point for building an interesting audio track. This will also give you greater control when you are assembling it. When you are planning the film consider what you think the audience should hear for every single shot and then start to collect these sounds. This could mean searching the Internet or sound effect CDs, but it could also mean re-creating all of the sounds yourself and recording them so that they can be added during the editing process. (In the film industry this is the responsibility of the **foley artist**.)

Key terms

Score: music which is written for a specific sequence (often atmospheric)

Foley artist: the person responsible for creating many of the film's sound effects

Once the sequence has been assembled, you should ask some of your classmates or a member of your family to look at it critically. Asking them specific questions will identify if there are any areas where you need to make adjustments and this will also be good preparation for writing your evaluation.

Web page

Almost all new films that are released will have a promotional website. This will be used to promote the film to audiences who are already likely to be interested in it. They can offer free downloads, merchandise and give opportunities to look at trailers and interviews with the cast and crew. Websites are carefully tailored to appeal to specific groups and the appearance and contents will differ depending on the film's genre and target audience.

Producing a website for the film you came up with for your pitch and pre-production task is a good way of pulling together several different pieces of practical work that you have already produced. Alternatively, you could come up with another film which is more suited to web promotion.

Below is a diagram for a basic film website. The boxes represent pages and the lines represent links.

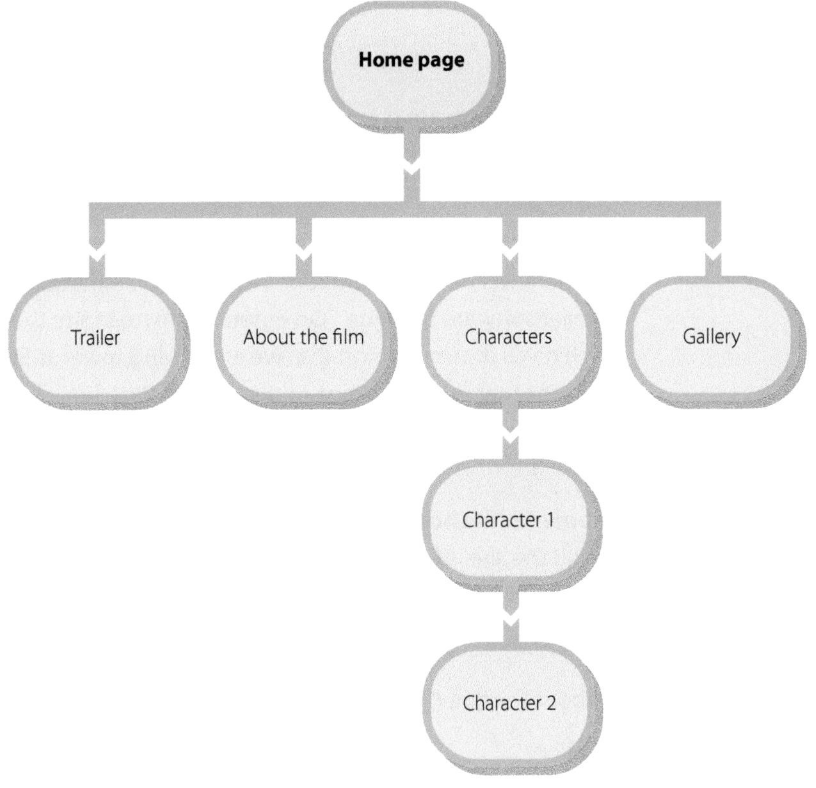

20 *The structure of a basic website for a film*

A good starting point is to undertake some close analysis of a couple of websites for current films. Case study 1, following, considers *The Simpsons Movie* website – www.simpsonsmovie.com. For each site you should look at every single page and consider how this enhances the experience of the audience/potential audience.

Activity 21

AO3 – Demonstrate planning, research and presentational skills

Think it through

- Look at three websites from films which are showing at the cinema now. For each of them, draw a diagram like the one above. If a page links to another, be sure to add the lines to show it does.
- What elements do all three contain?
- Which is the best and why?
- Which is the worst and why?

Case study: The Simpsons Movie

The Simpsons Movie

The first page we are presented with on *The Simpsons Movie* (2007) website contains only the title artwork. This has been used across all of the film's marketing and the website is trying to make use of, and reinforce, this familiarity.

Title pages like this which require you to click to enter the site usually indicate that there will be flash animation (web-based animation produced using Flash or a similar software package). On entering the main site there is a short animation which gives the impression that we are driving towards Springfield. The familiar Simpsons theme tune begins to play and as Bart Simpson enters the frame we stop on a high angle view of Springfield. For the audience, this almost creates the feeling that we are watching an episode of *The Simpsons*.

Key Terms

Home page: the first page you see when you visit a website

Avatar: a computer user's representation of him/herself

We arrive at the **home page** and this is the main page that we use to navigate around the site. At the bottom of the page , there are several options that are common to most film websites:

- Login/My Account
- About the film (DVD)
- Gallery
- Video
- Games
- Mobile
- Downloads
- Partners (sponsors).

There are several further options that can be accessed by using icons on the home page. These include the option to create your own Simpsons' **avatar** (an online character representing yourself) and to tour Springfield. This gives a level of interactivity with the characters and places.

Login/My Account

Many websites require you to log in to access all of the features. This is usually a very quick procedure which involves giving your name and email address. For the distribution company, this is an excellent way of getting the contact details of potential audiences (who are obviously already interested in the film). For the user, the benefits of creating an account include the ability to save progress/scores on games and save other features such as the avatar.

Case study: The Simpsons Movie

About the film

This page contains further information on the characters and production notes. This is the same kind of material that would be given to the press in the form of a press pack but would also be of interest to avid fans eager to know everything about the production. Publicity material is used further in the Gallery, which makes use of stills from the film.

Video

This offers different versions of the trailer for *The Simpsons Movie*. This is another common feature of promotional websites.

Games

The games offered make use of Flash. As *The Simpsons Movie* is animated, it is easy to come up with games that use the characters. Both 'Wrecking Ball' and 'Ball of Death' are based upon events that take place in the film.

Mobile

In recent years, more and more film websites offer exclusive material which can be downloaded to your mobile phone. In the case of *The Simpsons Movie*, this includes wallpapers, ringtones and screensavers. To access these, the user must text a specific code to the number given.

Features like this allow fans to make their passion for the film clear to others; the advantage to the distributors of having *The Simpsons Movie* theme tune played on buses and in classrooms cannot be overlooked as it is a constant reminder of a film on release.

Downloads

Further downloads are offered which allow you to tailor your computer workspace with Simpsons-themed screensavers, wallpaper and icons. In most cases these make use of existing artwork such as poster images or stills.

At the bottom of the home page there are a series of links to other websites such as The Simpsons official website. The other links relate directly to merchandise, and Simpsons DVDs, T-shirts and the film's sound-track can be bought with ease. The distribution company understand the merchandising potential of a film like *The Simpsons Movie* and are keen to capitalise on this. Selling directly through the website removes the need for a 'middleman' to sell the items and could ultimately lead to greater profits for the distributor.

Making your own website

Once you have looked at a range of film websites, you should have an idea of what things you need to include. If you want to include pre-production work (teaser posters, merchandising) you can do so, but this should be in addition to the two to three web pages you are required to design for the task.

Case study: The Simpsons Movie

While design skills are useful here, you are trying to show that you understand how websites are used in the promotion of films, and the content should be your primary focus. Most sites will have pages dedicated to some or all of the following:

- synopsis
- gallery (images/posters)
- production diaries
- information on characters
- information on stars
- games.

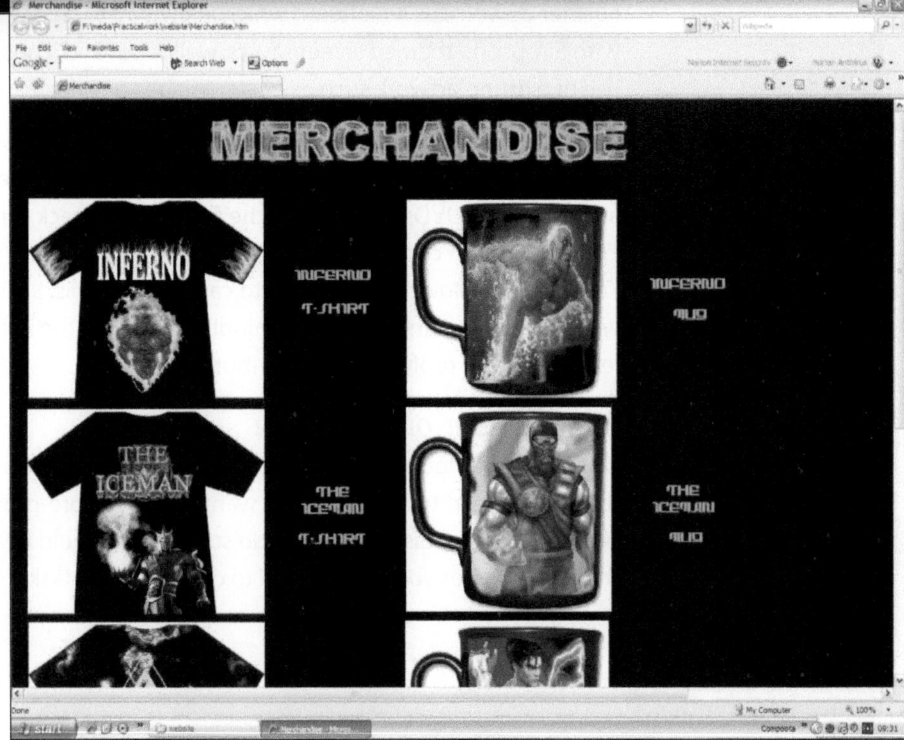

Case study: The Simpsons Movie

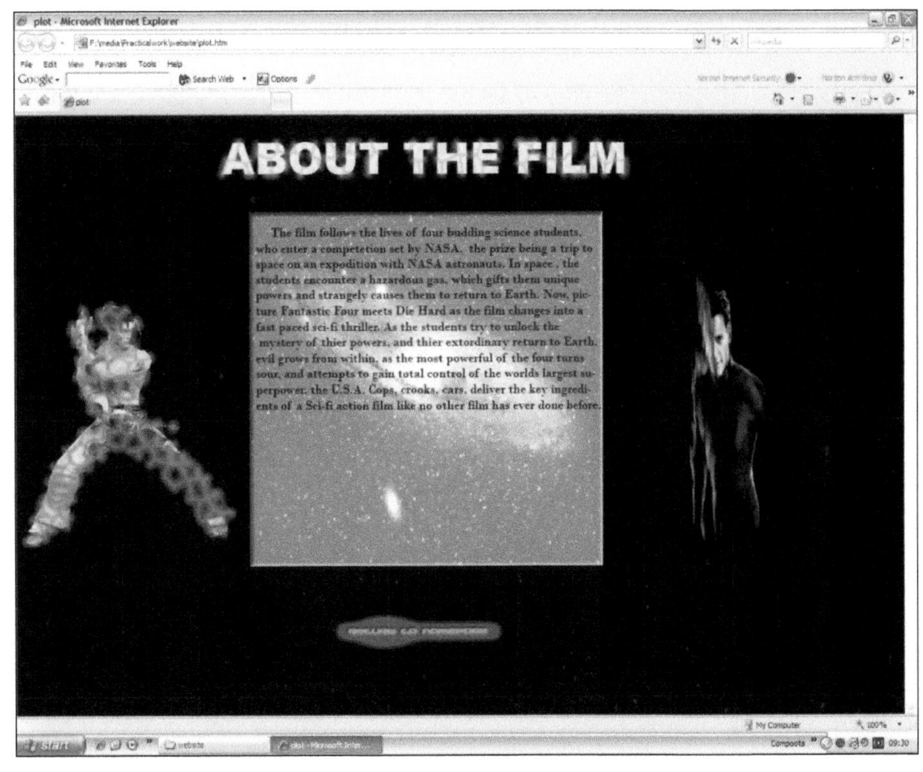

21 *Examples of website pages designed by a student (Source: Faizal Malek)*

You should try to produce two to three different pages from this list. You may also want to include a home page.

Websites contain a mixture of words and images and you must make sure that these are appropriate to your target audience. The best websites produced for this task are likely to contain:

- **original artwork** – the logo produced for the film
- **original images** – these could be stills or production photographs
- **an appropriate theme** – the use of background colour, fonts and layout must be suitable to the type of film you are trying to promote.

You should also attempt to replicate the conventions of a real website by making hyperlinks (which take you to another page).

Assessment practice

Produce a home page and at least one linked page from a website for a new film.

Poster campaign

Posters may be the original item of film promotion, as the origins can be traced back to the earliest days of film exhibition and the 'now playing' placards which would stand outside cinemas.

When a film is released, the poster may be the most visible promotional item.

Activity 22

AO2 – Explore, respond to and reflect on a range of films and topics

AO3 – Demonstrate planning, research and presentational skills

Think it through

- Look at a film poster for a film currently on release (the film's official website should be a good place to find this).
- Write a summary of how the following are used:
  - Images – what are the main images? How is colour used? What size are the images? How are the images combined?
  - Text – what different kinds of information are on the poster? What is the significance of the fonts that are used? How is the text incorporated with the image?

22 *Spot the difference! Two posters used to promote* Rush Hour 3 *(2007)*

You must produce between two and four posters. These should not be posters with slight variations in the layout, but different posters linked by similarities in the artwork (logos etc.). You should aim to include original images and, as these are the main feature of most posters, you must carefully plan how you will use them to build audience expectations.

Posters will often focus on the stars of the film. You could choose to produce a series of posters, each focusing on a different star.

If you are going to successfully replicate a professional poster, then repeating this exercise for several posters will be a useful way of examining the typical form and conventions. You may want to look at more examples from a genre similar to the one in which you are working as generic codes are a key feature in promotion through posters.

In the last chapter we discussed the way that a teaser poster will usually focus on one of the following:

- the star
- the genre
- the basic premise.

A poster which coincides with the release of the film is more likely to do all three. You should consider what signifiers you could include to make the stars, genre and basic premise clear to your prospective audience.

Key terms

Tag line: a memorable phrase that sums up a film, e.g. 'In space no one can hear you scream' from *Alien*

Stars and genre can be shown clearly through images; the premise may be a little more difficult. For this reason film posters often include **tag lines** which are short sentences that give an overall idea of what the film is about. In some ways it may be similar to the logline you created, but it is likely to be much shorter and may not include any reference to either the characters or the events.

Examples of some great tag lines include:

- *Shrek* (2001): 'The greatest fairy tale never told'
- *Monsters, Inc.* (2001): 'You won't believe your eye'
- *Bee Movie* (2007): 'Born to bee wild'

Most film posters will contain a tag line somewhere. Look for examples of tag lines for films which are currently on release. It is worth gathering these as it will help you to come up with your own. You should also look at the placement of the tag line on the poster as this will give you ideas for where and how big your own should be.

Location and format

Posters can be displayed in a variety of different places from magazines to billboards. You may want to produce a portfolio of different posters which are designed to be displayed in specific locations as this will lead to a greater level of variety in the items you produce.

Activity 23

AO3 – Demonstrate planning, research and presentational skills

In small groups

- Think of the different places where film posters could be placed.
- For each of these locations, think about the possible advantages.
- You should also try to think of any disadvantages for the locations you have listed.
- Share your list with the other groups.

Poster format

Producing posters in different sizes which reflect industry practice is a good way of showing that you understand the importance of considering where they are to be displayed. For example, a large poster on an underground station wall may contain quite a lot of information as people have more time to read it. Posters on the escalators may rely more on images as travellers rush by…

You may not be able to print out your poster in actual billboard size, but scaling down common sizes (retaining the size ratio) will provide more variety in your folder:

- **One sheet** (68.6 cm x 101.6 cm) – this is the most common size for portrait film posters and is the dominant format in the USA.
- **Quad** (101.6 cm x 76.2 cm) – traditionally more popular in the UK, this poster is in landscape format.
- **T-side** (731 cm x 64 cm and 117 cm x 117 cm) – this poster shape is designed specifically for the side of double-decker buses in major cities. Its gets its name from the 'T' shape it produces when the two rectangles are placed together.

***23** An example of a billboard*

- **Bus stop** – posters may be scaled up to the size that fills the side of a bus stop. These may be referred to as '6 sheet'. They are placed at busy bus stops where they will not only be seen by passing drivers but also by those using public transport.
- **Billboards** – billboards are frequently used to advertise films in key urban locations. The standard size of a UK billboard is '48 sheet'. There is also an extra wide billboard referred to as a '90 sheet'.

There can be various custom sizes ranging from the back of a double-decker bus to the entire side of a tall building. You should consider if your film could be promoted in this way to reach its target audience.

Assessment practice

Produce a poster campaign (two to four posters) for a new film using original images.

Stills

Film stills or publicity stills are an important part of getting a new film promoted; they are included by newspapers and magazines when they are reviewing a film. The images are 'licensed' for reproduction (meaning that the press can use these images without breaching copyright law).

They are not simply screenshots (images taken directly from the film) but will have been taken by a still photographer on the set. For this reason, stills can also include images that don't relate to the narrative.

As you can see in the publicity still below for *Kill Bill* (2003), the director, Quentin Tarantino, appears alongside the characters.

***24** A publicity still from* Kill Bill *in which the director, Quentin Tarantino, appears*

The best stills should give as much information about the film as possible and they are carefully constructed.

As stills rely on images to create the story, you could approach them using the skills that you have developed when analysing mise-en-scène.

Activity 24

AO1 – Demonstrate knowledge and understanding of how films communicate

Write it up

- Look at the still image below from *Hairspray* (2007), issued as part of the film's press pack. Make notes on how meaning is created through the following:
  - setting
  - costume
  - figure movement and expression
  - props.
- Even though this event may have taken place in the film, careful planning will have gone into posing the photograph.

***25** A publicity still from* Hairspray

When the film is complete, the distribution company will have a range of film stills to choose from. In most cases they will pick between five and ten images that they will reproduce and distribute as part of the press pack.

Captions

Film stills are usually supplied with a caption which could explain what is going on in the specific still or make reference to the film in general. Traditionally, this would have been included at the bottom of the image supplied, although it is more common today for a 'high-res' (high resolution) image to be supplied electronically via email or the Internet, with the caption supplied separately.

Traditional film stills

Traditionally, film stills tend to be printed onto 10 in x 8 in (25.4 cm x 20.32 cm) photographic paper. They come in both portrait and landscape and can be in colour or black and white.

As well as the image, a printed still will usually have a short caption (one or two sentences) directly under the image.

The logo for the film and the production/distribution company are also common, along with copyright credits for the photographer and company.

Getting started

You need to carefully plan the ideas about your film that you want to convey. Try to produce a series of stills which convey different information. One approach may be to consider whether the still is going to convey ideas about:

- **characters** – giving an insight into the type of character
- **narrative** – showing a particular event that happens within the film.

You may wish to create three stills with different purposes. For example:

1. one to show the protagonist
2. one to show the antagonist/villain
3. a still representing a climactic sequence from the film.

Once this has been decided, you need to plan the following:

- **Location** – where are you going to take the picture? Why has this location been chosen? Does the location need to be dressed in any way?
- **Characters** – how many people will be in the shot? What clothing will they be wearing? How will they be posed? What will their facial expressions be like?
- **Genre** – can you include any features which indicate the film's genre?
- **Props** – do the characters need any specific props?
- **Lighting** – does the shot need to be lit in a particular way?
- **Shot** – what distance will the shot be taken from (close-up, long shot etc.)? What angle will the shot be taken from (low, high etc.)?

When taking the photograph, you could try to take a couple of shots from different angles. A digital camera will make this easier as you will be able to instantly review the shots and decide if adjustments are needed. Remember, professional publicity stills are carefully framed and always clearly in focus.

Once you have selected the best images to represent your film, you will need to write appropriate captions for each of them.

Assessment practice

Produce a press pack containing four items and at least two stills for a new film.

Magazine article

Magazines, and the press in general, help to keep the public informed of films that are in production, due for release or currently at the cinema. The marketing team for the distribution company (who are responsible for promoting a film) will work hard to get as many magazines talking about their new film as possible. They will set up days where the stars can be interviewed by a number of different publications and will supply material to the magazines free of charge. The content in dedicated film magazines will rely heavily on information supplied in this way.

A full-page advertisement in a magazine like *Empire* could cost around £8000, whereas a double-page interview with a film star where the film is frequently mentioned would not cost a thing.

Activity 25

AO3 – Demonstrate planning, research and presentational skills

Think it through

- Choose a film that is due to be released this/next month. Look through film magazines (or any other magazines which contain information on films). Collect all of the information on that film that you can.
- How much coverage did that film receive in magazines?
- How might each item encourage a potential audience to go and see the film?

When using magazines that are not specifically about films, the publicity team will try to make sure that information about their film appears in publications with an audience similar to the target audience for the film.

Most coverage that we see in magazines is positive. If an article is over-critical of a star, they might not get an interview with them in the future! Magazines often rely on stars to sell copies, using them on the front cover to draw in fans.

The main types of coverage that magazines give to films include:

- interview with the star
- profile of the star/director
- in-production report
- reviews.

Activity 26

AO1 – Demonstrate knowledge and understanding of how films communicate
AO2 – Explore, respond to and reflect on a range of films and topics
AO3 – Demonstrate planning, research and presentational skills
Think it through

- Find an example of each of the four types of coverage listed above for the same film (you may need to look at several magazines).
- For each of the articles answer the following questions:
  - Is the article positive or negative?
  - What angle does the article take? (What is it discussing?)
  - Do they make reference to any other texts?
  - What is the main focus (the film, the star or the director)?
  - Do you consider the source to be reliable?
  - Did you find the comments useful?

If you chose the magazine option for your production activity, you should aim the article at an audience you know. For this reason, the brief suggests that the article should be written for a school/college magazine. You must include a minimum of two appropriately captioned images.

Every idea you come up with should relate to the examples that you have analysed, as this will make it easier to evaluate. It will also make your understanding of the chosen format clearer.

Assessment practice

Produce a magazine feature on a new film with at least two original images.

Knowledge check

In this chapter you have learned the processes involved in the production of your own short film sequence. You will have explored how to produce a web page for your imaginary film and the ways in which posters are created and exhibited. You will also have looked at what is involved in producing a press pack for a new film and how to produce a feature for a film magazine based on the production of a new film. The questions below will help you to check your knowledge and understanding of these areas.

1. Which essential features contributing to the creation of meaning should be considered when making a short film?
2. What features are usually included on the 'home page' of a web site?
3. What is an avatar?
4. How might the location of film posters affect size and content?
5. What are 'stills' and why are they important in terms of film promotion?

Films referenced in the text are listed below. Films that students must watch in order to complete the activities are shown in **bold**.

300

Airport

Airport '79

Airplane!

Alive

Alien

Amelie

A Night To Remember

Anita And Me

Armageddon

Back To The Future

Bee Movie

Bend It Like Beckham

Bhaji On The Beach

Black Sheep

Black Water

Casablanca

Casino Royale

Clueless

Crash

Cry My Beloved Country

Dante's Peak

Daylight

Deep Impact

Die Another Day

Earthquake

East Is East

Enchanted

Final Destination

Ghosts

Godzilla

Gone in Sixty Seconds

Goodbye Lenin!

Hairspray

Hero

High Noon

Independence Day

Indiana Jones And The Kingdom Of The Lost Skull

Kill Bill

Lord Of The Rings

Misery

Monsters, Inc.

Mrs Doubtfire

Pan's Labyrinth

Pirates Of The Caribbean

Platoon

Poseidon

Rabbit-Proof Fence

Raiders Of The Lost Ark

Rambo

Ratcatcher

Revenge Of The Sith

Road To Perdition

Romeo And Juliet

Rush Hour 3

Scream

Shrek

Spider-Man

Spirited Away

Star Wars

The Blair Witch Project

The Bourne Identity

The Constant Gardener

The Core

The Day After

The Day After Tomorrow

The Devil's Backbone

The Full Monty

Thelma and Louise

The Matrix

The Mummy

The Other Boleyn Girl

The Perfect Storm

The Poseidon Adventure

The Ring

The Simpsons Movie

The Sixth Sense

The Swarm

The Towering Inferno

The World's Fastest Indian

Threads

Titanic

Tomb Raider

Transformers

Tsotsi

Twister

United 93

Volcano

War Of The Worlds

Whale Rider

When The Levees Broke

White Chicks

World Trade Center

X-Men: The Last Stand

Yasmin

Index

Note: Page numbers in **bold** indicate where definitions of key terms are to be found. Film titles are in *italics*